Glimpses *of* Black Life
ALONG
BAYOU LAFOURCHE

Glimpses *of* Black Life ALONG BAYOU LAFOURCHE

Brief Stories of How Black People Lived, Worked, and Succeeded During Challenging Times

CURTIS J. JOHNSON

AND

EDITH A. JOHNSON

CLAUDIA JOHNSON CELESTINE

ODILE JOHNSON HUEY

WALTER E. JOHNSON

Library of Congress Control Number: 2012921193
ISBN: Hardcover   978-1-4797-4753-5
               Softcover   978-1-4797-4752-8
               Ebook   978-1-4797-4754-2

The contents of this book are based on oral history, folklore, and information found in the public domain.

This book was printed in the United States of America.

To order additional copies of this book, contact:
Xlibris Corporation
1-888-795-4274
www.Xlibris.com
Orders@Xlibris.com
119959

CONTENTS

PART TWO

Family Life: Simple Pleasures

PART THREE

Hometown Heroes

DEDICATION

This book is dedicated with deep love, admiration, and appreciation to the memory of our parents, Eddie and Elzena Pinkins Johnson, both of whom contributed to the fullest to their family, their church, and their community; to the memory of our youngest sister, Carolyn, who helped us to better understand the joys of Christmas; and to the memory of Walter and Odile, our older brother and oldest sister, both deceased, and to Claudia, our next-to-oldest sister, who were true role models who helped to shepherd the younger three siblings toward positive life accomplishments.

And to Sarah Johnson and Henry Weil, August and Antoinette Rodrigue Pinkins, Alphonse and Nellie Johnson, Ozema and Usele Rodrigue, and Virginia Pinkins, and to the many family members and friends, forerunners of African, American Indian, Creole, French, Jewish, and Spanish descent who, in some way, were principals in the creation and sustainment of the Eddie and Elzena Pinkins Johnson Family.

PREFACE

When a society or civilization perishes,
One condition can always be found.
They forgot where they came from.

—Carl Sandberg

D URING THE EARLY 1980s, my family discussed the idea of writing a family history journal or some such document that would contain interesting and relevant experiences that were central in our lives during our earlier years. We envisioned the plight of our children's children wondering who their forefathers were, what they did to earn a living, how they lived, and what contributions they made to society. We considered the lack of documentary evidence that proved our ancestors existed four generations past. We pondered the situation in which the Joad family found themselves in Steinbeck's *Grapes of Wrath*. Realizing they would have to leave behind *family* items because of a lack of space in their old, well-used truck during their travel from Oklahoma to find work in the fruit orchards of Southern California, Ma Joad thought, "How can we live without our lives? How will we know it's us without our past?"

About that same time, I read in a training journal that we are 90 percent more likely to achieve our goals in life if we remember them by writing down on paper our plans for life and reviewing and updating them periodically.

The same can be said about history. Much of our history is lost to us and to other generations because we too often fail to commit our memories to writing. Unless we *write it down* and pass it on to follow-on generations, chances are we will be prone to eventually forget it. How else can we be reminded about the treasures of our past? And what can be more important to us than our culture, our traditions, our heritage, and *our lives?*

We decided the time was right for our family history to be written, and we drafted and mailed out a questionnaire and collected information from family members. Linkages spanning more than 150 years would be shared, enjoyed, preserved, and continued for generations to come. We wanted future generations to know *we did not forget where we came from*!

In 1985, my siblings and I completed our family history book entitled *How We Will Know It's Us: Biography of a Black South Louisiana Family*. Copies were printed for family members and friends of the family. The book was copyrighted but not published. In addition to specific information about families and family members, the contents included general information about our hometown area such as our early childhood years, folklore, home remedies, what we did for a living, working in the rice and sugarcane fields and *making grinding*, our educational experiences, and many other events such as penny parties and other social outlets, the games we played, baptisms, wakes and funerals, the cuisine being from a merger of cultures, family homesteads, school days, and additional short stories about our experiences during our childhood and later years. Much of this history is repeated in parts 1 and 2 of this manuscript.

As I thought more about these features of our family book, I realized that my family's experiences were much like the experiences of many other families who lived in the general area that included *parishes* that surrounded *Bayou Lafourche*. Specifically, common local culture, customs, traditions, and living experiences were basically the same in communities throughout the Bayou Lafourche system and other areas as well.

Although somewhat *folksy* in content, this work focuses on aspects of what life was really like for Black people in the region during the one-hundred-year period roughly from 1875 to 1975.

We hope you will enjoy the journey!

CJJ

ACKNOWLEDGMENTS

T HE PAST HAS been traditionally charted for us in writings, pictures, art, and oral history. Most of the contents of this manuscript were created from oral history learned in short and extended conversations and verbal and written question-answer sessions with family members, friends, neighbors, and folks who worked and lived in communities throughout the region. Our firsthand experiences and those of our immediate and extended family members and friends who grew up with us also account in large measure for the manuscript.

The information presented in this volume was made possible by too many sources to acknowledge each one individually. We are indebted to all contributors whose names and shared information appear throughout. However, we would be remiss if we did not recognize with gratitude the special efforts of the following helpers.

Sources in Saint James:

Rev. Joseph Thomas and Erwin Octave for their descriptions of historical events; educational, religious, and social institutions; and working conditions in the parish;

Herman Nicholas, who provided information about early family life, the economy, and miscellaneous historical experiences;

Lloyd Edwards, who scheduled interviews, helped to record names of veterans living and those buried in West Saint James cemeteries; and Raymond Walters, now deceased, for providing names of veterans of American Legion Post 565.

Sources in Ascension:

Larry Christy, who provided names of veterans of American Legion Howard-Johnson Post 557, assisted with the collection of names of deceased veterans located in East Ascension cemeteries and provided historical information on education, businesses, and other social issues;

Clarence J. Brimmer, Jr., who gave freely of his time to collect names of veterans living and those buried in cemeteries in Saint James, Ascension, Assumption, and Lafourche parishes;

Kathe Hambrick-Jackson, for sharing historical documents that highlighted education and family businesses;

Olevia Batiste-Rogers, for providing information about early family life, education, and community activities in the greater Donaldsonville Area;

Lois Julien Nicholas, who shared names of businesses, schools, clubs, and community affairs in Modeste, West Ascension Parish;

Janet Cloudet, who offered names and locations of cemeteries in East Saint James Parish; and James "Mailman" Smith, for helping identify veterans from Ascension and Saint James parishes.

Sources in Assumption:

Hilda Worley, who contributed a wealth of history about the early-years economy, education, businesses, social institutions, and other living experiences;

Earl Burd, who spent many hours gathering names of deceased veterans in Assumption and Lafourche cemeteries and provided names of early businesses and social outlets;

Earnest Harris, who provided names of veterans, past and present, all members of American Legion Marion and Skidmore Post 585;

Mary Bell Terry, for providing the history of the Israel Academy in Belle Rose; and Marcus Southall, who gave the names and locations of cemeteries in the parish.

Sources in Lafourche:

Rev. Lloyd Wallace, now deceased, who provided historical revelations on education, the economy, race relations, and names of professionals and businesses in the parish;

Irvin Jones, who offered information about veterans, businesses, C. M. Washington High School, and community activities; and Gerald Theriot, for contributing the names and locations of cemeteries and the names of past and present members of American Legion Raymond Stafford Post 513.

I also wish to thank the following:

Heidi Hartwiger, for her keen editorial skills and text suggestions;

Michael Ottavian Hall, for the professional sketches and cover design that bring bygone years to life;

Al, Sheila, and Kelly Knight, whose computer graphics skills assisted with the family lineage charts and artwork;

Reggie and Simone Bowens, who helped with text arrangement and artwork manipulation and layout;

Kyle Barrè, my grandnephew, for his technical assistance in computer diagnostics and program application;

Dr. Kirk A. Johnson, my son, for his many editing efforts and helpful recommendations;

Elizabeth "Libby" Johnson, my wife, who, in so many "little" ways, helped to bring the writing to fruition; and to all family members and friends who helped in any way with this manuscript and our first family biography, *How We Will Know It's Us.*

CJJ

ARTWORK

PART ONE

The Mississippi River—Bayou Lafourche Region

INTRODUCTION

I N THE MOVIE, *Hush, Hush Sweet Charlotte*, a scene takes place in a kitchen where a meat cleaver swings downward, cutting off a human hand as it contacts the chopping block. The site of the production was the Houma House, an old plantation mansion located in Burnside, Louisiana, on the east bank of the Mississippi River across from Donaldsonville, my native town. One of the biggest historical *monuments* in the Donaldsonville Area was the juncture of the Mississippi River and Bayou Lafourche, or *the fork*, as the French who settled the area referred to it.

The word *bayou* is derived from the American Indian word *bayuk,* meaning "river." Bayou Lafourche is the world's longest bayou, stretching over 110 miles from the Mississippi River in Donaldsonville southward through Ascension, Assumption, and Lafourche parishes (counties), emptying into the Gulf of Mexico at Fourchon City.

Two additional monuments that graced the area during my early years were the hundred-year-old grand live oaks, some with their huge lower branches resting comfortably on the ground and decorated with live Spanish moss, and the elegantly symmetrical cypresses that graced the landscape and were plentiful and favored for building timbers and other materials (siding for houses, garages, and sheds and for building fences, etc.).

This area of Louisiana is steeped in American history, beginning in 1803 with the Louisiana Purchase, the Western territory the United States bought from France for $15 million. Louisiana became the eighteenth state of the Union on April 30, 1812.

My family lived in the small community of Port Barrow, a small village that was adjacent to and separated from Donaldsonville by Bayou Lafourche (and later became the west side of Donaldsonville). There were distinct communities indigenous to the small town that served briefly in 1830-1831 as the capitol of Louisiana. The small town of Darrow was separated from Donaldsonville by the river and connected by the Bisso Company ferry boat system that was powered by steam and paddle wheel that connected the east and west riverbanks. Throughout the Bayou Lafourche System are small towns and villages located on both the east bank and west bank from Donaldsonville to the entry of the Gulf of Mexico.

In many instances, the area was no different from most in southern Louisiana, with Burma Shave signs lining the highways, billboards advertising Clabber Girl as *the* baking powder for mothers to use, reminders of the need for security during a time of war on signs posted on billboards and utility poles, and the popular saying, "Kilroy Was Here" graffiti. In many other respects, however, the region was distinctly *different* from many others.

Part 1 offers insight into some of the more interesting circumstances related to our living during the earlier years and attempts to lay a brief foundation of an unusual area in South Louisiana. We will briefly examine the impact of the Great Depression on the economy and the national and regional industries that helped to sustain families during this difficult time. Information is provided about the Civilian Conservation Corps (CCC) Camps, the Works Progress Administration (WPA), and the impact of the sugarcane and rice industries as well as truck farming, sharecropping, and the seafood trade on the local economy. The role of welfare commodities is also explained.

The region's uniqueness is revealed as we look back to earlier days, reflecting on the region and its people; Black businesses; the cuisine as a merger of cultures; health care and home remedies; its baptisms, wakes, and funerals; the folklore; woodcutting as an "industry"; its neighborhood grocery stores and *lagniappe*; seepage water and tadpoles; fish fries, chicken dinners, and penny parties; its cultural and social aspects and outlets; its special institutions; and more.

> *Don't lose your head*
> *To gain a minute;*
> *You need your head,*
> *Your brains are in it.*
>
> —Burma Shave

The Region

Referring to the strip map below, the area described as the *Mississippi River—Bayou Lafourche Region* includes three parishes (Ascension, Assumption, and Lafourche) situated along Bayou Lafourche and Saint James Parish. Although Saint James does not actually border on Bayou Lafourche, it is included in the focal parishes because of its close proximity to the bayou, its bordering on Ascension, Assumption, and Lafourche and its location on the Mississippi River.

On the east bank of the river, the area's townships and villages stretch from Geismar in Ascension Parish to Gramercy in Saint James Parish and Modeste in West Ascension to Vacherie in Saint James Parish. Bayou Lafourche communities include those from Donaldsonville on the west bank in Ascension to Golden Meadow on the east bank in Lafourche Parish and Port Fourchon on the west bank. Although there were few known Blacks living below Golden Meadow before the mid-1920s, our information includes Fourchon since we believe the thirty-five miles between the two towns would have made little if any difference in how people lived and prospered.

To understand the region is perhaps to better understand the importance of the river and the bayou to the economy and that of the extended communities of the quad-parishes. To outsiders, the river served as a major communications network connecting towns and industrial complexes from Canada to the Gulf of Mexico and beyond. The bayou played the same role in communities from Donaldsonville to the gulf. To the people of the area, these waterways were major sources for their livelihood. It meant fishing, shrimping, catching and cutting wood for fuel, entertainment aboard steamboats for the more affluent and jobs for housekeepers, laundry workers, cooks, and general laborers. The bayou was a major commercial tributary for farmers, watermen, wholesalers, and retailers of the area. However, because of the rapid flow of water from the river that was damaging the banks along the bayou, the water flow was dammed in 1905 in Donaldsonville and was not reopened until the early 1950s.

CURTIS J. JOHNSON

The Economy: Impact of the Great Depression

The Great Depression began during 1929 and was exacerbated by the collapse of the stock market in October of that year. This action was quickly followed by banks, corporations, and business closings that, in turn, led to loss of life savings, investments, and jobs by large numbers of people. In addition to the staggering number of Wall Street investors being ruined, newspapers and radio accounts recorded the economy as being the most severe in the history of the country.

Newspapers carried stories about people starting "small businesses" on street corners in large cities, selling pencils, apples, and hot dogs and offering shoe shines and service skills for homes and businesses such as janitorial chores, window washing, gardening, and other handy work.

For more than two years after the start of the depression, little progress was recorded in moving the economy forward; that is, until the presidential election of 1932, which played the pivotal role in the creation of many jobs for people throughout the country. In his nomination speech, then-governor of New York, Franklin D. Roosevelt, outlined the framework for what would become the Civilian Conservation Corps (CCC) upon his election to the White House.

CCC Camps

Not long after his election, President Roosevelt implemented the CCC program in 1933 that immediately began employing young men in jobs that focused on the environment. Included in this program were such tasks as preventing soil erosion by planting trees in forest areas and constructing ditches, swales, and dams for improved drainage. Additional jobs available were in building roads and parking facilities in public areas, installing telephone lines, and maintaining beaches and other projects related to conservation.

A number of young men from the quad-parish area took advantage of this work program by signing on. Initially, the workers lived in "camps," where they ate in dining facilities and slept in tents provided free of cost to workers who were paid one dollar a day. "Of the $30 a month, five were paid to the workers and the rest of the money sent home to help take care of the family," Mrs. Worley, a retired school teacher and native of Assumption Parish, volunteered. By the end of the first year, the tents had been replaced by wooden structures with tin roofs, much like the homes used by people who lived in the surrounding areas.

CURTIS J. JOHNSON

Of the seventy-five CCC camps located throughout Louisiana, two were located in our general area in Gonzales (Ascension Parish) and Thibodeaux (Lafourche Parish).

The WPA

Within several years after the start-up of the CCC projects, another federal work-intensive program emerged under the Roosevelt Administration as the Works Progress Administration (WPA), a further means of reducing the continuing high rate of unemployment. This program differed from the CCC in that its jobs centered on the construction and repair of public school facilities, hospitals, and other facilities deemed by the federal government to be important to the livelihood and health and general welfare of the American people. Levee repairs, construction of paved roads and sidewalks, and construction and maintenance of drainage ditches were also jobs that were heavily manned by WPA workers.

"You couldn't buy a job during the Depression years," stated Rev. Joseph Thomas of Saint James Parish. He added, "For my first job as a young man, I was getting fifty cents a week. Some folks picked [Spanish] moss and sold it to families to stuff their mattresses. So the WPA was a godsend program that paid $1.50 for one day. This was a time when you could *make* [buy] groceries to last a week for a large family for $5.00."

"In Assumption, there were no limits to the WPA projects that involved the workers," stated Mrs. Worley. Now living in Donaldsonville, she reported that one such project was the digging of a "sizeable" canal by WPA workers using hand shovels. "Workers were proud to be employed in the program and were given a paper sticker plaque that measured about four inches square and read, 'NRA—We Do Our Part,' as an incentive to the workers. NRA stood for National Recovery Act. They were asked by the project director to place the plaque in a front window of their house as a recruiting effort," Mrs. Worley stated.

There were few opportunities available outside of the WPA and CCC to the working public during these years. Periodically, the oil fields in Lafourche and Terrebonne parishes hired laborers in the manufacturing of natural gas and petroleum products. As the sugarcane industry expanded, and during the harvest season, mostly laborers were hired, although jobs as equipment operators and mechanics were available periodically at refineries in Saint James, Ascension, and Assumption parishes.

Had it not been for these two work-intensive programs, the CCC and WPA, it remains questionable today whether many families would have made it through these extremely hard times.

Our father was fortunate to have maintained his job throughout the Depression years, except for a period of healing as a result of a work-related accident. He worked for the Elray Kocke Service, Inc., as a heavy truck driver. His job also involved loading and off-loading lumber, heavy boxes and crates, bags of cement, and other building construction and oil drilling materials. On one occasion during an off-loading incident in 1932, a heavy box fell on his left leg and broke it several inches below the knee. Unemployment insurance that today's workers enjoy was not a federal government requirement at that time.

One of the traditions of the region included reaching out by its people to help others in need, in spite of economic conditions and their very low-income status even before the start of the Depression. An example of this tradition is illustrated by relatives, neighbors, and friends during a time of need involving my family in 1932.

After the accident, our dad was laid off without any source of income. Our family of seven (parents and five children at that time) did not qualify for welfare because of his job that paid about $22 take-home pay per week. There was no minimum-wage law then, and wages were left to the discretion of the employer. However, as custom dictated, neighbors and family friends helped as best they could by sharing homegrown fruits, vegetables, chickens, and meat during hog-killing season. He maintained a list of the names of donors and their contributions made during his recovery. I believe the list represents the gifts he received during his entire recuperating period, considering the multiple gifts noted by several of the donors. Also, chances are that the list did not contain the names of donors of vegetables, because sharing vegetables was an ongoing, everyday regional tradition, especially to families in need. His handwritten records showed the following notations:

Feb 27, 1932

Donated

Buck Johnson	oranges, camel cigarettes 1 cigar
August Pinkins	2 cigars cigarettes 2 pack
Isiah [Pinkins]	cigarettes 2 pack 1 dollar money
Kirmet Hubbard	fifty cents in money
Kirmet Hubbard	35 cents in money
Lawrence Pleasant	35 cents in money
Sam Clark	oranges cigarettes
Sam Clark	10 cents in money
Rev Johnson	25 cents in money
Emily White	10 [cents] in money eggs
Mathiew Joseph	10 [cents] in money eggs
Margret Freeman	05 [cents] in money
Virginia Hawkins	05[cents]
Louise Lively	15[cents] in money
Elizabeth Ridrigue	tea cakes
Elizabeth Pinkins	oranges
Dr J. S. Brazier	fruit
Sissie Randolph	10[cents]
Kirmit Hubbard	25[cents]
Buck	1 pack cigarettes
Eddie Pinkins	1 pack cigarettes

During the pre-World War II period, thousands of Louisianans out-migrated to job opportunities in other states. At the onset of the war, word spread quickly that companies in California were hiring workers to manufacture war equipment. Similar notices were received that the Chicago stockyards and Detroit automobile manufacturers were also hiring. It wasn't long before hundreds of workers from the region were resettled in these and other places with jobs for the first time since early 1930s.

Worley, now living in Donaldsonville, stated that as the economy began recovering somewhat from the Depression, work opportunities for Blacks in Assumption were sparsely scattered about the parish. "Jobs were limited to mostly laborers during the sugarcane grinding season and rice field maintenance and harvesting. Strawberry pickers traveled to Hammond and Ponchatoula for the harvest in early spring. The Texas and Pacific Railroad Company hired laborers periodically to lay and repair rail tracks and buttresses. The sawmill in Plattenville hired one or two laborers, on and off," she said.

A native of Saint James, Edwin Octave, Jr., said that during the early 1930s when Huey P. Long (a.k.a. *Kingfish*) became governor of Louisiana, he began to help poor farmers, Black and White. "Operating on the theme of *Every Man a King,* the Governor was able to start a loan program in the amount of $750 for farmers to buy mules and horses and needed tools and equipment to start and maintain sharecropping and truck farming businesses. As it turned out, these loans became grants, since the recipients did not have to repay them. For the first time ever in South Louisiana, Black farmers were able to hire on field hands to share in the workload," he stated.

Making Grindin'

South Louisiana has had a rich history for growing and refining abundant sugarcane crops for more than two hundred years. When Jesuit priests first brought sugarcane into South Louisiana in 1751, little did they know that the foundation was being laid for an industry that would become one of the leaders in growing Louisiana's economy for the future. During the earlier years of cultivation, the average yield of sugarcane in Louisiana ranged from sixteen to twenty tons per acre. The state crop averaged around three hundred thousand tons of sugar per year and was a source of livelihood for five hundred thousand people.

The sugarcane industry continued to grow and prosper through the nineteenth century in South Louisiana with few distractions beyond too much rain during the growing season causing low sucrose levels that resulted in reduced market value. There were occasional minor disputes between workers and plantation managers; however, all combined would not measure up to the blatant slaughtering of humanity that occurred in 1887, as noted below by Stephen Kliebert:

> One of the most interesting, and probably least known events in Louisiana history is the Thibodaux Massacre of 1887, the second most bloody labor dispute in U.S. history.

Cutting Sugarcane

CURTIS J. JOHNSON

Although most of the blood-letting occurred in the environs of Thibodaux, the strike encompassed a larger area. The strike affected sugar plantations in St. Mary, Terrebonne, and Lafourche parishes. These parishes make up an area known as the "sugar bowl." Thibodaux is the parish seat of Lafourche.

The plight of the sugar cane worker in 1887 was one of back-breaking labor and meager pay. Most field hands were paid approximately 13 dollars a month. They were also paid in script. Script was basically a coupon redeemable only at the company store owned by the planter. The store's prices were normally marked up 100%. You can see that the worker usually wound up being indebted to the planter. Louisiana law stated that if a worker owed money to a planter he could not move off the planters land until the debt was paid. This law essentially reduced the plantation laborer to the status of serf.

In 1885 the Knights of Labor was successful in organizing railroad workers who worked for the Charles Morgan Railroad and Steamboat Company. The company owned a stretch of tracks that ran from New Orleans to Texas. The railroad passes through the communities of Des Allemands, Raceland, Schreiver, and Morgan City on its way to Texas. The K. of L. felt that the sugar cane workers were fertile ground to expand their organization. In 1886 a L.A. (local assembly) of the K. of L. was established in Schreiver, La. for sugar cane workers. It was the [sic] probably the first assembly of a labor union that allowed both black and white members to join. During a time when a strict caste system was imposed this was a hell of an achievement!

In late October, 1887 LA 8404 (Schriever local) presented a list of demands to L.S.P.A. The L.S.P.A.'s (Louisiana Sugar Producer's Association), members included local sugar planters. The workers wanted elimination of scrip, a small increase in their daily wages, and payment every two weeks. The planter's association rejected the demands. The planter aristocracy ruled Louisiana at this point in time. They worked for many years to deny poor whites and blacks access to education, and better working conditions. They were not about to cede any of their power now.

"The Knights of Labor scheduled a strike to commence on the 1st of November 1887. The strike began during the crucial harvest period known as "grinding." On November 1st workers in St. Mary, Lafourche, and Terrebonne parishes refused to work, and refused to vacate their cabins that were plantation-owned. Attempts to evict

tenants by local sheriffs were unsuccessful. The sugar planters were faced with the possibility of losing their crops to a freeze if the strike persisted. On the same day the strike began, the planters association called on the governor to send them help in the form of the state militia. Governor McEnery (1881-1888), who was himself a plantation owner, had no problem in ordering the state militia to the embattled region. The first militia companies arrived in Schriever, Louisiana from New Orleans on the first of November. They made the short trip to Thibodaux where they intended to store their equipment which included horses, rifles, and a Gatling gun in front of the Lafourche parish courthouse. The courthouse is a beautiful antebellum Greek Revival structure which still serves as the parish courthouse to this day.

The two militia companies that arrived in Thibodaux were not the only ones to take part in strike-breaking. Other companies were sent to Houma and Lockport. Some 10,000 plantation workers took part in the strike. Most of the strikers were black, but nearly 1,000 were white.

The militia companies sent to the region worked with local judges in evicting strikers from plantations, and provided protection for "scabs" sent in to replace the strikers. When striking plantation workers were faced with soldiers armed with Springfield rifles they offered little to no resistance. They heeded the orders to leave the plantations. Many congregated in the black section of Thibodaux.

Problems arose when white scabs were fired upon in Terrebonne parish. Strikers, who were forced off plantations, were believed to be involved in firing into sugar mills in Lafourche parish.

Pickets were placed in around the city of Thibodaux. The "pickets" were composed of white civilians from Thibodaux, and neighboring parishes. They were no doubt horrified by the rumor spreading around town that black strikers intended to burn the city down.

The struggle came to a head when two white picketers were fired upon while at their posts in a black section of town. The two picketers survived, but the incident enraged the white population of Thibodaux. White vigilantes rode through the neighborhood firing their weapons and wreaking havoc. The strike had degenerated into a race war.

Strikers and their family members were rounded up by vigilantes. Many were told to "run for their lives," before being summarily executed. On the morning of November 23, 1887 anywhere between 30 to 300 black strikers were killed. A company of militiamen known as the Shreveport Guards is considered to have taken place in the massacre. Another attempt to organize sugar cane workers in southeast Louisiana would not occur until the 1950's.

The area sugarcane harvest, or *grinding* season, was much more than the process of crushing the stalks of cane with machinery to extract the juice from which sugar, syrup, and molasses would be made. It also represented an opportunity for jobs to many Blacks, some migrating in from distant areas and living in *boarding houses* in and around the sugarcane-growing communities. The grinding season meant a seasonal job for those who had developed a good work record over several years. To some, it represented the only means of income for the year. To all, especially children, it meant seeing huge trucks and railcars moving tons of sugarcane to area refineries every day.

The season began in early to mid-October and extended into January, sometimes into February, depending on the amount of rainfall during the growing season and time of harvest. Harvesting sugarcane was labor-intensive and hard work, with men and women often working ten-hour days, six days a week.

Cane cutting was a job relegated almost exclusively to Black laborers that included older children and young and old adults as well. The process involved using a cane knife designed expressly for that purpose. The *shucks* or bladelike leaves were removed with the knife's blade and hooked end; the stalk was cut near the ground, and finally, the stalk was cut off, or *topped off,* and discarded with the remaining shucks, since the sweet juice was contained mostly in the lower part of the stalk. The cut stalks were then laid across the rows where they had grown and were burned slightly to remove the remaining leaf fragments. Laborers then loaded the cane stalks onto horse—or mule-drawn carts and carried the cane to a loading platform where the bundled stalks were hoisted by a block-'n'-tackle rig into cane trucks and taken to sugar mills where the grinding process occurred.

The cane fields had to be maintained from the time the cane was planted until the harvest. Seed cane was planted end to end in rows to become the following season's harvest. Maintenance involved cutting grass from around the young stalks and cultivating the rows with hoes. "*Hoeing cane* [chopping grass from cane rows with a hoe] was another job that provided work for laborers who were paid $1.85 a day. A row of cane measured nine acres long, and you could only do two rows in a day," Worley said.

Workers at the mills labored around the clock in twelve-hour shifts in some locations. Some lived in shacks on the plantations. In many cases, boarding houses were provided for transient field and mill workers. Here, workers slept and ate their meals during the grinding season. Workers who lived in the area were picked up each morning and carried to the worksite and each evening they were returned to their homes on trucks provided by the plantation.

A typical day in the cane fields began at dawn with workers repeating the cutting and stacking process down long rows of sugarcane stalks standing seven to eight feet tall. At some time during midmorning, the workers rested, and some ate a meal brought from home in a small metal bucket. Others brought food purchased at the plantation store, which was usually operated by the farmer or plantation owner. After the meal and a rest period, the workers resumed working until "knocking-off time" in the early evening. There were reports of cases where workers did not receive take-home pay, supposedly because they used their entire salary on food and household items from the plantation store.

The sugarcane industry in Lafourche and Assumption was highly successful during the 1930s and 1940s because of the crop's high sucrose content, according to Rev. Wallace of Thibodeaux. "There was a high unemployment rate for the Blacks in the area, especially during the 1930s, even though the official rate for the state stood at 3.7 percent. The unemployment figures did not include Blacks at that time. Also, employers offered many part-time jobs such as cane harvesting to Blacks, thereby avoiding paying employment benefits. Consequently, almost 100 percent of the cane cutters were Black men, women, and teenagers," Rev. Wallace concluded. "Also in Assumption, many Blacks worked in the Supreme Sugar Refinery in various capacities, including drying, stacking, and loading sugar and molasses onto trucks and boxcars," Mrs. Worley added.

Occasionally, the Domino Sugar Refinery, the largest in the country for many years and located in Saint John Parish (adjacent to Saint James Parish), advertised for laborers, especially during the grinding season, according to Herman Nicholas, a native of Saint James.

It was not uncommon for entire families to work together in cane fields. Some workers left home to *make* (work) grinding on some distant farm or plantation. This meant being away from families for about three months, with an interim home visit made at Christmastime. Many Black children who lived on the plantations did not begin the school term until after the grinding season ended.

My family lived on the River Road paralleling the Mississippi River in Port Barrow, which served as a route from Lemanville cane fields to McCall's Evan Hall sugar refinery. Occasionally, loaded trucks passing by would invariably drop several stalks as the cane bundles shifted while turning at street corners. Children delighted in running behind cane trucks slowed down by graveled roads to snag a stalk or two of sugarcane. It was a great pastime—peeling away the tough outer layer and chewing the sweet juicy core of the cane *joints*.

The first sugarcane was said to be imported from Haiti during the early 1700s. Many improvements have been made to the process of planting and reaping sugarcane since its arrival in this country. However, one cannot talk about the sugarcane industry in South Louisiana without mentioning the man who invented the sugarcane-planting machine.

On November 19, 1964, Leonard J. Julian, a successful Black sugarcane farmer in Modeste, Louisiana, applied for a patent for the sugarcane planter that he invented. The patent application began:

> *This invention relates to a device for planting sugar cane. Such planting is carried out by laying stalks of cane, some six to eight feet long, in a furrow, and this has heretofore been done by hand, since there is no known machinery for picking up the stalks, which are irregular in length and thickness, and depositing them, properly oriented, in the furrow.*

With this introduction, the application, prepared by Julian and his legal team, continued to describe the intricate functions of each component of the machine using highly technical mechanical language. Two years later, the patent for the cane planter, dated November 22, 1966, was issued and the machine put in production. With the use of this remarkable implement, a farmer was able to increase his planting capacity hundredfold while appreciably reducing the number of field hands needed to do the work.

There were several other prominent Black sugarcane farmers in the region, including Murry LeBouf, Saint James (township), Walter Weber, Chopia, and Eric Hydel, Brookstown in Saint James Parish, and Dr. John

H. Lowery, the owner of the Africa Plantation in Modeste in Ascension Parish that was managed by Leonard Julien and Anthony Julien.

The Rice Fields

The rice fields provided another industry that depended heavily on laborers for its success. Rice was grown in each of the four parishes and was a staple eaten throughout the South. The warm climate, the availability of water sources, and the nutrient-rich soil were all elements that combined to make the area ideal for rice production. Modeste, Polo Alto, Paytivan, and McCall in Ascension and selected locations in Saint James, Assumption, and Lafourche parishes were the primary locations for *rice fields* during these years. However, "rice fields in Lafourche were not as successful as those in Ascension, Assumption, and Saint James because the fields in Lafourche could not retain water. Consequently, rice farming in Lafourche was eventually replaced by sugarcane," Rev. Wallace stated.

Rice was planted in shallow rectangular beds (*paddies*) surrounded on four sides by a twelve—to fourteen-inch-high dirt barrier to retain the six to eight inches of water needed for the growing season. The beds measured approximately eighteen feet wide by thirty feet long. Rice plants were nurtured until they were about eight inches high before planting time, at which time a single plant was pushed two to three inches into the mud that immediately engulfed the root system. As the plants grew, an irrigation system gradually added water to maintain a depth of about six to eight inches. From then until near harvesting, the water was maintained at that level. Before harvesting, the paddies were drained and the rice stalks were dried for cutting. Like the cane knife used for sugarcane, the sickle was a specialty tool used to cut rice. (It was also used in other locations to reap wheat, rye, and other similar grain.)

The rice industry, like sugarcane, required additional workers during harvest time. A cadre of year-round workers planted, irrigated, and cultivated the rice crops. Summer-hired laborers were brought in during the early growing stages to pull weeds from among the rice plants. This weeding process was known as *grassing rice*. During harvest, laborers would be hired to cut, bundle, and load the rice onto trucks, some with trailers, for delivery to the rice mills for thrashing, winnowing, polishing, and packaging for consumers' tables.

"Back in the late 1930s and early 1940s, young boys worked in the rice fields in Assumption. Rice needed plenty of water to grow, so water was pumped from Bayou Lafourche out to the rice fields. The boys would pull the grass out of the rice field and throw it into a *flume* (deep ditch) where it was carried to the woods for disposal. They were paid thirty-five cents a day," Worley stated. When the rice was fully grown, it was cut with a *reef hook* [sickle] and put onto shocks to dry. After drying, the rice was put on a tractor cart and taken to a rice thrasher that separated the rice from the straw. There, the rice was bagged and sent to the mill for market processing," she concluded.

During the summer, I *grassed rice* along with other teenagers and adults in Modeste. The process consisted of five to seven persons walking abreast in a single line across the flooded bed, stooping to pull Johnson grass and other weeds from among the young rice blades and carrying them to the *head landing* where the weeds were stacked to be hauled away in horse-drawn carts.

One of the most challenging aspects of working in rice fields was dealing with the poisonous snakes. Occasionally, one would see a water moccasin or canebreak rattler sunning on the head landing. I remember one episode where we worked in an area that contained a deep-wooded segment about a half mile to our front where the paddies began. As we got closer to the woods, a moccasin or two would be seen slithering over the head landing and into the paddy we were approaching. The closer we got to the wooded area, more snakes could be seen escaping to the sides as well as across the front partition. Yet strangely, most workers wore old tennis shoes or no footwear at all, and few wore rubber boots. No one was bitten to my knowledge during my two summers grassing rice.

In Saint James Parish, there were two Black rice farmers, Murry LeBouf and Eric Hydel. Although most of the rice industry was controlled by White farmers, the LeBouf and Hydel families were successful in their production and sale of rice. Octave recalled that some of the farmland used by several successful White rice farmers was owned by Blacks and rented to those Whites. "I was told by my father that, over time, the Black landowners would borrow money from the farmers who rented their land. However, when the White farmers called the loan to be paid and the Black land owners couldn't come up with the money they owed, the Whites seized their land as repayment for the loans," he stated.

Other Area Industries

Truck Farming and Sharecropping

Vegetable and fruit crops were also seasonal and served as another source of employment for many laborers in the area. Prosperous farmers who produced vegetables for the retail market used tractors and full-time workers to prepare the soil, plant seeds, fertilize, cultivate young plants, and harvest mature vegetables. During the growing phase, some outside laborers were hired to cut the grass from the vegetable rows using hoes while cultivating at the same time. At harvest time, additional laborers were required to gather the crops of pole and bush string beans, crowder peas, field peas, green peas and butter beans, cushaw squash (then called pumpkin by most folks in the region) and summer scalloped squash, *Irish* (white or Idaho) potatoes, tomatoes, corn, green peppers, hot red pepper, garlic and green onions, celery, okra, eggplant, and mirliton, also known as alligator pear, chayote, or cho-cho.

Tubby Ewen Produce Company in Donaldsonville was one of the major vegetable producers in Ascension. Ewen also farmed vegetables in Darrow, on the east bank of the Mississippi where I worked at age thirteen picking bush string beans for thirty-five cents a bushel. The trick was that you had to start picking at 7:00 a.m. and take frequent breaks to pick three bushels by 1:00 p.m. and stop for the day due to the beaming hot July and August sun. Believe me, three bushels was a day's work for me under such hot conditions. Most adults would pick four to five bushels.

Sharecropping was a method of farming for persons who had some land but needed more to achieve their farming goals. There were also landowners who had land beyond their needs or no longer desired to farm some of their land. These two parties would enter into a contractual agreement for the first farmer to rent the land of the second for a share of the revenues realized from the sale of the crops raised by the first farmer. This was a commonly used method of partnering that allowed small land owners to increase their income.

Vegetable gardening was practiced throughout the region in many families, even before the start of the Depression. Practically all Black families and low-income Whites had vegetable gardens as well as an occasional flower garden. There were several large vegetable farmers scattered about the Black communities: Eric Hydel (Jamestown) and Murry LeBouf (Brookstown) in Saint James, Leonard Julien and Anthony Julien and Sons (Modeste) in Ascension, Willie Randall (Bertrandville) in Assumption, and James Grant and Willie Williams (Thibodaux) in Lafourche.

Like many in the region, our family did many things to contribute to our food supply. In addition to vegetable gardening, we canned fruits and vegetables, raised chickens, ducks, geese, hogs, and on at least one occasion, a cow. Fishing and crawfishing and buying fish from our neighbor, Mr. Shad, also provided other foods we needed to maintain healthy diets. It was traditional for families to can local fruits and vegetable in pint and quart Mason jars. Figs and pears were made into preserves while peaches and blackberries were canned for later use in pies and cobblers. Butter beans, string beans, crowder peas, okra, corn, and tomatoes were also canned to carry us through the winter months.

The Seafood Industry

South Louisiana was the country's leader in crawfish, shrimp, and oyster production during the pre-and post-Depression years and for some years that followed. The seafood industry was labor-intensive in the sense that during these earlier years, machinery used for trawling, loading, and off-loading of catches was limited. The block-'n'-tackle, with its mechanical advantage, was one of the most-used hoisting implements of the period.

The majority of the seafood harvested for retail was taken from the Gulf of Mexico and transported inland by trucks using highway LA 1 and by boats using Bayou Lafourche. All of the oysters, blue claw crabs, and much of the shrimp and fish (flounder, red fish, red snapper, speckled trout), and scallops were caught in the gulf. Rivers, bayous, lakes, and ponds were sources for freshwater shrimp, trout, sun perch, catfish, striped and white bass, *buffalo* (a freshwater fish resembling the carp), garfish, *gasper goo* (also known as freshwater drum), bream, eel, *sac-a-lait* (crappie), shad, turtles, crawfish, and frogs.

An abundance of tributaries was scattered about the quad-parish landscape. In Saint James and Ascension, there were the Mississippi River and ponds between the river and the levee that were created by excavating dirt to build the levee system. Additionally, East Ascension had its Amite River and Alligator River. Lake Verret, a vast water reservoir, was located in Assumption. Lafourche, the largest of the four parishes, boasted nine lakes (Lake Jesse, North Lake, Round Lake, Catfish Lake, Lake de Cade, Lake Long, Lake Fields, Lake Salvador, Lake Boeuf), also Dufrene Ponds and Bayou Boeuf. All parishes had a series of small bayous and lakes that were known to produce fish, turtles, and frogs, all of which were used for food.

Seafood was plentiful and easily obtained. A seafood market could be found in most communities. And every community had at least one fish man who caught and sold from his cart, wheelbarrow, or arm baskets. Although money was scarce everywhere, the cost of seafood was considered reasonable. Some fish (shad, buffalo, gasper goo, and catfish) cost as little as ten cents a pound, while preferred types (trout, red snapper, flounder, and bass) cost as much as twenty-five cents a pound. The great quantity of seafood available in the market made the price affordable for even most low-income families.

Welfare Commodities

The federal social welfare system was a much needed resource for a large number of people in the region, mostly due to the lack of jobs.

Social welfare assistance during the 1930s was provided to eligible families in the form of both cash payments and food subsidies. Like today, eligibility for the assistance was based on family income and size. Our family was not eligible for welfare because our income was slightly above the required federal standard.

Our family and others with similar borderline eligibility status were indirect recipients, anyway, getting food items from neighbors and friends who received more than they cared to use or the items they did not want. Oftentimes, children would help older recipients with their deliveries and would be rewarded with a small share of the food items that included government surplus butter, American cheese, raisins, dried apricots, canned peaches, whole wheat flour, canned meats, powdered milk, corn meal, dried pinto beans, and peanut butter.

Some people would not have survived without food assistance during those Depression years.

The People

We can build a beautiful city.
Yes we can. Yes, we can.
We can build a beautiful city.
Call it out, and call it
The City of Man.

—"Beautiful City" from *Godspell*

In many ways, Donaldsonville, like the other towns in the region, was a *city of man,* a true melting pot of nationalities and cultures. Family names such as Buggage, Capello, Joseph, Dominique, LeBlanc, Sanchez, Julien, Kocke, Gibson, Matassa, Gomez, Boudreaux, Leavings, Landry, Sims, Marchand, Weil, Butler, Casso, Bourg, Dorsey, Sagona, Sims, Williams, and Augusta were common during the early years.

The racial and cultural makeup of those living in the region included Spaniard, Italian, American Indian, French, German, Negroid, Jewish, Creole, and Cajun folks of varying economic and social levels. The Creole culture resulted from the merger of French or Spanish and the Negro peoples. The presence of the Cajun culture was made possible by the Arcadians who settled in South Louisiana from Nova Scotia around 1765.

With a variety of people and cultures came a mixture of languages and expressions normally associated with international seaport towns. Many people were bilingual, some speaking several languages, including Cajun and Creole dialects. Some emigrants spoke only their native language. Others spoke Creole and Cajun words and phrases in addition to a common, regional English which included such phrases as "cut it half in two" (meaning to divide it equally), "hose pipe" (garden hose), "It's hot today, yea" (It sure is hot today), "crawfish paws" (crawfish claws), "I'm wore out, me" (I'm tired), and "buy a bread" (buy a loaf of bread).

Blacks in the area added another dimension—a sort of *patois*—to the local language by using a vernacular that allowed them to refer to Whites in the third person undetected by Whites. For example, "Miss Ann" meant "White woman," "the gray boy" or "Mr. Charlie" meant White man, "meet the mule" meant going to work, and "selling the mule" meant going into debt. Pig Latin (*Ig-pay'atin-lay*) was practiced mostly among teenagers and was used effectively to give messages to each other undetected in the presence of adults, especially their parents who did not understand this "strange way of talking."

Our family maintained contact with a substantial number of people from communities surrounding Donaldsonville, such as Darrow, McCall, Modeste, Abend, Lemanville, Barton, Smoke Bend, White Castle, Napoleonville, and practically most all other settlements within a twelve-mile radius. At that time, the lack of automobile transportation limited the distance and direction one traveled. Sunday afternoon rides to Smoke Bend in Grandpa Ogeese's horse-drawn cart were among the highlights of our preteen years. Grandpa and Grandma Annette and several of their Johnson grandchildren would visit with close friends and relatives there: the Leon Rodrigues, the Isaiah Johnsons, the Jancy Pinkinses, the Evelyn Billys, and others. We all welcomed and enjoyed the cool water and fresh milk stored in quart jars in the well of Jancy Pinkins and the chance to grind corn into grits and meal using Uncle "Buddy" Rodrigue's grist mill.

In our immediate neighborhood, we maintained close association with friends and neighbors: the Helen Mitchells, Cliff Josephs, Clarence Josephs, Arthur Augustas, Leatha Graves, Walter Ricardos, Lawrence Hubbards, Frank Brooks, Norah Leavings, Russell Leavings, and others. We believe all of these people played positive influencing roles during our developing years.

One of Donaldsonville's most famous persons was Pierre Landry, who was born in 1841 on the Prevost plantation. Records archived at the Amistad Research Project located at Tulane University in New Orleans provided this account:

> The Prevost plantation was located in Ascension Parish and had one of the largest slave populations in Louisiana that revolved around the sugar industry. Landry was the son of a white plantation laborer Roseman Landry and Marcelite (Prevost) Landry, a slave and cook on the Prevost plantation. He had two younger siblings, Antoinette and Julian.
>
> In 1854, Landry was sold in a public auction to the Bringier family. This family was very prominent in Louisiana during the antebellum period. They owned 35,000 acres of land in several Louisiana parishes. Landry was educated on the Bringier plantation in their primary and technical schools. He also received private instructions from Reverend W. D. Goodman and Reverend A. L. Atkinson during this time period.

Water Well

After the Civil War in 1866, Pierre Landry moved his family to the town of Donaldsonville, Louisiana, which had the third largest black community in the state. Within his first year living in Donaldsonville, he founded two black schools, constructed a house for his family, and conducted a prosperous business, becoming an influential leader in the black community, as well as in Ascension Parish. He served the community in various roles including as a lawyer, architect, judge, superintendent of schools, juror, tax collector, president of the police jury, parish school board, postmaster, and justice of the peace. In 1868 he was elected mayor of Donaldsonville and served for a one-year term. Landry was the first African American to hold a mayoral position in the United States. That same year Landry formed a self proclaimed faction of the Black Republicans Party in Ascension Parish. He established this faction in response to white carpetbaggers from northern states.

In 1872, Landry ran for a seat in the House of Representatives in the state of Louisiana, with the help of Blacks and a significant number of white voters he won the election by a landslide. During his term in the House, he created numerous bills in support of African Americans, one of his more important victories came when his bill passed to establish New Orleans University, which became the third Black private college in Louisiana. In 1874, he was elected state senator where he served until 1880. During his term, he was one of two black members to dine with President Ulysses S. Grant in 1875. Landry also serves on the Ascension Parish School Board, served as a member of the police jury, and edited a Christian paper, The Monthly Report, during his term as senator.

Landry began gradually relinquishing his control of the Republican Party and increased his duties in the Methodist Church. He became pastor of St. Peter's Methodist Episcopal Church in Donaldsonville 1878. He was elected presiding elder at the Baton Rouge District in 1881. Landry was then elected presiding elder of the Shreveport District in 1885, and in 1889 he became pastor of St. Paul Methodist Episcopal Church in Shreveport. At the annual Methodist Episcopal conference in 1891 he was elected to the highest position in the Methodist Episcopal Church, a Presiding Elder of the South New Orleans District.

Landry served as a principal and dean of several high schools, including Gilbert Academy in Baldwin, Louisiana from 1900-1905. Gilbert Academy was a nationally recognized school that had its beginning in 1885 as an agricultural and industrial college for recently *emancipated Blacks. The college had been under the administration of the Methodist Episcopal Church and, in1919, the school merged with New Orleans University, and was renamed Gilbert Academy High School.*

Racial relationships, like in most other southern towns, have come a long way for our region from the White Only and Colored Only signs in doctor's offices, hotels, public restrooms, and restaurants, signs that were explicit reminders that Blacks were relegated to second-class citizenship. However, there were exceptions to the negative racial rules of the time. There were neighborhoods, such as ours, where Blacks and Whites lived in relative harmony, lending a hand or an ear or a dollar when needed. Our family and other Black families within a radius of six blocks from our house shared excellent relationships with most White families, including the Acostas, the Belefores, the Capellos, the Capones, the Dominiques, the Mattassas, the Morrises, and the Rivets. Without these kindhearted people and others like them, the road to national desegregation would have been continually filled with barriers.

Life was different for Blacks who worked and lived on the plantations. Lloyd Edwards, a native of Assumption and a retired teacher and industrial plant department manager, talked about a standing rule that was enforced at the Church Plantation located on Highway 308 between Plattenville and Napoleanville in Assumption. Every day during the work week near five o'clock in the afternoon, bells would ring throughout the plantation, and the foreman would ride around on his horse to warn Blacks who did not live and work there, "The gates will be closing at five. Make sure you're gone by then." Like so many so-called sundown communities throughout the Jim Crow South, these rules made it clear that any nonresident Blacks who remained on the plantation after dark could be subjected to harassment or worse.

Occasionally, a racial slur in the community would result in a fistfight among young people. Racial insults among adults were not uncommon, usually with the Blacks being on the receiving end. In cases where fistfights resulted, it was usually the Black who was charged with violating some "peace code," which was enough to cause the violator to spend at least a few days in the city jail, a situation which was dreaded by most. The occasional sound of the leather strap biting into a body and piercing screams and pleads for mercy were convincing enough for the passersby to fear ever going to jail.

Rev. Thomas talked about an incident during the early 1930s when the post office in Saint James was robbed. "The sheriff and his men came with the dogs to my daddy's house. They searched the house looking for evidence from the robbery but found nothing. But they took him to jail anyway where he stayed for thirteen days, then they released him. Although the postal system came under the jurisdiction of the federal government, the handling of this case by the local sheriff's office went unchallenged." Rev. Thomas added that two of his brothers who were living in California at that time wanted to sue the sheriff for the false arrest; however, their father chose not to pursue that option, and with good reason: such action would have resulted in the father being ordered out of the parish, forever.

Several other people told of racially motivated incidents where Blacks were severely mistreated by Whites. Edwards described a case where his uncle, John Edwards, Jr., was severely beaten in College Park and left on a trash pile by several White men. A White family passing by found him and called the sheriff's office. Edwards stated that his uncle suffered brain damage that resulted in recurring seizures for the remainder of his life. The beating resulted from a love triangle where John Edwards and a prominent White man were suitors for the hand of the same Black woman.

A more serious incident was described by Rev. Lloyd Wallace. "During the early 1960s, I saw a Black man hanging from the middle of the Labadieville Bridge. He had been accused of raping a White woman. A group of White men went to his house and dragged him outside. They beat him, gouged out his eyes, shot him, cut off his genitals, tied them around his neck, and hanged him on the bridge for everyone to see. Years later, a White man on death row in New York City confessed to the rape. He said he had dressed in black face when he attacked the woman but said he could not die with that issue on his conscience. The city gave the victim's family $2,000 in reparation."

A story involving a candidate for sheriff in Assumption who was friendly with and well liked by Blacks throughout the parish was related by Mrs. Worley. "Because of this good relationship, however, some White parish residents built him an expensive house as an incentive for him to stay out of politics. They didn't want a sheriff who catered to Blacks," she explained.

As a teenager, one of my Saturday evening routines included stopping by Nelson's Playhouse after a movie and meeting a girlfriend and several other mutual friends for sodas, chatting, and dancing. Eventually, I would walk her home where we would spend fifteen to twenty minutes talking on the steps (her father was very strict!), then I would leave for my house across the bayou. One such evening as I walked home, I approached a small bridge over a ditch at the same time a White couple approached the bridge from the opposite direction. I could see their faces by the streetlight behind me. The man was obviously intoxicated, as the woman held on to his arm, assisting him in walking. I stopped on my side of the bridge to allow them to pass. As they stepped across the bridge, the man looked at me and loudly mumbled something as he swung to hit me. I moved back and his swinging motion threw him off balance and he fell into the ditch. He yelled, "You bloody nigger!" or words to that effect. I knew I would be in trouble if I tried to help him and I thought he might be carrying a gun, so I started running to my house that was only two blocks away. My instinct, however, guided me in a roundabout way so that no one would be able to follow me home. I ran seven blocks, almost circumnavigating my house, arriving there from the opposite direction after walking the last block so as not to draw attention. Everyone at home was asleep when I arrived, and I quietly and quickly undressed and slipped into bed. At about that time, the police sirens started and continued for about ten minutes.

I learned the next day at school that my friend Preston Landry had left his girlfriend's house on my side of the bayou about the same time I left my girlfriend's house from his side. He was walking to his house on the opposite side of the bayou when he was stopped by a White man who brandished a pistol and asked him where he was coming from. At that time, another automobile arrived; and when the driver, another White man, recognized Preston as the son of Ulysses Landry, Sr., who the man knew as a fellow worker at Leo Cafiero and Company, Preston was allowed to proceed to his house.

As an afterthought, I suspected Preston was stopped for two reasons: first, I had left the scene of the incident with the drunken man, running in the direction where Preston was stopped; and second, although he was a bit taller, we carried a similar build and complexion and both wore a moustache, all supporting the well-used saying, "They all look alike to me."

The Black Business Community

St. James Parish

"During the 1930s, Jamestown was the center of activities in Saint James Parish. Attractions in the town included two grocery stores, a service station, two nightclubs, two dance halls, and a baseball park," said Carrol Cayette, a Jamestown native and retired U.S. Army lieutenant colonel. All of the businesses mentioned were owned by people of color.

The Ernest Cayette, Sr., family was a typical Creole family during the Depression years. The members consisted of father Ernest; mother Alphfosine; oldest son, Arthur Johnson; followed by Ernest, Jr.; Ida Mae; Carrol; and Harden. Each family member remained employed during those years when most people were without jobs. The family relied on a strong work ethic that sustained them even before the Depression years. Cayette explained, "My father, Ernest, Sr., was widely known for his entrepreneurial and diverse talents. He managed all aspects of a building that housed a bar and grill equipped with slot machines, a dance hall with a jukebox, a barbershop where he worked as the barber, and a cigar-making shop. My mother was known as a 'wise person' and was a certified midwife.

"I worked in the cigar shop along with Ernest, Jr.; Harden; Ida Mae; and sometimes our mother, stripping and drying tobacco leaves imported from Dominican Republic, Cuba, Kentucky, and Virginia. Our father was a licensed cigar-maker who actually molded and shaped the cigars in a press with twenty molds. He made two types of registered cigars, *Owl Special* and *Red Bird*. It was then my job to wrap the cigars in cellophane paper, and Harden completed the process by placing on the label band containing the name of the cigar and the location of the factory. Two drivers would deliver the cigars to locations throughout the area, including Baton Rouge and New Orleans.

"Uncle Jack Cayette was the manager of the ferry boat system that carried passengers across the Mississippi River from Battaux on the west bank to Convent, the parish seat, on the east bank. The one-way charge was ten cents for each passenger."

St. James Parish Black businesses were located in most of the larger towns and villages. In addition to the businesses mentioned by Cayette, Calvey's Grocery Store was located in Jamestown. Movies were shown at the Bee Hive Hall in Jamestown. There were also Murphy Winchester Barbershop, Murphy Winchester shoe repair shop, John Cayette Drycleaners, Paul Calvey Grocery Store, and both Paul Calvey and Wallace Calvey, brothers, owned separate rice mills in Jamestown. Other businesses included beauty shops (Carol LeBeouf, Brookstown; Lillie Gubre, Vacherie; and Ermiley's in Lutcher), another barbershop (James Gordon's, Lutcher), and a dry-cleaning shop (Jack Wallace's, Lutcher).

Ascension Parish

One of the oldest businesses and the first mortuary in Donaldsonville (Ascension) is the Donaldsonville Marble and Granite Company. It was established in 1875 by Telesphore Francis, a Black businessman, who provided services to both the Black and White communities. Although Francis started his business in a stable, he built his first workshop in 1885 in the location known today as the Protestant Cemetery on Saint Patrick Street. Francis was the sexton for both the Ascension Catholic Cemetery and the Protestant Cemetery. He hired a German immigrant to cut inscriptions and designs by hand. Both sons, Willie and John Francis, were also talented at this craft. As part of his services to the public, Telesphore Francis rented his three large black Arabian horses that pulled a beautifully designed hearse for all funerals that ended in the two cemeteries.

According to *Our Roots Run Deep: A History of the River Road African American Museum*, by Dr. Thomas J. Durant, Jr., Willie Francis, Sr., the second oldest sibling of the family, born November 16, 1889, later took over the family business and developed it to great heights. W. A. Francis, Sr.'s children, W. A. Francis, Jr., and John Francis, took over the business in 1946 and carried on the legacy left by their father. Willie Francis, Jr., operated the business until 1973. John Francis went on to master the brick masonry trade, which he taught all of his sons. Willie Francis, Jr., became a master of the stone, vault, and tomb business. He perfected his craft and taught all of his sons valuable skills and a career of notable distinction. His youngest son, Stanley Francis, was one of the recipients of the trade secrets that were transferred down to the fourth generation of the Francis family.

Stanley Francis, Sr., began working with his father while he was in high school. During the earlier years, their work was devoted primarily to designing and hand-producing memorials for cemeteries. As an apprentice, he received training in the shop in every aspect of the business, including trade administration. "In addition to learning the trade, my father instilled customer service and excellence in everything you do. He believed that these features were vital and necessary parts of any business and insisted that they were incorporated in our daily work," he said. In discussing the types of work they accomplished, he mentioned several memorials that the company created in Donaldsonville, including the Veterans' Monument located in the Louisiana Square (Town Square), the Fort Butler Monument, several large monuments in the Ascension Catholic Cemetery, along with cornerstones at many of the area churches. He stated, "We also built a monument to a great musician who educated many teachers who taught what they learned from the famous Claiborne Williams." Together, he and his father constructed a new building in 1973 in order to provide for a larger work space and an indoor display room.

The father of two children, Stanley Francis, Sr., inherited the monument portion of the business from his father in 1976. His brother, William Francis, who has two children, inherited the concrete vault section, now known as Mount Olive Vault Company in Donaldsonville.

Stanley Francis, Sr., is the manager of the business along with his wife, Gayle, who creates computer graphics, designs, and inscriptions for memorials and monuments. When asked if either of his children or his brother's children were interested in maintaining the family business, he said that his children were not presently interested; however, he hoped that some family member will come forward to keep alive the legacy of the Telesphore Francis family that began over one hundred years before.

Also in Donaldsonville, much like all other towns in the region, talented Black craftsmen and craftswomen were available to do almost everything imaginable in the home, some for a small fee. There was Joe Batt, a house painter and wallpaper hanger; Angie Leavings and Margarite Ricardo, cooks and bakers; Joe Smith, maker and seller of a unique popcorn and peanut confection; Pa Sam Clark, woodcutter and salesman, vegetable gardener and salesman, and dray team delivery service; Isiah Johnson, horse and buggy vegetable salesman; Ferdinand LeBlanc, house painter; Manual Lewis, moss gatherer and salesman; Eli Simms, butcher; Bessie Woods, kindergarten and piano teacher; Ms. Frazie, midwife; Martin LeBlanc, carpenter; Magnolia Ricardo, seamstress; Rev. James W. Ricardo and sons, Joseph and Walter, all construction contractors; and Cousin Edith, a nurse.

Henry Frazier and Vic Arthur, jitney taxi service, had clients in Donaldsonville; and George Mulberry's Taxi Service served the greater Gonzales area.

Rev. Mansfield Lawson's was the only shoe repair shop in town and served everyone in town and the larger surrounding area. Hambrick Funeral Home (Darryl Hambrick) and Purple Shield Funeral Home (Robert Lawson and Oscar Rawlins) served clients in East Ascension and East Saint James; Brazier's Funeral Home and, later, Demby & Son Funeral Home served Ascension, Assumption, and Saint James. Butler's Funeral Home (Modeste) had clients in Iberville Parish as well as in Ascension and Saint James.

Several barbershops were located in Gonzales: Stewart Barber Shop and Holmes Barber Shop (Wilbert Holmes), Modeste (Alfred Chatman), and Donaldsonville (John Schomberg, Homer Richard, and Mickey Landry). Beauty shops were operated by Mildred Dupard (Modeste), Holmes Beauty Shop (Brenda Holmes), Berdie Dominique, Sadie Schomberg, and Christina LeBlanc (Donaldsonville).

Dry-cleaning shops were operated by Earl and Sarah Nixon (Nixon Cleaners) and Herbert and Mable Bea (Busy Bea Cleaners) in Donaldsonville.

East Ascension Parish

Harold Hambrick, Sr., started in the funeral home business at an early age, beginning his official training immediately after finishing high school. He passed the state Board of Embalmers and Funeral Directors examination in 1941, the same year he married Mary Ellen Clark Hambrick.

At the age of twenty, he became the manager of Campbell's Funeral Services branch office in Clinton, Louisiana. He was also manager of the East Louisiana Burial Insurance Company. His funeral director's job was interrupted a few years later when tuberculosis caused him to be hospitalized for seven years. During his rehabilitation, he became a professional photographer and soon took a job as a medical photographer at the Southeast Louisiana Hospital in Mandeville.

After a successful career in medical photography, Hambrick moved his family, which had grown to five children, to California for better educational opportunities. While in Los Angeles, he worked for the Los Angeles Police Department and Los Angeles International Airport. Religion and civic responsibility were important in Hambrick's life, and he was actively involved in his church and children's education.

He met the Rev. Martin Luther King, Jr., and was involved in the civil rights movement through his church, Victory Baptist Church, which was the headquarters for the Western activities of the Southern Christian Leadership Conference (SCLC).

In 1969, he returned to Louisiana after being recruited by Purple Shield Funeral Service and Life Insurance Company in Gonzales. He was named manager of the year twice.

He established Hambrick's Family Mortuary in 1973, and his new facility opened in 1975. As a carpenter, Hambrick did most of the construction himself, and his son George designed the plans for the business.

Mary Ellen Clark Hambrick, cofounder of the mortuary, was a licensed practical nurse for fifty years. She was the first Black nurse at the local public hospital and eventually worked at the two area hospitals, the Hansen's Disease Center in Carville and local nursing homes. She was a home health nursing supervisor and trained nurse's aides.

[The senior Hambricks have passed on since the business started in 1973; however, all of the Hambrick siblings are involved in the family business. Darryl took over the reigns of the family business after his father's death in 1991. He returned to town after a successful career with a California securities exchange firm and also operates Hambonz Piano Room in Donaldsonville. Donald, who returned recently after a law career, helps with the business and is involved in many community service projects. Harold, Jr., who worked in public relations for thirty-seven years, is an accountant, business consultant, and CEO of the Los Angeles Black Business Expo. George, who still lives in Los Angeles, is the executive vice president of a research and software development company. After leaving IBM, Kathe returned to Ascension Parish after her father's illness and became the founder and executive director of the River Road African American Museum in Donaldsonville. She served as the national president of the Association of African American Museums.]

Assumption Parish

Most Black businesses in Assumption were reported as "slow" during the Depression years and as "thriving" in practically all years following, including the war years. Some of the businesses scattered throughout the parish during the 1930s through the 1960s are noted below:

> Dry-cleaning shops were owned and operated by Joseph Blanchard (Napoleonville), Risley Muse (Paincourtville), and Ernest Nelson (Napoleonville);
> The "motto" for Dan Coleman's barbershop (Labadieville) was, "Shave and a haircut, two bits!" Other shops were operated by Willard Parker (Bertrandville), Bud Sheffie (Napoleonville), and Lawrence Skidmore (Napoleonville);
> Two blacksmiths served the parish from Bertranville (Moses Williams) and Labadieville (Arthur Granger);
> H. P. Williams was the owner of the funeral home in Bertranville that bore his name. Years later, the business was known as the Williams & Southall Funeral Home. Bedman Charles worked for the T. X. Landing Funeral Home, a White establishment, he worked only on Black remains, however;
> Katie Whickham was the director-owner of the Whickham Beauty School and Salon in L'il Texas, located near Napoleonville; and Groovardy Pollard of Labadieville was known as the "ice man" who sold ice in the greater Labadieville area.

Lafourche Parish

Small Black businesses in Thibodaux provided services and goods mostly to the Black community. Taxi service was provided by three cab owners (Frank James, Mike Dubois and Isaac "Papa" Jones). Dubois also provided ambulance service. These taxi drivers traveled to New Orleans several times each week transporting residents to doctors appointments "because Blacks were treated badly on the Greyhound busses," said Irvin Jones, a native and resident of Thibodaux.

Within a year after the Depression began, Nolan Billups built the Nolan Billups Cleaners on Lagarde Street in Thibodaux in 1930. His was the first Black-owned cleaners in the parish. The shop was managed by Billups, assisted only by his wife, Bettie, for a number of years. The business developed a comfortable customer base after the Depression; and having the business mind that he did, he built a second dry-cleaning shop in Houma, some twenty miles south of Thibodaux. The Houma enterprise was managed by Harold James. The two men worked closely together, and occasionally, Billups would travel to Houma for a day or two helping James with backlogs and would return home each day to work in the Thibodaux shop. By this time, business was reportedly "booming" in Thibodaux. However, the shop was destroyed by fire several years later. As he became older, Billups sold the Houma shop to James, allowing him to dedicate his entire time to the Narrow Street shop that he had built onto his house.

Billups was well known throughout the community. He was constantly working and, according to his daughter, Vaneesa Billips Evans, a confirmed workaholic who was dedicated to customer service. "Customers would call or knock on the door after closing hours or on Sundays, knowing that my dad would willingly open the shop to help them out," she said. Her dad would pick up and deliver clothes each day of the week. He was known for the heavy starch and fine creases he would iron into jeans that would allow customers to wear them three to four times, sometimes with some crease remaining in place. Her father was a member of the Freemasons, and her mother was an Eastern Star member. They both were also members of Allen Chapel Church.

Nolan Billups, Jr., was working full-time in the shop when his father died in the early 1970s. Nolan Billups, Jr., and Vaneesa Billups assumed ownership of the business, with Billips, Jr., becoming the manager. According to his sister, Nolan Billups, Jr., "was well-liked in the community, even more well-liked than our dad was. He was an astute businessman, and the business boomed because of him. He had a way that attracted people; everybody loved him. He was a member of the Kingsmen Club that was affiliated with the Mardi Gras krewes. He was indeed a special person."

Other Black businesses that provided goods and services in Thibodaux included these:

- Irvin's Barber Shop (Irving Jones) that served the community since mid-1970s.
- Blacksmith George Robinson, known for excellent service, was well respected by area Whites who also used his services;
- The Harlem Theater, owned by Paul Hill, also the owner of the Mayfair Club;

- Four dry-cleaning shops that served the entire parish and were owned and operated by Nolan Billups (opened in 1930), Wilson (1935), Hanny Jones (1938), and Jessie Joseph (1955);
- Joseph Stone, Dennis and Williams, and Southhall funeral homes that provided mortuary services throughout Lafourche, Terrebonne, and Assumption;
- Sharecrop farmers included James Grant and Willie Williams;
- Two restaurants operated by Rezona Lee and Mrs. Antonia Hill's Mayfair Club, the latter opening in the early 1930s; and
- The first general store opened by Joe Gilbert during the early 1930s.

The Cuisine: A Merger of Culture

No matter where you go on this planet, the mention of Creole and Cajun cooking will normally get anyone's attention. Those who have sampled it will eagerly talk about its qualities. Those who have only read or heard about it will try to satisfy their curiosity by questioning the "what," "why," and "how" of dishes such as gumbo, jambalaya, and crawfish *bisque* (stew). Now, just as during our childhood, most of us still enjoy the foods in our households as they were prepared one hundred years ago.

References are made to a merger of cultures in South Louisiana as being responsible for the notoriety associated with its cuisine. Several distinct nationalities and cultures shared in developing certain foods. In and around the Mississippi River—Bayou Lafourche Area, the Spanish, the Italian, the American Indian, the French, and the Negro. The Creoles and Cajuns added two additional dimensions to the uniqueness of the cuisine. Although all foods were savored, it was the Creole and Cajun cultures that most influenced the ingredients and methods used in preparing the foods that most area people cooked and enjoyed.

History is filled with stories about the important role food has played in all cultures since the beginning of time. However, in the case of Creole and Cajun cultures, food is perhaps the most talked-about social subculture.

South Louisiana, and certainly the quad-parish area, held three distinct farming advantages over other areas in the state: (1) extended growing seasons; (2) rich, fertile soil; and (3) warm, humid weather, all of which were necessary for growing vegetables and herbs and spices.

Family at Table

What We Savored and Enjoyed

Like many mothers of the day, ours operated the household on an extremely fixed budget. Yet on a typical day, she demonstrated magic in providing three meals a day for a family of eight for about fifty cents. Much of our food was homegrown and right from our backyard, the gardens of Grandpa Ogeese's, Uncle Eddie Pinkins, or neighbors and friends. In addition to green and yellow vegetables including *peppergrass*, we ate rice, dried beans, jambalaya, Irish potato stew, fried chicken (homegrown), crawfish dishes and other seafood, stews, gumbos, and soups. Gravy was made for many dishes to extend the quantity and add flavor, and was usually served over rice. Stews were made from chicken, beef stew meat, *sweetbreads* (hog organs such as hearts, kidneys, lungs, pancreas, etc.), and *trimming*, the strips of lean cow belly. Tripe simmered in tomato or brown gravy served over rice was simply delicious.

During the early 1930s, our family had several cows (one at a time) that provided fresh milk and cream that measured four to five inches in the top of the milk bottle. We made clabber and cream cheese for the household. Uncle Eddie Pinkins and Noah Leavings later supplied our milk for a small price when our cattle-raising days ended.

We bought commercial food items from one or two of the neighborhood grocery stores. Our mother's shopping list would be easy to remember: ten cent portions of coffee, sugar, dried beans, rice, and two loaves of French bread. These items would be supplemented with chicken or salt meat that was on hand. Given our mother's instinct for using herbs and spices, we all enjoyed her meals. She made Sunday meals special with fried chicken or pot roast, homemade soup or okra gumbo, *petits pois* (tiny green peas), potato salad complete with homemade mayonnaise, rising bread, candied sweet potatoes or sweet potato bread, or bread pudding, tea cakes, or hand-cranked ice cream. The food could not have been better!

An abundance of fresh foodstuffs in the Pinkins's household gave Grandma Annette what she needed to be the excellent cook that she was. Her ingenuity and the availability of local herbs and spices provided her family with endless mouth-watering dishes. Her catfish-head *court bouillon* (stew, "'coo-be-yon") and her garfish *boulets* (bullets, "bu-lay") always resulted in guaranteed good eating. The cornmeal dumplings in mustard greens and blackberry dumplings that she fixed brought lasting memories of pleasant dining. The pot likker from the mustard greens was as much a prize as the dessert that followed. A demitasse of freshly made coffee with chicory that ended the meal was the crown fit for any king.

The Secret? The Roux and the Seasonings

The foundation for many routine and special dishes was the *roux* ("roo"), the basic gravy for soups, gumbos, pot roasts, smothered liver, court bouillon, and seemingly, everything. Although a simple-looking procedure, even master cooks were careful to ensure the mixture did not burn or even become too brown. There was a fine line that separated a perfect roux from a burned roux. One's total attention was needed for this most important part of the cook's responsibilities.

Spices and seasonings used in making gravies and other dishes included *shallots;* celery; green and dried onions; garlic; red, white, and black pepper; parsley, bell Peppers; and *sassafras,* all used in balanced abundance. Tomato paste or tomato sauce was used to make red gravy. Gumbo was simply not eaten before *filé* ("fee-lay") was added. The filé thickened the gumbo and added extra spice to the dish. Red pepper and garlic were used freely in preparing most meat dishes, and most of the herbs used were grown in backyards.

Another important aspect of food preparation were the pots and pans used in the process. For rouxs, sauces, and gravies, the heavy iron skillet and Dutch oven were basic utensils found in practically every kitchen.

The basic roux was made in several easy steps:

Ingredients:

1 heaping teaspoon shortening or lard
2 rounded tablespoons all-purpose flour

After melting the shortening or lard, the flour is added, stirring in a circular motion until the mixture becomes dark brown in color. Because the burner must be hot in order for the ingredients to become the rich brown color desired, much care is needed to prevent burning. Once completed, spices and other ingredients are added to vary the taste in making sauces and gravies for which South Louisiana is now famous.

CURTIS J. JOHNSON

When the roux foundation was in place, the cook was ready to build on the remaining steps in creating a distinctly delicious dish.

"Sangaree" and Other Refreshing Beverages

With both the temperature and humidity hovering high on the charts from June to November, many ways were sought to cool and refresh the body. Air conditioning had not yet come to the area during the early forties, and few electric fans could be found in houses. Some people complained that using energy for a cardboard or cloth fan simply added to the body heat. Cool, soft rainwater found in shaded cisterns was always refreshing. Sipping a glass of iced lemonade was another way to cool off.

Next to lemonade was cool fresh milk. Stored in iceboxes or water wells, fresh milk was a staple in most households. Other beverages in our household included homemade root beer, sodas (occasionally), and punch made with leftover syrup from canned fruit. As noted earlier, sangria, or "sangaree" as we called it, was a special beverage that was sold at fish fries or served on special occasions. Hot eggnog was served only at Christmastime, making it even more special.

Freshly dripped coffee with chicory was enjoyed by most adults and some children. As children, we enjoyed *café au lait* (half coffee, half milk, "ca-'fay-olay") at breakfast time. Most adults sipped a cup of hot coffee throughout the day, hot temperatures notwithstanding. It was traditional to serve coffee to visitors, neighbors, or anyone who dropped by. The most delightful aroma of freshly brewed coffee was enjoyed in our community from morning until late at night.

The Great Gumbo!

Not since the invention of potato chips by a Black chef in 1865 has an appetizer been so revolutionary as gumbo. It was also served as a main dish for years in most area families. That tradition continues today.

If you ask any of the older cooks for their recipe for gumbo, you'll probably get a typical "I just add what I have on hand" response. That is precisely what our mother did as did most mothers in creating a pot of gumbo. Starting perhaps with a chicken or turkey carcass, ingredients were added to make one of the most famous dishes ever.

Seasonings

CURTIS J. JOHNSON

The word *gumbo* actually comes from the Congolese word *guingombo*, which literally means "okra." Okra is used in the recipe to add taste and color and to thicken the dish. In gumbo dishes where okra is not used, filé is added as the thickening agent. Most cooks used both.

Our family made filé from leaves of the sassafras tree just as the Choctow Indians in South Louisiana did centuries before. The leaves were dried thoroughly on the hot tin roof of the shed. On a flat surface, we used a rolling pin to crush and pulverize the brittle leaves to a powder. The finished product would be bottled and became our filé supply for the winter, and to be shared with other family members and neighbors.

Gumbo came in many variations: shrimp gumbo, sausage gumbo, filé gumbo, chicken gumbo, okra gumbo, seafood gumbo, and combinations of any of these. All of these gumbos were served over rice.

One word of caution about making gumbo: it is best prepared in a porcelain pot to prevent it from turning a dark, unappetizing color.

Lost Bread, Rising Bread, Corn Fritters, and Flap Jacks

Just as in many other countries, bread has long been a staple in the American diet. In our neighborhood, the aroma of hot loaves from the local bakery—even after the bread had been delivered to neighborhood grocery stores—caused one to wonder how anything could smell so appetizing. Even stale French sliced loaves had a special place at the breakfast (and sometimes supper) table in the form of *lost bread,* also known as *Pain Perdu* or French toast.

The notion that breads were at their very best when freshly baked was common throughout the region. Family cooks and bakers took great pride in their ability to bake breads to share with neighbors as well as for their dinner table. They knew that a lot of care went into the process, and care required time. The wood stove with its oven did little to make baking chores easier, let alone time-saving.

A good portion of the five or six hours our mother spent preparing, cooking, and serving meals each day was devoted to preparing some type of bread: flap jacks, corn fritters, biscuits, corn bread, or rising bread (yeast bread). Making the perfect match with these items in our household were the homemade preserves (figs and pears), home-churned butter, and cane syrup from one of the area's sugar refineries.

Seafood Platter

CURTIS J. JOHNSON

Savory Poultry and Dressing

We "grew" (raised) leghorn chickens for eggs and Wyandottes, Yellow Buffs, Dominics, Plymouth Rocks, and Rhode Island Reds for meat. Much of the time, the chicken inventory in brooders and on the yard would exceed a hundred, in different stages of growth. Eggs were selected with care for setting hens, and baby chicks were treated with special care. Startena and Growena were names for the chicken feed folks used until the chicks became spring chicken size. They were then fed cracked corn. In spite of the large flocks we had, some would be lost to heavy rains, cold weather, disease, and occasionally, to scavenging rats or possums. Some of the spring chickens were fried for meals while some were left to replenish the flock. Hens would be used in their second year for stewing or gumbo.

We had many meals of fried chicken and biscuits, chicken that was finger-lickin' good long before Colonel Sanders introduced his famous recipe.

In our family, we used several methods for killing chickens, including wringing their necks and chopping off the head with a hatchet. Our brother, Walter, I believe, invented a third method that we used successfully for years. The process involved throwing a three-foot length of broomstick at the flock while kneeling. If he aimed carefully, he broke at least one neck with each throw. Although this method may have been looked upon as inhumane, it worked well, and we considered it expedient at the time.

We also raised ducks and geese from time to time, fowl that was prepared for special holiday meals.

Crawfish and Seafood

A small lobster look-alike, the crawfish has for many years provided the basis for the most unique-tasting dishes in Louisiana. History has it that during earlier times, Indians guided their *pirogues* (canoes, "'pee-row") through the bayou networks in search of the delicate-tasting crustaceans.

Prepared in a variety of ways, crawfish were plentiful and free for the taking. Men would travel to some hot spots down the bayou and return with sacks filled. The catches that could not be used for one or two meals, since refrigeration was limited, would be shared with friends and neighbors.

The crawfish were washed thoroughly in clean water, scalded, and the tails peeled for cooking. A favored dish was a stew made with the tails and claws, a roux, several herbs and spices, and some of the fat shaken from the head of the crawfish. Fried crawfish, boiled crawfish, crawfish stew, crawfish bisque, crawfish gumbo, crawfish *étouffeé*—all of these dishes are still considered a treat by South Louisiana natives and the unseasoned visitor as well.

The Mississippi River, Bayou Lafourche, the ponds, lakes, and other bodies of water provided catfish, shad, sac-a-lait, turtles, *choupique*, gar-like fish, shoo-frogs, buffalo, gasper goo, and other fish indigenous to the area. River shrimp were plentiful and preferred by some people over saltwater varieties. Shrimp from the Gulf of Mexico were also plentiful and inexpensive. Likewise were crabs that were taken from the lakes near places like Thibodeaux, Pierre Part, Raceland, and the gulf.

Hog Killing Days

Several men in most communities were known to be skilled butchers, and whose skills were in high demand from approximately December until April. Each butcher may have had a different flair, perhaps, but were expert at not only the slaughtering phase but the butchering, crackling-cooking, and headcheese—and sausage-making phases as well.

Our family raised at least one hog each year in our backyard and usually scheduled the killing so as not to interfere with the school schedule. Uncle Eddie (Pinkins) was our butcher, and my siblings and I were excited about being his helpers. Almost everyone helped by

- catching the blood and stirring it with a large spoon to prevent coagulation before making red *boudin* (sausage made with hog's blood, herbs, and spices, "boo-'dan");
- heating and pouring water over the carcass to aid in scraping away the bristles;
- cutting the belly fat into small chunks (to render lard and cracklings); keeping the fire going under the huge cast-iron wash pot used for cooking the cracklings;
- chopping and grinding green onions, celery, and bell peppers for red and white *boudin* (sausage made with hog's liver, herbs, and spices), and regular sausage;

- boiling and picking meat from the head to make hogs head "cheese"; and more.

Hog-killing days were as exciting as Christmastime, and almost as enjoyable. Traditionally, portions of the fresh pork were wrapped and delivered to family members, immediate neighbors, and a few friends. It was customary to eat practically the entire hog except for the bristles. Even the hooves were used to make "tea" for various illnesses. The heart, lungs, kidneys, tail, feet, and of course, chitterlings were all *gourmet* food to us.

Hog killing in Saint James included clever ways of preparing and storing the meat and sausages. Herman Nicholas stated that there were traditionally two "killings," one at Christmastime and the other during February. He explained the storage process for sausage and meats as follows: "After the sausage was prepared, we would hang the strings of links from the clothesline and, periodically, pricked each link with a pin to allow the fat to drain into a pan. The next step entailed coiling the strings of links in a large tin can and packing the can with lard made from cooking the cracklings to prevent spoilage. The various cuts of meat for salting would be placed in large tin cans and covered with a generous layer of salt. After several hours, we would drain off the liquid that was drawn out of the meat and add more salt. This process was continued until most of the liquid was extracted from the meat."

Another locally made "favorite" sausage, andouille ("ahn-do-wee"), is made of chopped pork, green peppers, onions, and other choice seasoning stuffed in casings made from the stomach and large intestines of the hog.

Mirliton and Other Vegetable Dishes

Called "*cho-cho*" in the Caribbean and "alligator pear" in South Louisiana, mirliton ("mel-e-ton") was a sought-after vegetable that is shaped like a pear and tastes like summer squash, but better. It remains a favored vegetable in our family. A pleasing feature about this squash is that it is vine grown and requires only a trellis (or fence or tree) to support its vines and fruit. Equally pleasing is that two crops were usually harvested from the same vines each year. No mother had to admonish her child to "eat your vegetables" when mirliton was served.

Hog Killing Days

CURTIS J. JOHNSON

A versatile support dish, rice was served with stews, gumbos, in casseroles, and as main dishes such as "dirty rice" and jambalaya. Dried beans were not served as frequently as rice but seldom without the white staple companion. Red beans and rice, white (navy) beans and rice, pintos and rice, limas and rice, black-eyed peas and rice, crowder peas and rice, field peas and rice: all combinations that graced our dinner table.

We planted and "dug" sweet potatoes. We supported Kentucky Wonder pole beans with stakes from young willow trees that grew along the river's edge. The aligned rows of red tomatoes, light green lettuce, dark green spinach, creamy white scalloped squash, purple eggplant, red and green beet tops, and multicolored honeysuckle trailing on fences gave the family garden the rainbow quality that was always pleasing to see. Composted horse and cow manure was the fertilizer we used. The manure, coupled with just the right amount of rainfall and warm temperature, accounted for a perennial cornucopia of super quality fruits and vegetables. Surpluses were canned in Mason jars to serve during the cold months when most fresh vegetables were not available.

As children, red-ripe tomatoes taken from the vine and dipped in a light salt and black pepper mixture (in your hand) was a tasteful treat, especially while standing next to the plant. A baked sweet potato was an inviting snack at any hour of the day or night, and homegrown peanuts roasted in the fireplace during chilly winter nights were always welcome.

Pralines, Tea Cakes, and Homemade Ice Cream

It is said that the praline was invented during the seventeenth century by a French pastry chef in the chateau of the Plessis-Praslin. As the story goes, one day the chef noticed a kitchen boy nibbling on almond bits and scraps of hardened caramel syrup from the bottom of a used dessert pan. The chef was so impressed by the idea that he made up a confection from these ingredients that was served at dinner that night. It made such a great hit with the guests that the chef quit his job at the chateau and opened a sweetshop featuring the praline, which was named after his employer.

The French influence, in concert with the other cultural influences in South Louisiana, accounts not only for the many known gourmet dishes but also for the array of pies, cakes, cookies, tea cakes, and other pastries. Joe Smith's popcorn-peanut block, our sister Carolyn's pralines, Angel Leavings's cinnamon rolls, our mother's bread pudding, Marguerite Ricardo's decorated shortcake cookies, and our aunt Henrietta's pecan fudge were all products of these cooking influences that would be challenging if not impossible to match anywhere in the world.

Homemade ice cream was another "highly celebrated" dessert. Volunteering for the ice cream detail gave us a chance to taste the product when the freezing process was completed. When the crank became too difficult to turn, the container was opened to check the rising frozen custard for possible overflow or to test to ensure saltwater had not seeped in during the churning. Everyone agreed: the best-tasting ice cream, however, was the spoonful sneaked from the paddle while our parents weren't watching!

Crawfishing or Catching the Mud Bug

Jo Stafford sang of "jambalaya, crawfish pie, filé gumbo." Either of these South Louisiana dishes would be menu items at special events or anytime at the family dinner table. Crawfish dishes were passwords to good eating. And crawfish were free for the catching.

Crawfish, or crayfish as they are biologically known, were plentiful in the region. "*Mud bugs,*" as they were called by some, not only provided food for the table but also served as an income source for some. Generally, crawfish were found on the edges of ponds or ditches where water remained year-round.

In the spring, homemade and commercial crawfish nets were placed in locations where crawfish were known to thrive. As in crabbing, the nets were placed at the bottom of the water. After a short waiting period, nets were slowly raised, with one or more crawfish clinging to the bait tied to the bottom of the net. Commercial fishermen used baited wire cages similar to shrimp traps and salted shad for bait. Water sources for catching crawfish were the rice fields in Peytavin, although the edges of ponds and ditches were respected breeding areas. The crawfish season extended from June to mid-September. Following the rice harvest, the fields retained much of the water that had been used for irrigation; and combined with the residual rice stalks, the dormant water provided ideal breeding grounds for the crustaceans.

Crawfish

We used a simple trapping system: two people walked abreast in a rice section, moving slowly through the shallow water, flushing the crawfish to the other end of the section where the crawfish would attempt to cross over the three-foot-wide dirt barrier. Here, they would be quickly—and carefully—snatched up and tossed into a croaker sack or metal bucket in one swinging movement. Lightening fast, the crawfish claws were strong, and the larger ones could draw blood from a finger that was slow in moving out of danger.

As the summer came to a close, the shell of the crustaceans hardened, and the females began to lay eggs that would provide the *crop* for the next year. The crawfish began to burrow into the mud for winter, remaining there until early spring when the waters began to warm. Crawfish would again be seen seeking food near the shoreline and edges of ponds and ditches that, in turn, signaled the start of another season.

Health Care and Home Remedies

An influenza pandemic spread over the country during the fall of 1918. My older relatives recalled "people dying like flies." Hundreds of households in our area were affected in some way by the dreaded illness. The Pinkins family was not spared the inevitable tragedy. Two of our mother's sisters, Lydia and Laura, died from the flu, nine days apart. On the night of her death, a conversation between Aunt Lydia and Grandma Antoinette was witnessed by a third family member who captured the conversation in writing so that the other members would know that "Lydia had made her peace with the Lord."

Not only was our area impacted by the Spanish flu, as it was called, it caused the deaths of millions of people around the globe. American soldiers were said to return home from World War I during the fall of 1918 and through the spring of 1919 "in time to die from the flu."

Health care services for Blacks during the 1920s, 1930s, and 1940s were limited to occasional visits to doctors' offices in cities and towns and by doctors making *house calls,* that is, going to the patients' home to provide treatment in the more rural areas. There was at least one White doctor in most towns who also served the communities surrounding the town. In larger towns and cities, more than one doctor was usually available to accommodate the larger number of patients. Mostly families that were able to pay out of pocket for services or were members of *benevolent* societies or clubs sought services from doctors.

Black Medical Professionals

There were also a few Black medical doctors and nurses located in the quad-parishes during this same time. Dr. John H. Lowery was one of three Black medical doctors who served Black communities in the Ascension area during the 1920s and 1930s. Although his specialty was pediatrics, he also provided services to family members for routine medical needs.

The other medical doctor in the Donaldsonville area was Dr. Luther C. Speight, Sr., who was also a Methodist preacher. His son, Luther C. Speight, Jr., was an educator in Donaldsonville and Bogalusa. Drs. Ellis Williams and Kevin Stevens served the Black communities in the Prairieville-Gonzales area.

The Brazier Drug Store located in Donaldsonville was owned and operated by Dr. Sidney Brazier, pharmacist and businessman. During the late 1930s, he started the Brazier Funeral Home. His wife, Emily, owned and operated a beauty culture school and salon. According to Mrs. Olevia Batiste Rogers, a native of Donaldsonville and a retired high school teacher from the Chicago Public School System, "The drugstore soon became a tourist attraction with the addition of the beauty school that created the ambience of a big city salon. This exposure gave additional vibrancy to the prominent Railroad Avenue, where most of the town's businesses were located."

According to records at the African American River Road Museum in Donaldsonville, Dr. Emma Wakefield, a native of Thibodaux, received her medical certificate from the State Medical Board in 1897. She was said to be among the first women to study medicine and the first Black woman to receive a medical diploma. Her performance on the medical examination was one of the best recorded. Rev. Wallace noted that one Black medical doctor, Dr. George C. Bryant, served the entire parish of Lafourche and a large client base in Assumption during the mid-1920s. The first football stadium at C. M. Washington High School was named after Dr. Bryant.

In Saint James, Dr. Ernest Ezidore established his practice in the Lutcher and Gramercy areas and served patients in both the east and west banks and parts of Saint John Parish. Octave explained a unique system that was established in Saint James to alert the itinerant doctors who made house calls. "The family that needed medical attention would tie a white cloth on the gatepost. If the needing family lived down a lane, the family would tie a white cloth on a post at the entrance to the lane and again at the gatepost where the sick person lived. It worked every time," he said.

Practically every community had a midwife who primarily delivered babies. However, some would also treat the sick in communities where trained medical personnel were not available. Carroll Cayette, a native of Saint James, stated, "White doctors seldom delivered babies in the Black community. This was done by midwives. Doctors were called on when birthing problems arose. My mother was one of those who delivered babies, charging $3 per head." In the Donaldsonville Area, Ms. Frazee was one of the best known midwives in the business.

According to the 1936 book, *History of the Town of Napoleonville* by Sam K. Gilbert, a report by the Assumption Public Health Unit noted, "Health services were provided by Mrs. Stewell, Parish Nurse, who mostly gave shots at Saint Vincent Society Hall. A special colored nurse, Marguerite White, R.N., paid by Social Security, has been detailed to work exclusively among the negroes [sic] of the Parish" (p. 40). There were two Black registered nurses who accompanied children to the Charity Hospital in New Orleans to have the children's tonsils removed. These were Mrs. White and Mrs. Stevens.

<u>National Negro Health Week</u>

Worley shared a copy of an article that appeared in the *Napoleonville Pioneer* issue that was dated March 17, 1934. The article was entitled "National Negro Health Week" and read as follows:

> *The week beginning Sunday, April 1st and ending Sunday April 8th has been designated National Negro Health Week and the United States Public Health Service has called upon us to assist in carrying out this program throughout the whole country.*
>
> *This period is important not only to the negroes [sic] alone but to our white people as well. They are in our very midst, in many instances in our very homes as servants and nurse maids for our children and it is but the part of self protection, to say nothing of the betterment of the negroes [sic], that we try to improve their health. Not alone are they in our homes but they are in and [sic] the stores and other public places, we rub elbows with them in a hundred ways that we scarcely notice, so*

it therefore falls upon us as duty to them as well as to ourselves to assist in every practical way to improve their health conditions.

The prevention of disease as well as the curing of the sick among them should be one of our first concerns, for only too often disease starts among them and spreads to our own homes as well as among the laborers in our families. So, let us one and all take an interest in the National Negro Health Week, April 1st to April 8th.

> P. M. Payne, Director
> Assumption Parish Health
> Unit

Black public schools marked National Negro Health Week by having visiting nurses from the Public Health Service show training films featuring stories about tuberculosis, mumps, and chicken pox and advice about what families should do in the event children contracted these diseases. The nurses also distributed several mimeographed health-related handouts. Periodically, students at Lowery Elementary and High Schools in Donaldsonville were treated to short skits on the seven food groups recommended by the government as essential for good health. In one such second-grade skit, I played the role of Freddie Fresh Bread and held a cardboard cutout of a loaf of French bread that was my height with holes for eyes, nose, and mouth. I had about ten words to say, but seeing all the students and teachers as I stepped onto the stage made me forget several words in the script.

Our mother had no medical training whatsoever; however, folks from our community would come to our house to get her at all hours of the day and night to care for a sick relative. She treated children as well as adults and the elderly using the home remedies noted below. People would come for her late at night to care for someone who was very ill or thought to be "on their dying bed." In the case of the latter, she carried a small mirror in her purse to check the sick person's breathing by holding the mirror directly under the patient's nose. A foggy mirror indicated that the person was still breathing. Although many offers were made, she refused to accept money for the help she provided. Some folks "paid" her with chickens year-round and pork during hog-killing season.

Home Remedies

The medicine man who healed with herbal remedies was revered in Africa, in Turkey, and on the reservations of Native Americans and elsewhere. Perhaps for the same reasons used by those natives (knowledge, cost, availability), people in our area, including our family, depended largely on native herbs for medicinal purposes. The saying "What goes around comes around" is truly applicable here. Many people today are turning to herbs as the natural cure for many common ailments.

Beyond iodine, castor oil, Epsom salt, and rubbing alcohol, little commercial medication was to be found in medicine cabinets. Most bathrooms did not have cabinets anyway. A large wooden cigar box or small dried apricot or raisin boxes served adequately.

Herbs native to the area and simple household items were used effectively in treating many health problems for adults and children: chest and head colds, colic, rheumatism, fever and aches of all kinds, and cuts and bruises. In spite of the area's notoriety for herbs in the cuisine, more were used for home medical problems than for cooking. Some of the more commonly treated ailments and the herbs and home remedies used in counteracting them were these:

Chest Cold: ~ Application of beef tallow or Vick's salve rubbed into the chest area and laying a piece of heated flannel cloth on the chest
~ Steaming sassafras root tea
~ Lemon tea with tallow
~ Several drops of coal oil in a spoonful of sugar

Stomachache: ~ Peppermint tea
~ Baking soda or baking powder in water
~ Steaming sassafras root tea

Diarrhea: ~ Chewing (and swallowing) several lumps of Argo starch

Fever: ~ Plantain or elderberry leaves soaked in cold water or vinegar and applied to the forehead
~ Solution of vinegar and baking soda applied to entire body in a rubdown

Indigestion: ~Baking soda or baking powder in water

Constipation: ~Dandelion tea, cooked peppergrass

Colic: ~ Rubbing fresh garlic on the throat area

Chicken Pox
Sores   ~ Application of sulfur mixed with lard

Mumps: ~ Rubbing throat area with oil from canned sardines

Although most ailments were taken seriously, one injury in particular was treated with attention and concern. Foot cuts on rusty metal and stepping on rusty nails brought about special care to prevent lockjaw. The clean and simple tetanus injection today was preceded during earlier years by a ritual that took more time and effort but worked well just the same. Rust in wounds was known to be deadly and was well respected in every household. The treatment featured *smoking* the wound.

The cut or puncture was cleaned with coal oil, turpentine, or rubbing alcohol. The next step—the smoking—was primarily done by using a joint of dried cane reed, one end dipped in coal oil and lighted. The flame was doused after a minute or two, leaving a slow-burning smoke-producing pipe through which the smoke traveled to the wound. The process took eight to ten minutes, with an occasional hot foot resulting when the reed was held too close. After the smoking, a thin piece of fatty, salted meat was applied to cover the area, wrapped with string and left intact for four or five days. Of course, substitute measures and ingredients were used. When the reed was not available, a hollow, dried length from an elderberry tree worked well. In the absence of salt meat, a thin layer of creosote applied to the bandage was used. A second readily available substitute was a wad of moist tobacco, which was thought to have "pulling" powers to rid the wound of its infectious potential. This "pulling" sensation was actually felt by the patient, and provided release of tension in cases of lockjaw.

Catching the common head or chest cold for some people was as certain as the changing of the seasons. Occasionally, the medication would vary, but the eventual "knockout punch" was castor oil. Nothing tasted worse than a tablespoonful of warmed castor oil! Peppermint candy helped to neutralize the aftertaste. Later when the family budget

Medicine Cabinet

CURTIS J. JOHNSON

allowed, a glass of orange juice mixed with the castor oil made the ordeal somewhat tolerable. The best feature of having a cold was staying home from school for a day to facilitate the repeated trips to the outhouse and the tender, loving care given by our mother.

In our family, each member had to have a "spring cleaning." The memory is still vivid of our father preparing a pitcher of cold lemonade, lining up the drinking glasses near the pitchers, and stirring one teaspoonful of Epson salt in each glass, a treatment that tasted bitter and caused diarrhea. As the warm spring days approached, each child would warn the other, "Don't let Daddy give you a glass of lemonade—unless you see him make it!"

Faith Communities: Baptisms, Wakes, and Funerals

In addition to religious and spiritual practices and teachings, the church served as the center for social, educational, and cultural growth for the people of the communities as well. The church-sponsored programs and activities (Sunday school, Sunday and weekly religious services, some with breakfasts and dinner following, prayer meetings, Bible study, committee meetings, youth programs such as BYPU (Baptist Young People Union), church revivals, church anniversaries, pastor's anniversaries, and various ministries providing community help and others) were also considered "social" opportunities that brought people together. Churches served as the first school facilities for Blacks throughout the region. Some churches also featured youth athletic programs, summer camps, and sponsored Boy Scouts and Girl Scouts Troops and Cub Scouts and Brownie Scout Dens.

Regardless of the religious denomination, practically all churches sponsored and encouraged clubs that were designed mainly as fund-raisers to support church ministries, programs, and other purposes. The Board of Trustees, the Deacon Board, or similar governing body suggested fund-raising for other church needs beyond regular church service collections.

As an example, at my family church, Mount Triumph Baptist, there were three or four clubs that competed to raise the most money during a given period of time. Names like *Willing Workers, Star of David,* and *Sunshine Circle* were used to motivate their members to work hard every other month to sponsor a fund-raising chicken dinner, fish fry, or penny party, where everything on the menu cost from one to five cents and games were played. These activities also served as the only social outlet for many area people.

Our maternal grandmother, Annette Pinkins, was a pious and devout Christian. She was a founding member of Saint Catherine of Sienna Catholic Church that was built in Donaldsonville in 1925. She was active in the Saint Ann Society and the Altar Society, organizations whose members maintained the various linens used on the altar and other places in the sanctuary and vestments worn by priests and altar servers. On late Saturday afternoons, she cut beautiful flowers from their garden and sent them by my older sisters to the women who decorated the altar at Saint Catherine's for Sunday masses.

Before Saint Catherine, there was no separate Catholic church for Black parishioners in the Donaldsonville area. Blacks attended the Ascension Catholic Church on Mississippi Street, where they were directed to sit in the back of the sanctuary. Because of abuses from White church members, especially the youths who threw trash and spat on them from the choir loft, Grandma and her family left the church, refusing to be subjected to continuing indignities. The family began attending services in the Baptist community. It was between that time and the start-up of Saint Catherine Church that our mother and several of her siblings were born into the Baptist faith. My siblings and I were, in every sense of the words, *brought up* in the Baptist community.

"St. James Catholic Church was the only Catholic church in the parish," said Octave. "Pews were *sold* to parishioners at $10 to $25 per year. People who didn't have that kind of money would be charged 10¢ each Sunday. The last two pews in the back of the church were designated for Black parishioners. However, when the church was full and more Whites came in, Blacks who had not paid the 10¢ would have to give up their seats to the Whites and stand in the back of the church," he concluded.

There were several religious rituals that stood out as features of the black community. Chief among these were Protestant public baptismal ceremonies in the Mississippi River, wake services, and funerals for those of all faiths. A significant number of Black Catholics made up the religious community, although the vast majority of Blacks were Protestants, with the Baptists having the highest numbers of that group. These denominations differed in their rituals; however, there was a common spiritual bond that tied them closely together.

Batiste-Rogers recalled the excitement of tents being erected on Second Street (Babin Alley) and Elizabeth Street in her community. She said they knew that Mother Cook and Reverend Jackson were about to begin their sanctifying services. "The air would become permeated with sounds from tambourines and drums and songs and dancing," she added.

Baptisms

The Mississippi River was the source of the baptismal water for most Saint James and Ascension Protestant churches that were within walking distance from the river. Some churches had fonts built within the sanctuary for the baptismal rite.

Baptisms were held on Sunday morning. Our family church was located six blocks from the river, which became our site of choice. On the day before the event, several leaders of the church would prepare the baptismal site by staking and roping off an area near the river for safety. Following a special early-morning church service, the baptismal processional, led by the pastor with the candidates dressed in loose white gowns and centered among the church elders, stewardesses, and choir members, would begin walking toward the river. Interested bystanders joined the procession along the route, all singing appropriate hymns as the group moved slowly through the streets and over the levee.

Upon arriving at the water's edge, the pastor blessed the proceedings, as scripture readings, prayers, and songs were expressed according to the baptismal rite. Joined by a deacon in waist-deep water, the pastor spoke from the book of Matthew about the trek of John baptizing in the Jordan River. As each candidate was led into the water, the hymn "Let Us Go Down to Jordan" was sung. The pastor would place his left hand on the candidate's back and, raising his right hand to the heavens, say, "Obedient to the Great Head of the church, I now baptize you, Sister Gomez, according to your word, in the Name of the Father . . ." While holding the candidate in the small of the back with one hand and using the other to cover both the mouth and nose of the person, and with the aid of a deacon, the preacher submerged the entire body momentarily, quickly bringing the person to their feet. The crowd expressed shouts of "Praise God!" and "Yes, Lord!" Another hymn was started as the newly baptized was led from the water. The next candidate was then led to the preacher, and the process repeated. Dripping and chilled by the water, the baptized were wrapped in blankets and taken home to prepare for their first noon church service as a new Christian.

Baptism Scene

CURTIS J. JOHNSON

Wakes

Death seemed to have had a particular advantage over many people since it was not clearly understood. To say that it was the final stage of life would not be convincing to most Christians, who believed in the hereafter. It is perhaps because of these and other reasons that sympathy was showered on the family of the dead. A black bow was hung on or near the front door of the house, signaling the death of a family member. The bow remained in place until the day following the funeral.

The ritual of wakes followed a tradition of many years of showing respect for the dead, of "staying *awake* while the dead slept," the old folks would say. Tales of dead people coming back to life in the funeral parlor or during church services would spread around communities periodically. In any event, the all-night ritual was the order, being another form of social expression practiced for years in the Black community. Where the dead had held membership in one of the benevolent societies, members of the society were assigned three-or-four-hour shifts to assure members remain awake all-night with the dead.

Catholics held wakes in the home of the dead. The Rosary prayers, led by the priest or close family friend, were recited by members representing the Holy Name, Saint Ann, Sodality, and Altar Societies. In the Protestant community, wakes were conducted in the home or the church.

Following the evening services for Protestants, light refreshments were served. As a general rule, meat was not served at wakes as a matter of respect for the dead. Cheese and crackers and coffee were the usual fare. The aroma of coffee with chicory and evaporated milk was a constant reminder to those remaining after eleven o'clock that a refuge for the living could be found in the kitchen annex. And there were those who preferred the more "sociable" refreshments. They could be seen heading to the neighborhood beer garden periodically to be "refreshed."

Funerals

A traditional method of notifying a community of the death of a resident was the pealing of a church bell in a slower-than-normal cadence. The bell tolled once in about every 6 to 8 seconds, continuing for about 5 minutes. It was important in the Black community to learn about a death quickly, and that funeral arrangements be made as soon as possible. There was a good reason for this.

There were no undertakers in the Black community during the early-to mid-1930s; therefore, embalming service was not available. "Consequently, a body would have to be buried within twenty-four hours after death," said Rev. Thomas. "Shortly after death, the body would be washed by family members and the individual would be dressed in church clothes. A wooden coffin would be brought to the house where the body would be placed and carried to the church for the wake. A funeral would be held the next day. The cost would be something like $27, at least that's what my daddy's funeral cost," he added.

Funerals were extremely sad occasions. In the Catholic community, the service began with the pall (a large white cloth) being placed on the casket, followed by an appropriate prayer by the priest. A reading from the Old Testament and one from the New Testament were read by the lector. The Gospel was read by the priest, followed by a homily (short sermon) that focused on the deceased and the family. Communion was then offered, followed by a prayer. Holy water was sprinkled on the casket, the concluding prayer offered, and a hymn sung as the casket was carried from the church. On average, the church service lasted about an hour.

The ritual for Protestants was extended and lasted from one and one-half to three hours, depending on "the kind of Christian life" the individual lived. The better the Christian, the longer the funeral, it seemed. These services were characterized by highly emotional eulogies and sad hymns that told about *a home in the sky, rest for the weary,* and *beyond the river*. The pastor would remind the family of former members who had preceded them in death, and how they would all be together soon, and what they would do when they all met in heaven. Most sermons were aimed at the kind of life the deceased had lived and what his or her final reward would be, regardless of the religious denomination.

All funerals were usually well attended. Almost everyone in a community knew each other, usually by name. It could be said that funerals were actually community services.

A listing of Black regional churches is below.

Aboveground Cemetery

St. James

First Baptist	Vacherie
First Community Antioch Baptist	Lutcher
Golden Grove Baptist	Gramercy
Greater Evergreen Baptist	Paulina
Hyliary Baptist	Vacherie
Israelite Baptist	Lutcher
King David Baptist	Lutcher
King Triumph Baptist	Lutcher
King Solomon Baptist	Lutcher
Lutcher Chapel United Methodist	Lutcher
Mt. Calvary Baptist	Brookstown
Mt. Olive Baptist	Jamestown
Mt. Olive Baptist	Paulina
Mt. Triumph Baptist	Chapmanville
New Zion Christian Center	Gramercy
Phillipian Baptist	Convent
Pilgrim Baptist	Convent
Pleasant Hill Baptist	Convent
Prevailing Faith Baptist	Lutcher
St. James Catholic	Battaux
St. James United Methodist	Lutcher
St. Joe Baptist	Lutcher
St. Luke Baptist	Moonshine
St. Matthews Baptist	Paulina
Youth Pilgrim Baptist	Convent
Zion Travel Baptist	Convent

Ascension

Christian Assembly Full Gospel Baptist	Gonzales
Do Right Baptist	Gonzales
Ebenezer Baptist	Darrow
Emanuel Baptist	Klotzville

First Baptist	Smoke Bend
First Pilgrim Baptist	Donaldsonville
Greater Mount Pilgrim Baptist	Donaldsonville
Hopeful Baptist	Gonzales
Hopeful Triumph Baptist	Darrow
Little Zion Baptist	Gonzales
Mt. Bethel Baptist	Abend
Mt. Calvary Missionary Baptist	Galvez
Mt. Gillian Baptist	Prairieville
Mt. Moriah Baptist	Abend
Mt. Olive Baptist	Darrow
Mt. Pilgrim Baptist	Donaldsonville
Mt. Salem Baptist	Donaldsonville
Mt. Triumph Baptist	Donaldsonville
New Mount Calvary	Modeste
Nazarene Baptist	Donaldsonville
New Saint John Baptist	Gonzales
New Saint Peter's Baptist	Darrow
Progressive Baptist	Gonzales
St. Catherine of Siena Catholic*	Donaldsonville
St. Luke African Methodist Episcopal (AME)	Donaldsonville
St. Mary Baptist	Modeste
St. Matthews Missionary Baptist	Donaldsonville
St. Phillip Baptist	Modeste
St. Paul Baptist	Gonzales
Second Mount Olive Baptist	Smoke Bend
Shiloh Baptist	Galvez
Shiloh Baptist	Port Vincent

* Blacks also attended Ascension Catholic Church during the earlier years, although it was a White church that allowed Black attendance.

Assumption

Bright Morning Star Baptist	Napoleonville
Canaan Baptist	Plattenville
Evening Star Baptist	Napoleonville
First Baptist	Napoleonville
First Israel Baptist	Belle Rose
Greater Israel Baptist	Belle Rose
Nelson Chapel AME	Napoleonville
Pilgrim Baptist	Paincourtville
Rose Hill Baptist	Belle Rose
St. Charles Baptist	Paincourtville
St. John Baptist	Napoleonville
St. Phillip Baptist	Labadieville
Virginia Baptist	Eveilville
Westley Methodist Episcopal	Napoleonville

Note: There were no Black Catholic churches in Assumption before Saint Benedict the Moor was dedicated on October 11, 1911. However, the following White Catholic churches allowed Black attendance:

Church of the Assumption	Plattenville
St. Ann	Napoleonville
St. Augustine	Klotzville
St. Benedict the Moor	Bertrandville
St. Elizabeth	Paincourtville
St. Jules	Belle Rose
St. Philemon	Labadieville

CURTIS J. JOHNSON

Bell Baptist	Thibodaux
Calvary AME	Thibodeaux
Morning Star Baptist	Raceland
Morning Star Baptist	Thibodeaux
Moses Allen Chapel Methodist	Thibodeaux
Mt. Olive Baptist	Gary
Mt. Zion Baptist	Larose
Mt. Zion Baptist	Raceland
Old Fountain Missionary Baptist	Thibodeaux
St. Joseph Co-Cathedral	Thibodaux
St. Luke Catholic	Thibodeaux
St. Paul Baptist	Thibodeaux
St. Peter Baptist	Thibodeaux
Third Zion Baptist	Raceland

Folklore: Customs, Traditions, Fads, and Superstitions

We all believed in stories about the pot of gold at the end of the rainbow, the tooth fairy, avoiding a black cat crossing your path, Santa Claus, and Ripley's Believe It or Not. We threw a pinch of spilled salt over our left shoulder to prevent bad luck, and during a thunderstorm, we always covered the mirrors in each room with sheets or blankets and sat quietly in a closed room. Covering the mirrors was thought to prevent the reflection of a lightning strike. Girls did not whistle ("Not a 'nice' thing to do!"). Umbrellas were not opened in the house, and hats were put anywhere in the house except on the bed. Some folks hung a horseshoe on a nail over the main entrance to the house for good luck.

Some of these beliefs were just as common in other parts of the country. On the other hand, there were some beliefs and behaviors that made South Louisiana a breed apart. The following is one such retelling of spectacular events, such as real-life ghost stories, as witnessed by respected community people.

Union Soldier at Door

CURTIS J. JOHNSON

Two people in our immediate neighborhood reported having "visions" in which they saw the ghost of a Black Civil War soldier standing guard over a buried treasure. One neighbor two doors away, Ms. Evelina Cross, told of frequent conversations she had with a particular Black Union soldier whom she saw standing next to her back door at night. She said he told her several times that a pot of money was buried in a certain spot near the place where he stood and that the money could be hers if she would dig for it at a designated time. She never tried.

Our immediate neighbors, the Elnora Cobb family, were similarly advised by a "ghost" who pinpointed the exact spot where they were to dig. They decided to attempt a dig and informed our family of their plan. (Their reason for telling us was so that no member of our family would make a "noise" during the digging, a condition mandated by the "ghost." At the designated time, we listened quietly at a window out of sight as the digging proceeded. Shortly thereafter, we heard sounds that resembled metal hitting metal, then the shuffling of feet, and running footsteps, followed by a door slamming shut. Then silence. Our curiosity was not satisfied until the next day when we were given a blow-by-blow account of what had happened. We were told that when the digging had reached about two feet, the shovel did hit a rectangular illuminated metal object resembling a small chest. Excited at seeing the chest, one of the two treasure hunters said something which caused the chest to sink deeper into the hole and out of sight. Immediately, they heard a loud noise ("like a windstorm") from the opposite corner of the fence at the back of the house. Looking up, they saw a "fiery bull snorting smoke" heading their way! End of expedition!

Voodoo Power

The power of voodoo (gris-gris or hoodoo) was well respected by most people, both religious believers and nonbelievers. Certain people in the area were said to have the power to place a hex ("fix") on someone, causing them grief, pain, sickness, and misery. Others were said to cast a juju or good luck spell. Similarly, still others were said to be able to remove hexes. These feats were available for a fee. Storytellers reported on endless mojo cases involving other causes.

There was a commonly accepted "protector" said to contain the power to ward off voodoo: pulverized brick. It was used to scrub down the wooden steps leading to houses. When asked, most people would deny any belief in voodoo. However, the number of households in the area with terra-cotta-colored steps told a different story.

Another commonly used protection was to burn a candle next to a lemon under the backdoor steps to ward off evil spirits. A chicken egg left on one's doorsteps meant that a "spell" of a negative consequence was intended for someone in that household.

As a rule, adults did not discuss "hoodoo" in the presence of children. Those who participated in this *art* often kept it to themselves. Local practitioners visited out-of-town service providers, or if service providers were local area folks, visits by practitioners would be made under the cover of darkness.

Nicknames

There were other customs and traditions that we recall as being regional and somewhat different when compared to places outside South Louisiana. One common practice was the use of a.k.a. names, or nicknames, usually a name that was used as the sole identity for many people in the community. Names such as Slim, Nonk, Snake, Tante, Cher, Ms. Shug, Tootee, and Ice Cart Joe were often used. It was surprising in many cases to learn a person's "real" name after a lifetime of calling him or her something else.

The Sociable Coffeepot

The Boston Tea Party was staged during 1773 in protest of high taxes and prices imposed by Great Britain. This action—dumping of a load of British tea into the Boston Harbor—gave birth to coffee that became the preferred drink for many. Long before the Party of 1773 however, coffee was enjoyed as a stimulating drink in northern Africa as early as the 7 BC. By the start of the twentieth century, the coffeepot had become the prize for social sharing on practically every kitchen stove in South Louisiana.

It was customary in most households to serve a *demitasse* of coffee with chicory in fine porcelain to visitors. The coffeepot was usually kept hot on the stove, prepared to refresh anyone who might stop by; it was shared by family members as well.

In our household, coffeemaking was a recognized ritual, taking up to twenty-five minutes to brew a small (quart) drip pot that required extra time because coffee grounds would swell when hot water was poured over them, clogging the drip holes in the basket where the grounds were held. Paper coffee filters were not yet in use, although some used cheesecloth for straining the dregs. Luzianne coffee with chicory was our chosen brand and type, the chicory adding to the brew a strong taste and a very black color.

I believe our parents were confirmed coffee addicts, as were most adults. For example, our father drank a cup of coffee at breakfast, took with him to work a quart-sized thermos for sipping coffee throughout the morning on the job, had coffee with lunch at home, finished the coffee left in the thermos during the afternoon, and had a fresh cup as soon as he got home from work in the late afternoon. He consumed several more cups before bedtime.

As was the case for children in many households, my siblings and I drank café au lait with French bread and homemade butter or fig preserves for breakfast many mornings.

Dress and Grooming

Hair that was not too kinky was considered to be "good hair," and thought to be in vogue, along with skin bleaches and other skin care products by Madam C. J. Walker and others. Women and girls used Lucky Heart products including Hi Brown Beauty Cream. Available hair products for men and boys included Royal Crown Men's Pomade, Murray's Pomade, and Dixie Peach Pomade. Pressed or hot-combed straightened hair was fashionable for women. Men who straightened their hair wore the conk, resulting from using a mixture of lye, egg and white potato.

For everyone, no formal outfit was complete without a freshly washed and starched handkerchief. Girls wore colorful ribbons in their plaited hair to accentuate their starched dress, while boys wore starched short pants or knickers. Girls and women carried purses. Men carried pocket watches that were suspended on gold chains and kept in either a vest pocket or a watch pocket located near the top edge of pants. Men and women wore hats year-round. When meeting women on the street, men greeted women by "tipping" their hat, that is, by touching the leading edge of the brim without removing the hat. On the other hand, some men removed their hat several inches from the head while bowing slightly to the lady.

Storytelling

Older people enjoyed telling stories about interesting events in their lives. Some specialized in humor while others enjoyed telling stories, including those about ghosts. Every neighborhood had a storyteller.

A part of leisure time was devoted to risqué storytelling by men of all ages. For instance, they told humorous and rhythmical tales about a Black man named Shine aboard the *Titanic* when it sank in the Atlantic on April 14, 1912, and how he out-thought the Whites on board and outswam the sharks. There were many versions of that story. One often heard in our community started this way:

> *Gather 'round boys and let's get drunk.*
> *I'll tell you how the old* Titanic *sunk.*
> *The fifth of May was a hell of a day*
> *When the seaport news at the seaport town*
> *Was that the old* Titanic *went oozing*
> *down.*

Of course, there was much more to the story, which was spiced heavily with profanity. Different people, each with a slightly different lean to it, would recite several versions of this story while Shine was the central character in each version. Ironically, there were no Blacks on board the Titanic as passenger or crewmen when the ship sank.

Everyone tried to outdo everyone else in telling stories. Other entertaining stories were about Stagger Lee (who was said to be good with the gun and known for pulling one over on the *ladies of the night*) and the Signifying Monkey (who used strategy to replace his lack of physical strength to overcome the elephant). Men (and boys!) also spent time *playing the dozens*: seeing who could make the gravest insult about the other person's mother. For example:

"Boy, why you so black?"
"'Cause I'm in mourning for yo' momma!"

Fistfights were inevitable.

Several neighborhood boys tried their hands at storytelling, as with an often repeated tale of being followed by a six-foot-tall black-and-white cow walking six feet in the air behind them. Those boys lacked finesse and were brushed off. However, serious storytellers told about bone-chilling events and experiences that had universal appeal. Most communities had at least one serious storyteller. We certainly did.

One evening when I was about age ten, our family welcomed Miz Jones, an older family church member and friend who was invited by our mother to a chair close to the fireplace that was vacated by one of the children. She was able to relate an event in such a way that captured the total attention of all the children, even the most active ones . . . and adults, too. However, her method of looking around and making eye contact with each child present made her story more convincing to the children.

On this occasion and after some polite conversation, she shared a couple of lightweight stories that I considered to be believable. Then she began talking about an old grizzled man who was 7 feet tall, as strong as an ox with his body covered with hair, and who despised children! I don't recall all of the details but by the time she finished the story, my heart was racing as if it was trying to vacate my body!

Miz Jones thanked our mother for the coffee and tea cakes, and bade us good night. Our bedtime was less than an hour away. When it finally arrived, the thing that totally occupied my mind was "Daffalee," the name of the man in the story.

My brother Walter and I slept in the dining room, and I chose to sleep next to the wall (of course!). Sometime during the night and after I finally got to sleep, I was awakened by something heavy across my shoulder. I slowly moved the covers back to move what I thought was Walter's arm when my hand came in contact with a hairy arm that did not belong to Walter. The Lord knows that I was scared out of my head! I slowly pulled the covers over my head and, after what appeared to be an hour or more, I somehow fell asleep.

The next morning when I awoke, the first thing I looked around the room for was the hairy arm that was no place in sight. I re-examined Walter's arms and, although they were a bit fuzzy with hair, they did not qualify as the arm I had moved away during the night. Miz Jones proved to me that she was indeed both convincing and fascinating; and I immediately excused myself from the room the next time she visited. I was still clearly remembering the Daffalee story!

Zoot Suit

CURTIS J. JOHNSON

Fads

Of course, there were fads common throughout the region, such as the following:

- Teenage boys (and some men well into their twenties) wearing colorfully dyed shoes (chartreuse, blue, orange, pink, yellow, and bright red!) and navy pea coats.
- Girls wearing saddle oxfords and penny loafers.
- Wearing the zoot suit with its long coat and trousers with baggy body and peg legs at the cuff. It was *the* fashion for young men during the 1940s.
- High school students, mostly graduating seniors, sought each other's autograph.
- Using expressions such as "Hey now!" "Honey hush!" "Well all reet, then," "Solid!" "Hit the road, Jack!" "Give me some skin," and "Ooh-la-la."
- Families saving S&H Green Stamps gotten with purchases from most stores to redeem substantial prizes from participating stores.
- Calling a friend "brother-in-law" ("'brud-n-law") meant that he was a *good* friend, sometimes closer than a blood brother.

Wood Cutting: An "Industry"

Woodcutters in Saint James, Ascension, and parts of Assumption occupied practically every foot of unoccupied space along the Mississippi River bank that was not private property. Many of these artisans made a living from this often-difficult occupation. However, woodcutting was respected as another skill required to develop a needed household product to fuel cooking stoves all year-round and fireplaces during winter.

Many cutters kept several logs on hand throughout the year, although woodcutting was done mostly during the cooler months, away from the hot sun. It was during the spring that most of the logs were caught as they traveled downstream with the current and were brought to shore for cutting into firewood. This time of year coincided with the melting ice and snow in Canada and the northern states that bordered on the river. The melt caused the river to rise far above its normal level, and with the rising waters came the logs, heading for the Gulf of Mexico.

As the logs passed our area heading downstream, men in *skiffs* (flat-bottomed boats) would row out to the channel, inspect the drifting log (hardwood was preferred), nail a rail spike into the log, tie on with a length of rope that was attached to the boat, and begin rowing toward the shore with the log in tow. Occasionally, large logs would be abandoned due to their excessive weight in the swift current. Most times, however, one person was able to tow in a log singlehandedly. Once into the bank area, the logs were then tied together by salvaged cable or chain and left just above the water's edge or pulled up onto the near-level landing by horse and capstan.

When horses were not available, two or three men would turn the capstan while a helper placed chocks behind the creeping log to allow the men to rest. In cases where the riverbank slope was excessive, several helpers with *peaveys* (lumberjack leveler) would assist the capstan in rolling the log to its resting place. Flat boards and timbers were used in cases when logs were pulled (rolled) up the bank to the cutting area. Once in place, the log would be leveled and shored up to a comfortable level for sawing from a standing position by one or two persons on a timber saw—one pulling as the other pushed, alternating these motions. Logs were cut into two lengths: one for fireplace and the other for cooking and/or heating stoves. The blocks of wood would then be chopped into desired chunk size with an axe and stacked in half-cord (four feet long and four feet high) and full-cord measures if the stacks were to be sold or stacked in any fashion when the wood was for home use. The stacking allowed the sun and the air to dry the wood cut from "green" or uncured logs to facilitate burning.

Often, because of the steep slope of the area, woodcutters used a "slide" to move the cut logs up to more level ground accessible to carts to haul the chopped wood away. A slide resembled a large wooden oblong box. However, instead of wheels, two boards were used as gliders, allowing the "box" to be pulled relatively easily by a hitched horse.

Each year, erosion ate away the river's edge, necessitating the gradual relocation of the operation higher on the bank to a new cutting area.

Other changes to the river occurred over the years. One such change was that people stopped drinking water from the Mississippi as we did after working up a thirst cutting wood. Raw sewage and other pollutants have precluded that for a number of years.

Man Chopping Wood

Another fuel source for some folks in Port Barrow was "the tipper." This specially built stationary hydraulic mechanism was used to tilt gondola railcars filled with coal so that their contents could be transferred to much smaller railcars that carried the coal to barges and ships to be used as fuel.

Coal was used for fuel in potbellied stoves and space heaters in school classrooms. It was the only fuel used in blacksmith shops due to its intensive heating capability to "soften" (make red hot) iron for it to be shaped into horseshoes, plowshares, and other farm and commercial implements. Some folks used coal for fuel in their homes. They were allowed to pick up the pieces spilled during the "tipping" process. The coal was free for the taking; however, it was quite dangerous as a fuel because it created potentially deadly carbon monoxide.

Neighborhood Grocery Stores

The corner grocery stores were daily shopping places for food and household cleaning and maintenance items for most families of the community. They were well stocked with familiar brand names: Clabber Girl baking powder, Luzianne coffee, Red Ball sugar, Kite and Bull Durham tobacco, Octagon soap, Wing cigarettes, and Argo starch, to name several.

One reason for the daily run to the store was the lack of controlled refrigeration in most households. The icebox was used for refrigeration, mostly overnight, until the food could be consumed or until the delivery of more ice the next day. The icebox was the center of attraction in most homes during the hot season. In some locations, such as in my family, the hero of the day was usually the iceman who delivered the ice to your porch or icebox, whichever you preferred. For ten cents, you got a twenty-five-pound block of ice that would normally last the average family until another delivery the following morning. On Saturdays, folks doubled their order for ice, since there would be no home deliveries on Sundays.

At one time, five grocery stores were located within six blocks of our house. Though inventories were similar, each store had slightly different specialties—or maybe it was the same products offered differently. Whatever the case, we frequented each of these suppliers during the course of several days for one thing or another.

Although some of our grocery shopping was done at the Capitol Store and Midway Store, our major purchases were made on Saturdays at B. Lemann and Brothers, the area's largest department store. It was a one-stop shopping oasis for families from miles around and featured dry goods, household appliances, hardware, and grocery departments. People came from Modeste and McCall, Saint James and Souvenir, Bell Rose and Paincourtville in jitneys and horse-drawn carts to shop for bargains in cane knives, coal oil, pretty dresses, space heaters, coveralls, horseshoe nails, Bay Rum, and other household and personal necessities as well as food products. B. Lemann and Bros. was especially noted for its payment system. Sales clerks throughout the store would place an invoice and the customer's payment into a wooden capsule that moved along wire tracks to a centralized cashier. The customer's receipt and change would be returned in the same manner.

Lagniappe: A Great but Bygone Tradition

"Lagniappe, please?" I asked as the clerk handed me the small bag of rice, two loaves of French bread, and change. In response, she smiled and handed me several pieces of hard candy. She and I had just consummated a tradition that was widely practiced in parts of South Louisiana.

Although some stores in our hometown did not give *lagniappe* ("lan-yap"), all of the stores in our neighborhood followed the tradition of giving a small treat when purchases were made. Each store's offering had a different twist: One gave several pieces of candy. Another would let you choose from several types of candy. A third sometimes used a combination of the two methods. Adults were given a small additional amount of the purchased item such as coffee, rice, and sugar "for good measure."

The treat was a welcome reward for children for walking two to six blocks during the scorching summertime sun for some staple item our mother needed to prepare a meal.

My favorite place for shopping was not a grocery store. Variano's Meat Market gave as treats small servings of white boudin. Yum!

Unfortunately, lagniappe is no longer a part of the Creole-Cajun tradition, fallen by way of cultural changes.

What a pity!

Seepage Water and Tadpoles

The communities in Saint James and Ascension that bordered on the Mississippi River were affected every spring by seepage water. My family lived a block and a half from the Mississippi River. From our front porch during the high water season, we could see the booms and smoke stacks of cargo ships passing by beyond the levee. Thousands of families from Canada to the Gulf of Mexico shared that experience. But in our neighborhood, high water meant the hatching of millions of tadpoles throughout the area closest to the river in the springtime.

Every year in the spring with ice and snow melting in the north, the water level of the river in our area rose high against the levee and water "seeped" into ditches and dry pockets and depressions throughout the area. Low-lying areas were practically inundated, and many home gardens were destroyed by the accumulation of excessive amounts of water over several weeks' time.

Tadpoles grew in the seepage water. Drainage ditches held water for extended periods and were ideal breeding beds for frogs. Clutches of tadpoles could be seen everywhere and in various life cycle stages. Children caught and placed tadpoles in jars filled with water, after punching holes in the jar top to allow for air. Much of their free time was spent watching the little entertaining swimmers move about the jars or ditches. It was not uncommon for a mischievous boy to slip a tadpole or two down the back of a girl's dress. Sometimes and with rare luck, when the animals were kept in containers larger than jars, one or two tadpoles would develop into frogs. The unusual thing about this transformation was that the tadpoles were fed breadcrumbs and other foods that a tadpole would probably never eat on its own. It was miraculous that they survived at all!

Seepage water also served as breeding grounds for the dreaded mosquitoes that swarmed throughout the area. Because many houses did not have screened doors and windows, mosquito netting was used to enclose the beds to keep the pests out and ensure a relatively peaceful night's sleep. In late evening, it was common practice to spray insecticide in dark corners and under beds, even in homes with window screens.

The seepage water usually remained for a month or more or until the water level in the river returned to normal. We surmise that this stagnant water that perpetuated infectious mosquito breeding was the cause of many of the people's ailments of the day.

CURTIS J. JOHNSON

Tadpoles to Frogs

Fish Fries, Chicken Dinners, and Penny Parties

An often-used fund-raising social was the selling of home-style fish and chicken sandwiches and dinners in every community. Community groups other than church clubs, and even individuals, sometimes used the events as a means of raising money for civic, social, and sometimes personal use.

Tickets for dinners were sold for a nominal price (25¢) each entitling the holder to a "fish plate," usually consisting of fried fish (catfish, buffalo, *gasbagoo*, or freshwater drum), potato salad, green peas, and a slice or two of fresh bread. Another option was a fish sandwich, containing fried fish and potato salad on sliced bread, with the price of the sandwich costing much less than the plate. The fish served was usually caught in the nearby Mississippi River or the many bayous and other tributaries located throughout the area.

The chicken dinner usually consisted of fried or stewed chicken, green peas, potato salad, rice dressing, and bread. If stewed chicken was served, white rice and gravy replaced the dressing. Take-out orders for dinners were honored only if the ticket holders brought their plate from home.

Like penny parties, different dinner sponsors offered varying menus. Some sold sweets as an aside: cake, fudge, pralines, popcorn balls, and ice cream, all homemade, of course. Beverages included lemonade, root beer, and sangria ("sangaree"). Occasionally, home brew was sold discretely. If there was a player piano in the house, anyone available would play; and frequently, a sing-along developed during the course of the evening. There was one thing in common about fish fries and dinners: they were known for their delicious food.

The penny party was another form of socialization that was eagerly anticipated in the community. These neighborhood socials were held on lawns or indoors, depending on the weather. Spring was the best time of year for these fellowship opportunities, with Sunday afternoon being the usual day and time.

Chairs and benches would be scattered about the sponsor's yard or house and porch to accommodate conversation and provide laps to hold refreshments. Girls wore starched dresses, colorful barrettes in freshly done plaits, and black patent leather shoes. Boys wore short pants or knickers with short-sleeved shirts and Buster Brown shoes.

The supply of party refreshments was provided by the sponsor, with each contributing their "best dish"—ever colorful, appetizing, and delicious. Folks would come supplied with pennies to buy coconut and pecan pralines, chocolate and vanilla fudge, plain and iced cupcakes, homemade ice cream, popcorn balls, and sangria for adults for five pennies per serving.

Penny parties provided games and refreshments while ensuring the sponsors several dollars for church clubs and committees. In some communities, some parties were known for specialties, such as Ms. Shug's gatherings that featured a record player for dancing. On the other hand, Lula Rodrigue and Alice Joseph's party foods were perhaps the tastiest. All parties featured games for children, a favorite being Pin the Tail on the Donkey. Each try at pinning the tail cost a penny, with the winner usually receiving a small "prize" or several of the goodies being sold.

Penny parties were usually held to raise money for church groups, benevolent societies, young people's groups, and personal family use. Sometimes, when a family experienced some misfortune (accident, home fire, or illness), penny parties were given by friends and neighbors to help the needy family.

My family's biggest enjoyment came with those parties given at our house. Since we did not have grass in the yard, it was the children's job to sweep the yard and *banquette* (sidewalk, "ban-ket"), hang lights (occasionally), arrange chairs and tables, and freeze the ice cream. Volunteering for the ice cream detail gave one the privilege of tasting the product once the freezing was done. When the crank became hard to turn, the container was opened to check the rising frozen custard for possible overflow or to insure saltwater had not seeped into the custard container during the churning process. We all agreed: the best-tasting ice cream, however, was the spoonful sneaked from the paddle.

Other Social Outlets . . . for Children

In addition to church-related activities, there were other social doings for both adults and children, mostly for children. Fishing and crabbing outings, weekend baseball, movies, and nightclubbing were among the options for grown-ups. Many of the children's games were traditional and not as regional as the language, food, and customs. Softball, jumping rope, seesaw, hopscotch, and several others were included in our choices.

Hopscotch

CURTIS J. JOHNSON

There were no defined playgrounds for Blacks in the regional communities except for those located on school grounds. "The sidewalk and street games proved to be the best locations for competitive sports. The drive to win caused us to be extra careful in choosing playmates for our teams. The difficulty and rules for these games would change each time we met which, of course, was almost every day. This was acceptable with our parents because they always knew where to find us," Batiste-Rogers added.

As children, some of our favorite games included these:

Throw the Peg

This game required two or more players, each with sharpened wooden pegs (stakes about twenty inches long and as wide as your hand could easily handle). The game required stiff mud to allow the pegs (pieces of stove wood sharpened on one end) to stick fast into the ground. The object was to throw down the peg into the mud to knock over another player's peg. The player who knocked over a peg would, using his peg, bat the fallen peg as far away from the site as possible. The player whose peg was batted away would attempt to retrieve his peg and stick it into the ground before the batting player had a chance to stick his peg into the ground three times. If the batted player was able to achieve this, he eliminated the batter who must wait until the winner of the next round is declared to again enter the game.

Belt Line

Normally a boys' sport, this game was considered more fun with six or more players who lined up in two rows about six feet apart. Each player in the rows stood about six feet from the next with a leather belt in hand. The objects: (1) a "loser" would run between the rows of belt swingers, dodging as many hits as possible (for obvious reasons!) and (2) the players with belts would try to smash the runner's rear end as hard as possible. All players would eventually become a runner, and the runners who could not take the hits gracefully were usually the ones getting the most direct hits!

Boys Shooting Marbles

CURTIS J. JOHNSON

Shooting Marbles

A circle with about a four-foot diameter was drawn on level ground. Two or more players with shooting marbles ("taws") placed one or more marbles in the center of the ring. The object was for each player ("shooter") in turn to shoot at the pile of marbles, knocking as many as possible from the ring during the player's turn. Should a player's taw remain in the ring while knocking out one or more marbles from the pile, the player continued to shoot until he missed, or his taw went outside the ring as marbles were knocked from the ring to the outside, or he missed hitting a marble from the ring.

Razoo was an added attraction to some marble games. Razoo was a chance for a poor loser to try to recover some of his losses. At the "right" time during the game, while a lot of marbles were still in the ring, the loser would shout, "razoo!" which gave him license to scoop up as many marbles from the ring as possible. All marbles then became the target for anyone who could reach them. Mostly fingers and pride suffered in the process.

Penny Pitch

Two parallel lines about three feet long were drawn about ten feet apart on the ground. Several players stood behind one line and pitched pennies toward the second line. The player whose penny was closest to the line after all throws was declared the winner and collected all pennies. (Of course, some players would even try to "razoo"!)

Hoop Wheel

Usually a one-person event (for young children), it involves a small metal wheel discarded from a wagon and pushed along by a bent clothes hanger. The hoop at the end of the wire made by the bending formed a track that propelled the wheel as long as contact with the wheel was maintained.

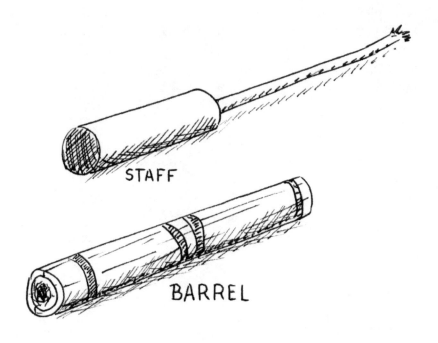

STAFF

BARREL

POPGUN

Pop Gun

CURTIS J. JOHNSON

Root the Peg

This game called for minimum imagination as several players tried to stick the blade of a jackknife with three open blades into a tree, log, or into the ground by throwing from a standing position. A variation of this sport was to spin the knife from one's knee with the other knee in the kneeling position to stick the blades into the ground. The player with the most "sticks" was the winner.

Pop Guns

These ingenious homemade toys were made with two components: a handle or staff and a barrel. The handle (plunger) was made from a length of mop (or broom) handle, a portion of which was carved to fit the barrel of the gun. Ammunition consisted of balls from the camphor (Chinaberry) tree.

The barrel was made from a length (six to eight inches) of elderberry branch with a diameter of about an inch. The core of the branch consisted of soft pulp that was removed by pushing a small metal rod back and forth through the barrel, forcing out the pulp. Assuming an eight-inch-long barrel, the handle portion was carved to a length to accommodate a child's hand, say three to four inches. The plunger portion was whittled down to fit the barrel with relative ease. The length of the plunger would extend to approximately one-half inch from the end of the barrel.

The staff portion of the handle was whittled with a pocketknife so that a good fit resulted when inserted into a corresponding length of elderberry "joint." A thin tassel was made by repeatedly scoring the end of the staff opposite the handle, and hitting the end with a blunt object to cause it to flare at the end. The resulting tassel formed an airtight vacuum to build up in the barrel when, after inserting one camphor berry into the full distance of the barrel, a second berry was inserted and thrust forward with the staff toward the first ball, propelling the first one toward a target with stinging force. The shooting caused a loud "popping" sound, thus the name, "pop gun." Small-scale wars with popguns provided youngsters with fun-filled but dangerous playtime.

Red Light

Another favorite game that was a big thriller for boys and girls was Red Light. One person turned their back to a small group of players, covering his or her face as he/she counted from one to ten. At the count of ten, the counting player (lead) would say, "Red light." The lead player would then turn quickly toward the other players to catch anyone moving after the announcement of "red light." Players caught moving would be eliminated. The object of the game was to become the last remaining player, who then became the leader.

Old Horse

A game of chance, the object was for one player to guess the number of pecans or peanuts or *jaw breakers* (a hard round candy) being held in the closed fist of a second player. The process:

First Player:	"Old horse."
Second Player:	"I'll ride him."
First Player:	"How many miles?"
Second Player:	(Guesses the number of pecans being held by the first player)

If the second player guesses correctly the number of pecans held, the first player is obligated to surrender the pecans to the second player. The obligation is reversed if the second player incorrectly guesses the number held. The players change roles after each guess.

Spin the Bottle

Spin the Bottle was a mature game at teen parties. The object was simple and easily achieved. Girls sat in chairs arranged in a circle. Each boy would be given a chance to stand in the center of the circle and spin an empty soda bottle on the floor. The girl who sat in the chair where the bottle opening pointed when the bottle stopped spinning became the object of a kiss by the boy in the circle. After each boy had a spin, they became sitters and the girls became spinners. If our parents had only known!

Boy Slapping Worn Tire

Other Pastimes

Boys made scooters from castaway roller skates and scrap pieces of lumber, while girls made mud pies and served them in plates and utensils they received from Santa during the previous Christmas. Girls also spent a lot of time with paper dolls and cutout clothing. Rolling used automobile tires was a fun thing to do for both young boys and girls. The children would enjoy "slapping" worn auto tires, running behind the tire, and keeping it rolling by hitting it with the open hand. Other games and sports included football, stick ball (ball often purchased with the coupons from Red Ball groceries), spinning tops, and an assortment of card games such as Spades, Tonk, and Pitty-Pat.

Entertainment facilities for teens were limited in most locations. "There were no teen designated facilities in Saint James," according to Octave. "There was a movie theater in Vacherie where Blacks were allowed to sit upstairs where it became very uncomfortable during the summer. Many teenagers took advantage of this when the temperature was more pleasant however," he stated.

Children were allowed to play on school grounds during nonschool hours in all parishes. In Donaldsonville, Nelson's Playhouse was the social center for teens. Practically all communities had at least one softball/baseball field.

Kite Making and Flying

Kite making and flying was one of the most enjoyable pastimes for boys, mostly, although a few girls made and sailed kites occasionally. Of course my sister, Edith, was one of them.

Kites were made in various shapes, sizes, colors, and for different purposes. The more talented folks used pictures of animals, Mardi Gras masks, and even life-sized self-portrait models.

Practically all of the supplies needed to make a kite were available at home or at our grandparents'. Kite making was as much fun as flying it, in my opinion. Walter taught me the art of kite making when I was about ten. We made several models together before I branched out on my own. He was five years older than I was and out of the kite-making business by the time he turned seventeen.

The kite described below was perhaps the simplest to make, and was the most popular model during my preteen years.

Boy Flying a Kite

Cypress fence pickets were the source for the wooden sticks for the kite frame. Pickets were readily available and were easily split to make straight thin strips for framing the kite. We used very thin twine for framing and flying the finished product. Paper served to cover the frame to keep the kite airborne, with the help of the wind. Two sheets of the Sunday funnies spot-glued onto the frame served the purpose and added color to the finished product. We made glue to attach the paper to the frame by adding a bit of water to about two tablespoons of baking flour. A tail made from strips of cloth tied together hanging from the bottom of the kite was used as a stabilizer to prevent it from continuously doing cartwheels and falling to the ground. Finally, a bridle made of twine was attached to the frame to facilitate the launch.

Materials needed include:
  a. 2 wooden sticks, approximately ½ inch wide, 1/8 inch thick and 24 inches long; 1 stick with the same dimensions but 18 inches long
  b. Spool of thin twine, length depending how high you intend to fly the kite
  c. Paper to overlap frame by 1 inch
  d. Glue
  e. 3 strips of cloth (1 inch X 18 inches)

Steps to building the kite:

  1. Using a piece of twine, tie the two twenty-four-inch sticks together forming a cross so that the length of the shorter wooden strip (eighteen inches) would be horizontal and divided equidistant from the longer vertical strip.
  2. Cut shallow notches (one-eighth inch) in the four ends of the two sticks. Using a ball of twine and beginning at the top of the vertical stick, slip the twine into the notch and tie the string tightly close to the end of the stick. Using that connection as the anchor, stretch the twine through the slot on the end of one of the horizontal sticks very tightly, wrap and tie the twine to the stick, and repeat this process until all four ends are secured. Attention should be given to stretching the twine so that there is a slight bow in the frame once all ends are tied.
  3. Lay the paper on a flat surface, ironing out the wrinkles with the hand. Place the frame atop the paper with the slight bow

CURTIS J. JOHNSON

of the frame on the paper. Cut the paper with scissors, leaving about an inch overlay all around, and glue overlap to the frame, ensuring that the paper is stretched to accommodate the bow. (If the paste is used, the paper should be completely dried before flying the kite to prevent tearing.)

4. With the bow side up, slip a twelve to fourteen-inch length of twine into each notch of the three top stick ends and secure each. Then gather the loose ends of the three strings and tie them together so that when the kite is held at eye level with the junction of the two original sticks, the three strings should then be tied together, forming a bridle.

5. Using a short piece of twine, connect one end to the tail and the other end to the bottom of the vertical stick.

6. Finally, attach the spool of twine to the bridle and go out and launch (wind permitting!) your flying creation!

If you preferred to see your kite flying in front of you or more overhead in the sky, the bridle was adjusted to reach the desired angle or height.

. . . And for Grown-Ups

Few communities in the region had social facilities for teens, and Donaldsonville was one of the few. As noted earlier, our facility was the Nelson's Playhouse, a restaurant—dance hall frequented mostly by mature teens.

Located next to the Harlem Theater, the facility became a Saturday night oasis with its standing-room-only crowd of youthful dancers eager to demonstrate or improve their boogie-woogie, slow drag, and jitterbug dancing skills. A colorful jukebox that played 45 RPM records for five cents for each selection or six selections for twenty-five cents provided the music. Here, we enjoyed songs by Louis Jordan and His Tympany Five ("Saturday Night Fish Fry" and "Don't Let the Sun Catch You Crying") and the Nat King Cole Trio ("Red Sails in the Sunset" and "Straighten Up and Fly Right"), and others. The Playhouse had booths along the walls, and music selections could be made from each booth. Teens from Saint James and Assumption as well as local teens patronized the facility. It was at the Playhouse that I saw black-and-white television for the first time in July 1949.

Folks used weekends for R & R (rest and recuperation) and to wind down from long and tiring workdays. Adult baseball games were played in most towns and were well attended, mostly by men. Some men and women chose the barroom or nightclub, also known as the *beer garden* or *juke joint*. These places of entertainment were typically furnished with small four-person tables and chairs, with several booths lining a wall, a jukebox, a bar that was usually well stocked, ceiling and/or window fans, iceboxes chilling bottled sodas and beer, and a small space for the dance floor. Neon signs advertised Jax or Falstaff or Regal as the beer choices, although the three brands were available in most places. On the walls, signs featured Coca Cola, 7-Up, and R. C. Cola. A half-pint or pint setup came with a bottle of your chosen liquor, a bottle of Coke or 7-Up and one or several ice-filled glasses along with a small container of ice. Often, beer drinkers insisted on holding on to their empty beer bottles on the table to serve as a measure of their capacity to drink others "under the table."

Adults had a wide choice of barrooms from which to choose.

- In Saint James, Cayette Bar and the Blue Swan in Jamestown were the choices of some folks, although Lillian's Bar in Freetown and the Ten Top Bar in Chapman Town were well accommodated.
- Ascension offered Buck's, Fontana's, the Shangri-La, and Bella's bars in Donaldsonville; Butler's Bar and Tom's Grocery, Bar and Gas in Modeste, Chatman Bar in Chapmanville, and the Sportsman Bar in Holm Solem; Johnson Bar in Gonzales; Bosie Nightclub in Prairieville; and Jenkins Bar in Hillaryville. Bea's Diner also served the Gonzales Area.
- Facilities in Assumption included Champ's, Rose Garden, and Monte Carlo's bars in Belle Rose; Jamison's and Willie Randall's in Bertranville; Ernest Hines in Napoleonville; and Booster Cheatham in Labadieville.
- Folks from Lafourche enjoyed the Silver Star Cook's Bar, Leonard Brown's Bar, and the Mayfair Club, all in Thibodaux. Built during the early 1930s, the Mayfair was the epitome of nightclubs in the region and was rated by some over the clubs in New Orleans. Patrons from the surrounding parishes made their way to Thibodaux to share in the glitter and great music and entertainment by Tina Turner, Etta James, Joe Turner, and other famous entertainers.

Beer on Ice

All clubs served food, with typical menus offering gumbo, sandwiches (fish, chicken, ham, oysters, smoked sausage, pork chop), red or white boudin, hog's head cheese, *cowan* (turtle soup), potato salad, red beans, and rice, with or without smoked sausage. The room was usually smoke-filled and dimly lit. Those who wished to hide their identity even more usually sat in the booths farthest away from the bar.

Some of these nightclubs also featured live entertainment, with a guitarist playing and singing the blues. Occasionally, the artist would also play a harmonica as well as the guitar. Some clubs presented small bands with excellent musicians from the area.

Disputes were common, often leading to fistfights. Sometimes, a knife or gun was flashed. In some instances, the owner also served as the bouncer and would move in quickly to quell a disturbance. Unlike in Western movies, drinks were never "on the house" at the end of a brawl.

Special Historical Institutions

"Watermelon, red to the rind!" yelled the vendor from the fruit and vegetable horse and buggy rig. "Bananas, dime a dozen!" In a sense, the horse-drawn cart of the vegetable man was one of the many "special institutions" of the region during the 1920s, '30s, and '40s. These entrepreneurs provided home delivery service and fruits and vegetables that were fresher and less expensive than any of the surrounding grocery stores.

Most communities throughout the country identified with famous people, buildings, statues and paintings of heroes, and other landmarks. The Black communities of our area boasted a variety of historical establishments: benevolent societies, social centers, business concerns, and schools. Several of these institutions are described below.

Benevolent Societies

In spite of her limited formal education, my maternal grandmother, Annette Rodrigue Pinkins, demonstrated excellent interpersonal and organizational skills. At a time when most grandmothers were busy about the home, she and several friends planned, organized, and formed the Ideal Benevolent Association in 1934 in Port Barrow. The main purpose of the organization was to provide financial assistance to its members and their families in times of sickness and death.

Grandma was the founding president. She was eager to assist with other association responsibilities, often taking minutes at meetings when the secretary was absent, even as she presided over the meetings.

Dues were supplemented by fund-raisers such as penny parties and selling dinners. A maximum amount for each member's expenses was established early on to ensure the solvency of the organization in order to benefit all its members.

All of the societies operated in a similar pattern with essentially the same purpose. As explained by Rev. Thomas, "That purpose was to care for the sick and bury the dead. In Saint James, we had about nine or ten benevolent clubs. In addition to paying doctor's care and medicine, some clubs also paid a portion of the funeral expense."

Rev. Thomas and Octave noted that in Saint James Parish, the Rising Sun Benevolent Society was founded in Freetown in 1908, the oldest in the parish. Other clubs or societies, as some were called, included Friends of Faith (Bay Tree), Rising Sun (Freetown), Pride of Brookstown (Welcome), Saint Joseph (Magnolia), Silver King (Vacherie), Lily of the Valley (Moonshine), Home Brothers (Grandell Plantation), Belle of Moonshine (Moonshine), and Young Soldiers (Magnolia). The Odd Fellows (Burden Lane) was recognized as a "secret club." A Prince Hall Freemasons Lodge was established and sustained over the years in East Saint James.

In addition to the Ideal Association, such organizations in Donaldsonville included the Old Folks Union, True Friends Mutual Benevolent Association, and the Odd Fellows and Knights of Pythias. In Modeste and Hohen Solm, two branches of the Willing Workers coexisted. In East Ascension were the Do Right Benevolent Society in Dutchtown, founded in 1919, and the Try Benevolent Association in Prairieville.

Clubs in Assumption were the Sons and Daughters in Belle Rose and the Friends of Hope in Bertranville.

In Lafourche, two clubs were located in Thibodaux, including the Odd Fellows, which began in the early 1930s, and the Young Men's Association that started during the early 1950s.

Harlem Theater, Donaldsonville

Prior to 1940, there were no separate movie facilities for Blacks and Whites in Donaldsonville. Black citizens were accommodated in the balcony at the Grand Theatre, the theater for Whites, located uptown on Railroad Avenue, where the temperature was often uncomfortable since the theater was not air-conditioned. Large area fans relieved some of the heat, but the noise from the fans sometimes distorted the sound from the screen. Batiste-Rogers recalled a specific advantage that we had over the Whites during the cooler months. "Although we had to enter through a side door and climb the stairs to the balcony, the balcony was comfortably warm, and the view was excellent!"

On July 19, 1940, construction on the Harlem Theater was completed. Located at the corner of Lessard and Albert streets, the building was constructed by Rev. Walter Ricardo, one of a few Black contractors in the area, who, with Dr. J. S. Brazier, owner and pharmacist at Brazier's Drug Store, and Claiborne Williams, the Black music professor and director of Claiborne Williams Brass Band, took part in the theater's dedication ceremony led by Sidney Harp, one of the White owners of the theater.

In addition to the physical facilities, the Harlem held the distinction of having on staff a living institution in the form of Arthur "July" Levy, the theater manager. His duties reached far beyond those of a typical manager. He was the head pacifier for crying children, bouncer on occasion for children and teens demonstrating improper behavior, and more. His presence at the Harlem became a permanent fixture, and at the announcement that "Mr. July is coming!" even the most undisciplined child would become immediately well-behaved.

The theater also served as a facility for high school graduations and a gathering place for community receptions for local military draftees en route to the induction center in New Orleans.

True Friends Hall

The center for social, civic, and also educational activities in the Donaldsonville area for many years was the True Friends Hall. The facility was owned by the True Friends Mutual Benevolent Association, founded in 1882 by ex-slaves, according to Ray Jacobs's guest editorial published in the December 21, 1989 issue of *The Donaldsonville Chief*. The article continued: "As was common practice all over the south, benevolent societies were organized to take care of certain [medical and burial] needs of ex-slaves. By resolution, on June 14, 1885, it authorized one L. L. Fernandez to purchase a lot on which they'd build a 'meeting place.' The present day True Friends Hall is that meeting place."

Ulysses "Nick" Landry, a Donaldsonville native and resident and member of the True Friends Mutual Benevolent Association for over thirty years, served as its president for six of those years. When asked what the purpose of the association was, he stated, "To honor the sick and bury the dead," short and simple.

Our Roots Run Deep: A History of the River Road African American Museum cites several significant roles played by the hall in the Saint James, Assumption, and Ascension parishes:

> *In the 1920s and 1930s, the True Friends Hall was a popular place for celebrity entertainers, including such legends as Fats Domino, Claiborne Williams, Tony Hudson, Leonard Julien, Joe Tex, and many orchestras and bands, both locally and nationally recognized. In February 1928, King Zulu and the famed Zulu Carnival Krewe, was the special guest at the True Friends Mardi Gras Ball in Donaldsonville. The king, headed by a brass band, paraded through the streets of Donaldsonville, which culminated with a grand dance at the True Friends Hall, where the king was presented. True Friends Hall also served as a center for civic meetings and social and political activities. A rally was once organized at the True Friends Hall after Martin Luther King, Jr. was assassinated. Julian Bond, a Civil Rights activist, attended one of the political rallies in the 1960s at True Friends Hall, according to attorney B. J. Francis, who was a student at Southern University at the time. When the African American members of the Catholic Church in Donaldsonville got tired of sitting in the segregated balcony of Ascension Catholic Church, the members of the True Friends organized fund raisers to help build St. Catherine's of Sienna Catholic Church, which opened in 1926.*

During the mid-1940s, the hall hosted a musical concert that featured a promising New Orleans jazz quintet, the Johnson Brothers. Born in Donaldsonville, the brothers (Ples and Ray) were master musicians as teenagers, and their sister, Gwen, was an accomplished jazz vocalist at age fourteen. Ray, who was fifteen at the time, launched his career that day at the hall. Hundreds of local teens and adults who attended the concert were fascinated by this talented team of young musicians, who went on to enjoy successful careers in music.

True Friends Hall

CURTIS J. JOHNSON

The hall was located adjacent to the Nelson Playhouse and Cafe on Lessard Street. Located within a forty-yard radius from the hall were the Harlem Theater, the Shangri-La, and Sullivan nightclubs. John Schomberg's barbershop occupied the room attached to the north side of the hall. This cluster of activities formed the social and entertainment center for Blacks in Donaldsonville and surrounding communities, including Saint James, Modeste, Belle Rose, Belle Alliance, and Darrow. As noted in Jacobs's editorial, aside from a meeting and dancing place, the facility served as a classroom for Saint Catherine Elementary School, which was located next door.

The hall has been closed for many years; however, efforts for its revival continue.

Ascension Parish Negro Fair Association and Fairgrounds, Prairieville

On the site of the once-active fairgrounds in Prairieville (East Ascension), a historical marker provides background information on the Ascension Parish Negro Fair Association, Inc., and the Ascension Parish Negro Fairgrounds as noted below:

Ascension Parish Negro Fair Association, Inc.

The APNFA, Inc. was established September 22, 1950 by concerned citizens in the Prairieville Area. The Association assisted and encouraged advancement of farming, livestock and poultry raising, literacy, athletics, domestic achievement and the general promotion of prosperity and progress in Ascension Parish and surrounding communities. On November 23, 1966, the name was changed to The Ascension Fair Association, Inc. which is sponsored by concerned citizens of Ascension Parish.

The reverse side of the marker displayed the following information:

Ascension Parish Negro Fairgrounds

On March 7, 1956, Tom W. Dutton donated 3.76 acres to help promote the educational, recreational and civic work being performed by the APNF Association, Inc. The property was donated for the purpose of establishing a site for the fairgrounds. Prior to 1956, the fair was held at Prairieville High School under the supervision of the assistant county agent, L. C.

Christy and Dennis Dorville, Fair Assistant President. Farmers from all areas of the Parish displayed Agricultural produce that was raised in the Parish. The fairgrounds activities also included group discussions, canning demonstrations, livestock judging, judging of poultry and eggs, judging of the best breeding of hogs and cows. The original officers of the Ascension P. N. Ass'n, Inc. were Dennis Dorville (Dorvel), President; John Cornish, 1st VP; James Roberson, 2nd VP; William Tillotson, Secy; Leo Christy, Treas.

Sponsored by the Concerned Citizens of Ascension Parish

Israel Academy, Belle Rose

The Israel Academy was the first school for Blacks in Assumption Parish. Established in 1890 in the village of Belle Alliance, the two-story wooden structure contained eight classrooms. The cost for the building was $3,556.20, an amount that was paid in full in six months and one day by the members of the First Israel Baptist Church of Belle Alliance. The founder and first principal of the school was Dr. Henry Clay Cotton and board members included George Harris, Thomas Davis, Mr. Frank (first name unavailable), and John B. Alcorn, who was one of the teachers. Dr. Cotton's successor was William H. Reed.

In 1931, the top floor of the academy building was heavily damaged by fire. Renovation resulted in a one-story structure. The academy was closed in 1940 with the opening of the Belle Alliance Junior High School (BAJHS) during that year.

It is not known if the academy was accredited initially; however, a spelling certificate by the State of Louisiana was issued to John Comeaux in 1937. Other teachers included Mercedes Amos, Leoneed Marie Scott, William H. Reed, Ms. Ellis, and Permilla L. Reed. Grades one through eight were taught, and subjects taught included English, reading, arithmetic, spelling, religious education, and vocational subjects. Students completing the eighth grade continued their education at Lowery Training School in Donaldsonville or McDonough 35 High School in New Orleans for those with relatives living in New Orleans.

Some classrooms in the academy facility were separated by partitions that could be opened into an auditorium with a stage for special programs.

From 1940 to 1950, the academy facility was used for the various First Israel Baptist Church activities and the neighboring BAJHS. In 1950, Rev. Alvin Charles Daniels and his wife, Mattie Foster Daniels, organized the church's first kindergarten program in the facility with seventy students attending. At that time, the school was known as the W. H. Reed Kindergarten. In 1970, the kindergarten program was assumed by the Assumption Parish School Board and the W. H. Reed Day Care was opened at the academy.

Some of the graduates from the academy who were successful after college included these:

- William H. Reed became the public school principal of BAJHS. He was also the pastor of First Israel Baptist Church. The high school in Napoleonville was named in his honor.
- Charles Lewis became a professor at Leland College (and later a professor at a college in Alabama).
- Permilla L. Reed taught English at BAJHS and W. H. Reed High School in Napoleonville.
- John L. Comeaux taught high school science and chemistry and was a successful businessman in tax preparation and copying services.
- Mercedes Amos was an elementary school teacher with the West Baton Rouge school system.
- Ethel Barnes Williams taught primary classes at BAJHS.
- Ms. Ellis taught first grade at BAJHS.
- Mattie Parker Perkins taught middle school in Assumption and Orleans parishes.
- Isabelle Wiggins LeBlanc taught middle school in Terrebonne Parish.
- Helen Douglas Crawford was an elementary school and home economics teacher in Franklin and Ouachita parishes.
- Percy Walker Brent taught accounting in Alberta, Canada, Pueblo. Colorado, and with the Job Corps in Missouri.
- Alberta Ausbrooks Holly became an elementary school teacher in Assumption Parish.
- Curtis and Agnes Anderson were teachers in the West Baton Rouge school system. Iran Douglas became a professional chef in the U.S. Navy and in San Diego, California.

The Israel Academy building is currently being evaluated by the National Register of Historic Places in Louisiana to determine the facility's eligibility for the National Register, thanks to the efforts of Mary Brent Terry, a native of Belle Alliance. She is a retired public school teacher and teacher coordinator for the Assumption Parish School System, a retired municipal clerk for the town of Napoleonville, and a retired manager of the Assumption Parish Schools Employees Credit Union.

C. M. Washington High School, Thibodaux

The only school for Black children in Thibodaux during the early 1920s was the small Negro Corporation School. At that time, grades one through seven were taught. Built by a Black social organization, the school operated until 1940 when classes were added to create the C. M. Washington Training School that offered classes through the eleventh grade.

The school was named for Mrs. Cordelia Matthews Washington, a Black woman, who campaigned for educational facilities in Lafourche and in two neighboring parishes, Assumption and Terrebonne. In Thibodaux, she campaigned for a school large enough to house and teach Black children. She died in 1937 at the age of sixty-two. Eight years after her death, C. M. Washington Training School celebrated its first graduation. However, a twelfth grade education would remain unavailable to the local community for a few more years.

On December 18, 1950, C. M. Washington High School (CMWHS) and the attached elementary school were dedicated. The school contained first through twelfth grades. Professor Robert M. Harris was the high school principal; and Mrs. Washington's daughter-in-law, Leola Washington, was the first principal for the elementary school.

Before integration of schools, C. M. Washington Elementary and High Schools were the only choice for many Black families who could not afford to send their children to private schools in New Orleans. The high school building became South Thibodaux Elementary after integration.

Retired CMWHS librarian and teacher, Jesse Weber, said, "Mrs. [Leola] Washington was given the Washington-Bryant Award for her lifetime of service. She was like a mother figure to the students in

Thibodaux." Ronnie Winston, a Thibodaux police officer, said, "In each of her students, Mrs. Washington inspired a sense of pride and commitment to service. We felt like it was a family, it wasn't just like going to school. She made you feel like you were part of something. She encouraged us to excel. She encouraged people to do the best they can." Washington sponsored school-wide May Day celebrations and field trips, when field trips were not part of the regular curriculum. Fund-raisers that she organized kept the school working, both Winston and Weber said.

Mr. Robert J. Bell went to Thibodaux on June 5, 1948, and began teaching veterans carpentry at the former Lawson Trade School. In January 1950, he began teaching industrial arts. In September 1967, he became the first Black teacher in Thibodaux to go into the integrated system when he was assigned to the East Thibodaux Junior High School. He retired from teaching in the Lafourche Parish School System in 1978 after thirty-three years' service.

C. M. Washington High School developed a tradition of graduating students who went on to successful careers throughout the country. One noted success story involves an alumnus, Dr. Harry Robinson, Jr., who was born in New Orleans, Louisiana, and raised in Raceland, Louisiana, where he attended Pitman and Kent Hadley elementary schools. The family moved to Thibodaux the year Robinson entered high school. He attended CMWHS and went on to graduate with a major in history and a minor in library science and received his BA degree from Southern University in 1964.

Robinson attended graduate school at Atlanta University and majored in library science. It is where Robinson researched volumes of African American history making him a legend in his field. He received his master of library science degree from Atlanta University in 1965. He went on to

- work as an archivist at Southern University,
- become a cataloger at Kentucky State University,
- earn his education doctorate in 1969 at the University of Illinois at Urbana-Champaign,
- head up special collections for Alabama State University,
- join Bishop College in Dallas as librarian and museum director in 1974, and to

- develop the African American Museum in Dallas into a nationally recognized destination for people from all over the world.

Robinson is the past president of the Association of African American Museums, the African American Library Association, and a member of the Institute of Museum and Library Science.

PART TWO

Family Life: Simple Pleasures

The family is a storehouse in which
The world's finest treasures are kept.
Yet the only gold you'll find is golden laughter.
The only silver is in the hair of Dad and Mom.
The family's only real diamond is on Mother's left hand.
Yet can it sparkle like children's eyes at Christmas
Or shine half as bright as the candles on a birthday cake?

—Alan Beck

INTRODUCTION

I N MANY FAMILIES throughout the region, all members participated in daily family life, and members related well together. Authority lines were drawn early in children's lives by parents who wanted the best for their children: a safe and secure environment, adequate shelter, positive attitudes toward life and people, and common courtesy and mutual respect among members. Additionally, there were strict family core values that were demonstrated practically everywhere: respect for self and all others, especially the elderly; a "good" education; honesty in dealing with people; integrity; being spiritual and having a family-church relationship; being sensitive to others; and honest work for a day's pay. Of course, there were exceptions to these values in some families; but for the most part, these were the generally accepted rules and expectations. To be sure, these were the conditions under which my siblings and I were reared.

Ours was a family of eight. In addition to our father, Eddie, and mother, Elzena, there were Walter (Walt), Odile (Dile), Claudia (Clau), Edith (Nook), me (Doc), and Carolyn (Ba'y), in chronological order. Our parents were married in 1925 with Walter joining the family in 1926.

My nuclear family was a fair representation of the average Black family living in the region during the early years. Like all others, we were affected by the Depression. On the other hand, and unlike many other families of the region, our father held his job throughout and beyond the Depression years, continuously working as a truck driver for Elray Kocke Service, Inc., in Donaldsonville. If ever there was a time for testing family core values, these were the "final exam" years.

This part focuses on the results of our family lineage research and details some of the more interesting notes about early family life throughout the region that we considered relevant. We looked back to the beginning years of the Pinkins-Rodrigue and Johnson clans, examining relationships and census biographies. Also included are accounts of the

Pinkins-Rodrigue and the Sarah Johnson homesteads and family life; what we did for a living; the celebration of Sundays and holidays; the impact of the *three Rs* and secondhand books; the music of our life; "the *revenoorers* are coming"; how we were disciplined; engineering the outhouse; coping with roaches, chinches, and mosquitoes; catching the *mud bug*; and family humor.

Researching the Census Records

In our first attempt at researching the census records of our maternal forerunners (August Pinkins family), our search took us back to Virginia Pinkins, our mother's paternal grandmother, who was born between 1843 and 1848 in Louisiana, and Ozema and Usele Breaux Rodrigue, our mother's maternal grandparents, who were born and reared in the Donaldsonville area during the mid-1800s. Immediately, we had established a family linkage with American slavery, a part of American history that has become more accepted in recent years as an integral part in the history of this country.

It is unfortunate that we were not able to find documented evidence relating to those other family members who lived during slavery. There is a chance that the evidence is there, and closer examination of the records will be needed.

In searching the files of the Census Bureau in Washington, D.C., we found records of many persons with names similar to those of family members. However, in comparing census records with oral history, we could not, without reasonable doubt, believe those census entries to be our relatives.

During our search of the National Archives files, we found an abundance of census records available for our area to begin the genealogy search, but it quickly became clear that our search would be limited in terms of applicable years. From 1790 to 1840, census records listed the names of free Blacks who were heads of households and slaves only by their given first name, age, and sex. During the census periods 1850 and 1860, names of all free members of households were listed. It was only with the 1870 records that Blacks were listed by name. This was because slaves were known by a given first name and the last name of the owner. Therefore, the names of slave owners would be necessary in order to research beyond the 1870 recordings. Unfortunately, we had no such names. However, an inspection of the 1870 records was the beginning of interesting and revealing information about the Rodrigue family.

Ozema Rodrigue Lineage

The census data for Second Ward, Parish of Ascension, Post Office Donaldsonville, State of Louisiana, which was authenticated in July 1870, listed an "Ozeme Rodrige," as a single, Black male, age twenty-one, whose occupation was given as a farm laborer. Other statistics included his birth in Louisiana and his American citizenship. According to the census, he could not read or write.

The following census records for 1880 for the same location showed an "Osamie Rodriguez," a Black male whose age was listed as twenty-nine. He was described as a laborer who could not read or write. His family included a wife, Ucile Rodriguez, a Black female, age twenty-six, whose occupation was that of "keeping house." Their children are noted as follows:

>   Daughter: Antoinette, mulatto, female, age seven
>   Son: Leon, black male, age five
>   Daughter: Victoria, mulatto, female, age four
>   Son: Paul, mulatto male, age one

This record combined with family oral history and the 1870 census to establish Ozema Rodrigue as the maternal family patriarch. However, several contradictory issues were discovered during further record search.

According to oral tradition, Ozema was a very fair-complexioned Spaniard who was a landowner in Ascension Parish. Although the records show Antoinette, Victoria, and Paul as mulatto, both parents are listed in the census as "black." The wife's name as later listed in the 1900 record is "Sarah."

We surmise that several factors contributed to these discrepancies. In reviewing the records, different writing styles are noted, ranging from calligraphy type to sub-satisfactory penmanship in instances. My opinion is that some of the census takers were uneducated people who relied on phonetic spelling for recording names, as witness the different spellings of "Ozema" and "Rodrigue." Perhaps the pronunciation of names by the census givers was in keeping with the dialect used even today by some South Louisianans, which to "outsiders" yearn for clarity. It is also questionable that a Black person being interviewed would identify the race of a child as "mulatto." One final opinion in this regard is that the census taker was authorized to record data from observation and by interpreting the information offered; therefore, the disparity between reality and opinion.

The 1900 census provided additional information about the "Ozema Rodriguez" household. Again, shown as the head of household, Ozema was listed as a Black male who was born in June of 1850. By then he was fifty years old and had been married for twenty-six years. He and both of his parents were born in Louisiana. His occupation was that of a "ditcher [ditch digger]," perhaps an occupation resulting from his not having attended school. He owned a mortgage-free house. Other members of the household included the following:

Sarah Rodrigue, wife; Black female; born July 1851; age forty-eight; married for twenty-six years; mother of nine children all of whom were living; born in Louisiana, as were both of her parents; occupation: laundress; she could not read or write.

Leon Rodrigue, son; Black male; born July 1875; age twenty-four; single; occupation: "ditcher"; could read and write.

Victoria Rodrigue, daughter; Black female; born April 1877; age twenty-three; single; no occupation; could read and write.

Paul Rodrigue, son; Black male; born May 1880; age twenty; occupation: "ditcher"; could not read or write.

Theodosia Rodrigue, daughter; Black female; born July 1884; age fourteen; could not read or write.

Ozeme Rodrigue, son; Black male; born February 1886; age fourteen; occupation: in school; could read and write.

Emanuel Rodrigue, son, Black male; born October 1887; age twelve, occupation: in school; could read and write.

Census Records

Ritta Rodrigue, daughter; Black female; born April 1890; age ten; in school; could read and write.

Ernest Rodrigue, son; Black male; born November 1891; age eight.

At the time of this census, Antoinette Rodrigue had left the household and was then married.

Virginia Pinkins Lineage

A careful look at the Ascension Parish census records of 1870 and 1880 failed to find information on the Pinkins predecessors—Virginia Pinkins or her son, August. According to an archives note, "most of the records for 1890 for all populations were badly damaged by fire in the Commerce Department building on January 21, 19__, and were disposed of. The remaining records did not relate to Louisiana." Therefore, the earliest records found that related to the Pinkins was the 1900 census.

The record for "Part of Ward One, Post Office of Donaldsonville, Parish of Ascension, State of Louisiana," which was authenticated on June 2, 1899, describes August Pinkins as a Black male, head of household who was born in October 1867, three years following the abolition of slavery. At this time, his age was thirty-two, and he had been married for nine years; he was born in Louisiana, as were his parents; his occupation was listed as that of a "ditcher." August could read and write. He owned the house in which his family lived, and it was free of liens. Other members of the family included the following:

Arnette Pinkins, wife, Black female; born October 1873; age twenty-six; born in Louisiana as were her parents; could both read and write.

Walter Pinkins, son; Black male; born February 1892; age eight; in school; could read but not write.

Eddie Pinkins, son; Black male; born November 1884; age five.

Ledia Pinkins, daughter; Black female; born December 1896; age three.

Laura Pinkins, daughter; Black female; born January 1898; age two.

Virginia Pinkins, mother; Black female; born March, 1832; age sixty-eight; widow; mother of three children; one child living; like her parents, she was born in Louisiana; occupation was that of "washerwoman"; could not read or write; spoke English.

Ten years later (census of 1910), there were four additions to the August Pinkins household:

Lillian Pinkins, daughter; Black female; age nine (born 1901).

Jimmie Pinkins, son; Black male; age six (born 1904).

Elzena Pinkins, daughter; Black female; age three (born 1907).

August Pinkins, son; Black male; age two (born 1908).

The Alphonse Johnson Lineage

The first record of the Johnson ancestors may have appeared in the 1880 census for the Third Ward, Subdivision 2, Donaldsonville, Ascension Parish, Louisiana. A listing was found for Alphonse Johnson (who, according to oral history, was Sarah Johnson's father), a twenty-four-year-old mulatto who was born about 1846 and whose occupation was that of a farm laborer. He could not read or write. His wife, Adeline, was shown as a twenty-year-old mulatto who, like her husband, was a farm laborer without reading or writing skills. Older family members knew Alphonse's wife as Daphne or Adele. The obvious question was, could it be that Daphne or Adele was a nickname for Adeline? If not, could it be the other way around? Or could the mix-up have been caused by some unskilled census taker? "Adele" did appear to be a possible derivative of "Adeline."

Further research of the following census documents for 1880 through 1900 did not substantiate family connections with Alphonse, as no such reference was found in Ascension Parish. The next census, however, did provide initial information that related directly to Sarah Johnson, mother of Eddie Johnson, my dad.

Alphonse and Daphne Johnson were said to have lived in the Gonzales area, with their six children:

Alfred Johnson, the oldest. His first wife was Mary Dorsey. He had two daughters, Mary and Theresa.

Sarah Johnson, born June 10, 1868; grew up in the Donaldsonville/Gonzales area; worked as a cook and housekeeper at Crescent Plantation in Belle Terre; had six children: Mable, Edna, Irving, Eddie, Caroline, and Royal; died on May 9, 1934; and is buried in the Mount Triumph Baptist Church Cemetery.

Ben Johnson, born in 1877, married to Peggy Coins who was also born in 1877; had seven children: Joseph, Severan, Arthur, Evelina, Hubbard, Pearley, and Earline; died in 1945, and is buried in the Mount Triumph Baptist Church Cemetery.

Clara Johnson Lewis, married to Manuel "Man" Lewis; had six children: Florence Lewis Woods, Vergie Lewis Gomez, Berdie Lewis Dominique, Ethel Lewis Williams, Raymond Lewis, and Amy Lewis.

Ophelia "Nellie" Johnson, married to Henry Howard; had seven children: Joseph, Westley, Ernest, James, Curtis, Herman, and Eveline.

Dora Johnson, married to Richard Parker. No descendants.

Alphonse and Daphne are said to have died 1909 and 1911, respectively, and are buried in the Gonzales area.

The thirteenth census for Donaldsonville showed Sarah Johnson and her children sharing the household of Island and Mary Ford. As head of household, Island's age was listed as fifty-seven, his birth year being about 1853. He had been married for thirty-one years and was born in South Carolina. He made a living as a farm laborer and could both read and write. His wife, Mary, was forty-five years old (born around 1865). Louisiana was the birthplace listed for her and her parents. She could read and write.

The Johnson family members, all listed as "cousins" to the Fords, included Sarah, who was thirty-five and listed as "single," notwithstanding the listing of her children as follows:

<u>Mable Johnson</u>, Black female; age thirteen; could read and write.

<u>Edna Johnson</u>, Black female; age twelve; could read and write.

<u>Earvin Johnson</u>, Black male; age six.

<u>Edda Johnson</u>, Black male; age four.

<u>Caroline Johnson</u>, Black female; age two.

Again, the spelling of common names such as Irving and Eddie were obvious challenges for the census taker.

Homesteads and Family Life

May the warm winds of heaven
Blow softly upon this home.
And the Great Spirit bless
All who enter here.

—Cherokee blessing

The quality of life for families in the Bayou Lafourche region was determined by financial means and the availability of goods and services. I recall the majority of the area Black families, including ours, were indeed financially poor and not knowing the difference in our case didn't seem to matter to us. What did matter, however, was that family members were healthy, happy, and aspired to close relationships among themselves, community neighbors, and others.

There were certain amenities that were either not available or not affordable during our formative years, services such as running water, the telephone, electricity, natural gas, and sewer. However, as these services became available and when financial means allowed, our family was able to integrate these services into our lives to upgrade our health and work standards.

Although many area low—to middle-income houses were built along the same architectural lines, most of them had one thing in common—they were built on foundations of concrete footings and bricks, cinder blocks, or concrete piers three to four feet off the ground as protection from the high water table of the area. Most of the homes had cypress clapboard siding and screen windows. Practically all had tin roofs.

The Pinkins-Rodrigue Homestead

Our maternal grandparents, August and Antoinette Rodrigue Pinkins, lived in a typical Cajun *bungalow* one block west of our house ("up the street").

Built around 1895, the Pinkins's house was a modest four-bedroom bungalow with a *banister* front *gallery* (porch) that was whitewashed once or twice a year. The house had dark green stained shutters at each window, a usually mowed lawn, colorful flowerbeds all around, and bountiful vegetable gardens.

The house was well furnished and clean. The traditional furnishings could be found throughout: wood stove and table and several chairs in the kitchen; an icebox, a *sideboard* (dining room furniture for holding tableware) and heavy oak table and chairs, and a *safe* (a dining room cabinet for storing food not requiring refrigeration), each bedroom had a four-poster bed, a rocking chair, a marble-top washstand with a ceramic basin and water pitcher, one or two kerosene lamps, an *armoire* (wardrobe), a white "granite" *chamber pot* (vessel for urination and defecation) with a lid and a marble-top dresser with a large framed mirror. The beds were comfortable with moss-filled mattresses and the bedstead shrouded with mosquito netting in each bedroom. In one of the front bedrooms was a hand-operated RCA Victrola record player with a stack of 78 RPM records, thick but fragile, that included Count Basie's "One O'Clock Jump," the Andrews Sisters' "Rum and Coca Cola," Nat King Cole's "Straighten Up and Fly Right," and the Mills Brothers' "Paper Doll." The coolest spot in the world in the hot summertime for children taking naps was on the linoleum floor in the front bedrooms near the shuttered doors.

The Pinkins patriarch, August, Sr. (called Ogeese by his friends), was a master gardener who supported the family with his gardening skills. His know-how was demonstrated in the upkeep of the lawns, flowerbeds, and the vegetable gardens that occupied the majority of the family land.

A Cajun House

Grandma Antoinette (called Teet by her friends) was an accomplished seamstress, making all of the bedcovers and window curtains by hand and, in some cases, with the help of a foot-pedaled Singer sewing machine. With the help of Aunt Henrietta, Grandma's youngest daughter, she maintained the interior of the house in splendid fashion. Linoleum and hard pine floors were kept cleaned and waxed. Dust from the graveled street was the number one housecleaning challenge for homemakers, yet her meticulous work ethic ensured the house was ready for inspection at any given time.

The family property measured 180 feet wide by 120 feet deep, a substantial land parcel for the time. Several unique features set the homestead apart from others in the neighborhood:

- Fruit trees (fig, Japanese plum, peach, tangerine, kumquat, orange, mulberry) and Concord grapevines.
- A wide (about six feet) concrete walk extending from the front gate to the front steps.
- An inlaid brick walk leading from the front concrete walk around the left side of the house to the side dining room entrance. (The walkway was plagued with cocoa grass between the bricks, which was removed by persistence and energy using table knives by Grandpa August and the grandchildren.)
- A whitewashed outhouse with three holes and seat covers, one specially made for children. The structure was well designed and included a sculptured, decorative exterior canopy that resembled the design on the house above the gallery. The structure also had two windows with shutters flanking each window.
- A concrete-lined drainage ditch for wastewater that started at the back of the house and emptied in the ditch that fronted the house at the street.

RCA Victrola

One of the outer structures at the home site was a combined utility barn, horse stable, and hog pen that was used for many purposes. At one time, the building housed Frank, the family dray horse, and several hogs; it was used for storing gardening tools and equipment, furniture, and vegetables. A separate closed-in portion stored food items used for the lunch program at Lowery Training School, the local high school for Blacks. Mr. E. C. Land, Lowery's principal, lived with the family from 1937 to 1941 and was allowed temporary storage space there while the new school was under construction. Among the wooden crates of food were raisins, dried apricots, prunes, and cases of powdered and evaporated milk and grapefruit juice.

My family was awakened one night in 1945 by loud knocks on the door. The light dancing through the windows signaled a fire in the neighborhood! The callers told us the barn was in flames!! Unfortunately, the fire was beyond the control of a bucket brigade. Everything was lost, including a hog that was being readied to provide the family's winter meat supply. We later learned that someone from the Sheriff Department said someone had intentionally set the fire. Evidence that gasoline had been used to start the fire was found at the scene. House fires, especially at night, had a frightening way of awakening a neighborhood and, like most tragedies, bringing people closer together.

The Sarah Johnson Homestead

The Sarah Johnson family lived with Sarah's cousins, Mary and Island Ford, who owned a home near Crescent Plantation on Highway 308 in Assumption Parish during the early 1900s. On December 9, 1912, Sarah Johnson, our father's mother, purchased from Clara Binnings Jeffery, a resident of Alexandria, Louisiana, a tract of land on Fifth Street in Port Barrow, Ascension Parish, Louisiana, for the price of $100. In the legal document that transferred ownership, the property was listed as "a certain lot of ground . . . described as lot No. 2 in Square No. 38, measures front on Fifth Street sixty feet in width, by a depth of 120 feet between parallel lines." After the purchase, a three-bedroom cottage was built and the Johnson family moved to their house in Port Barrow in 1913. The money to purchase both the lot and the modest house was provided by Henry Weil, the father of Mable Johnson Dorsey, Irving Johnson, Eddie Johnson, and Caroline Johnson Shorter.

The outside of the house was constructed of cypress clapboards that had a "natural effect" that never needed painting. Few of the houses in the area were painted, and many people preferred the "natural gray" effect enhanced by the weathered cypress. Dust generated from the graveled street, however, did not help the appearance of houses. Fortunately, vehicular traffic was mostly horse and buggy units that, in comparison, created far less dust than did automobiles that came later.

The yard surrounding the house contained fruit trees (fig, peach, plum) and nut trees (pecan, black walnut) and a quarter-acre vegetable garden. The traditional water *cistern* (large wooden reservoir) was located in the back of the structure. An attractive whitewashed picket fence lined the front of the property. Wire fences laden with *maypops* (edible aromatic vine fruit) and fragrant honeysuckle enclosed the remaining three sides.

In addition to the three bedrooms, the house contained a combined kitchen-dining room. The bedroom furniture included a four-poster large wooden bed, an armoire, a marble-top washstand with ceramic pitcher and basin, a chamber pot, a comfortable rocking chair, and one or two straight-back sitting chairs. The center of activities, the kitchen-dining room, contained a large oak table and several matching chairs, an iron wood stove, an icebox, a walk-in pantry large enough to store groceries and pots and pans, and a screened safe.

Port Barrow was sparsely populated around 1916. In some cases, several blocks separated neighbors. However, the Johnson homestead enjoyed several immediate neighbors. "*Tante* (aunt) Vick" lived immediately next door, while the Nelson "Piggy" Dixon family lived directly behind. The Johnson property was later extended by the addition of an adjacent lot. Grandpa Ogeese leased the newly acquired lot from the Johnsons to increase his vegetable production.

A typical day for the Johnson children included school at the Leland Academy for Uncle Irving, our father, Eddie, and Aunt Caroline, who were the children remaining at home. Aunt Mable was now married to Uncle Joe Dorsey and had moved to their house across from the Fords in Assumption Parish, while Aunt Edna had moved to New Orleans to work. At Leland, there were reportedly three teachers and "too many" students. The Johnson children enjoyed ample time for play after school and on weekends, and baseball was their favorite activity. Neighborhood boys visited the house daily, enjoying the Johnson boys' balls, bats, and gloves supplied by their father. Grandma Sarah cooked and did other domestic work for several White families in Donaldsonville to supplement the family income.

Social life for teens, other than church activities, included movies at the Grand Theatre on Saturdays and occasional dating. The children attended Sunday school, Baptist Young People's Union (BYPU), and regular church services at the Mount Triumph Baptist Church where Grandma Sarah was a member. The children also sang in the junior choir. By 1920, Irving had left the household for New Orleans to work while living with his sister, Edna. There, of course, the social life sparkled with parties and dances featuring such performers as the Peron Band, often referred to as the Guy Lombardo of the Black social scene.

In 1925, Eddie married and left the household at age twenty-two. He established a home for him and our mother, Elzena. Aunt Caroline, the youngest Johnson daughter, moved to New Orleans to work. Uncle Royal, the youngest of the children, also left the household destined for the New Orleans job market.

Grandma Sarah maintained the house through the Depression years of the early 1930s, until she became ill and moved in with my family in 1933. After she died in 1934, the siblings later sold the property.

Family Bloodlines

Miscegenation has been a sensitive issue for modern society to deal with, and it was frowned upon with disdain during earlier years. Even today, it remains an issue that many people are not comfortable discussing freely. During those same earlier years, however, away from the glare of the public, knowledgeable people admitted that racial mixing was simply another part of everyday life and, in the case of female slaves, a means of survival at times. The Johnson family can be used as a living example of miscegenation.

Merriam Webster's Collegiate Dictionary defines *miscegenation* as "a mixture of the races; esp., marriage or cohabitation between a white person and a member of another race." The term was derived from the Latin words *miscere* ("to mix") and *genus* ("race").

People from the area—Black and White—would ride by the Sarah Johnson household in buggies and could be overheard talking about those "little *mulatto* children," referring to our father and his sisters, Mable and Caroline, and his brother, Irving. *Mulatto* was an accurate description for them, as they were children of a White father and a Black mother.

Blacks of mixed parentage were placed in rigid categories, according to the makeup of their parents. The list below goes from lowest class to highest, as the amount of Black blood decreases proportionately from term to term:

Parents	Child
Mulatto and White	Quadroon
Quadroon and White	Octoroon
Mulatto and Mulatto	Casess
Mulatto and Black	Santo
Santo and Black	Mango

Recognizing the racial mixes associated with the Eddie Johnson and Elzena Pinkins marriage, it is reasonable to assume that my siblings and I would be a diverse mixture of a number of races, nationalities, and cultures. Grandpa August Pinkins was the offspring of a Black mother and a Creole father. The father of Grandma Antoinette Pinkins was a White Spaniard, and her mother's heritage included both American Indian and African American. Considering the mulatto status of Eddie and the mixed bloodlines of Elzena, it would seem virtually impossible to accurately classify Eddie and Elzena Johnson's grandchildren, considering the further racial diversities brought on by intermediate marriages. However, in the final analysis, classifying family members is not important to my family anyway. As we recognized this, we became more satisfied with who we are, rather than what we are in terms of racial bloodlines.

The Johnson-Pinkins Homestead

In 1925, the year our mother and father were married, Walter Ricardo, a local Black contractor, built the original Pinkins-Johnson house. A room that was added to the house in 1937 became the kitchen that transformed the shotgun architecture into an L-shaped one. In addition to the kitchen, the house consisted of a front screened porch, a living room, parents' bedroom, girls' bedroom, and the dining room that doubled as a boys' bedroom. The living room also doubled as a bedroom for two of the girls as they grew older. The bathroom was off the dining room but had no plumbing at the time. Later, a screened back porch was added, extending fifteen feet across the back of the house.

Throughout the years, the siding on the house was the typical painted cypress clapboards and corrugated tin was used for the gabled roof. The foundation for the structure was built on thirty-inch concrete piers, with brick steps at the front and wooden steps at the side and back entrances.

During the early years, the yard contained an *outhouse*, a utility shed, a storage shed, several chicken brooders, a chicken house with laying and hatching compartments, a cistern, two clotheslines, a hog pen, several stacks of firewood, a small vegetable garden, and cypress picket fencing on three sides with a more decorative three-foot-high white picket fence across the front. At one time, there were fruit trees (fig, pear, peach, grapefruit, and wild cherry), mirliton vines, a grapevine, and an assortment of other trees (pink crepe myrtles, pines, sweet olive, Japanese magnolia, camphor, and mimosa). Two neighbors' pecan trees supplied us with small but tasty nuts.

Family and Household Activities

Before electricity came to our house in 1934, fuel for cooking and heating was hardwood gathered by our father and, later, my brother and me, from the river. Our main lighting source was the *coal oil* (kerosene) lamp. The sewer system consisted of the outhouse, and bath and dishwater were dumped into a drainage ditch near the west side fence in our backyard and channeled out under the banquette (sidewalk) to a ditch parallel to the street. Kerosene was also used to start fires in both the cooking stove and the fireplace. Since we didn't keep fire burning in the fireplace throughout the night in winter, the temperature in the house would be virtually freezing at wake-up time, making it harder for anyone to get up from a warm bed to start the fire. Once done, however, the fire maker became the most secure person in the household.

A simple chore like taking a bath required extra effort and cooperation from family members to help fill and empty the washtub. During the summer months, the temperature of the water in the cistern was ideal for bathing. During winter, water was heated on the kitchen wood stove. Since the kitchen was the warmest place in the house, bathing was more comfortable there. Several of us didn't seem to mind bathing after someone else, using the same water. It was a resourceful (and convenient) thing to do. With the purchase of portable kerosene heaters, the bathroom was eventually used for baths during the colder months. The addition of the kerosene cooking stove followed, later.

Boy Taking Bath in Washtub

During late elementary and throughout high school days, Odile, Claudia or Edith would invite a friend over to spend the night periodically. The fun and fellowship generated in the small but uncluttered house was magnetic. Regardless of its size and whatever family relationships existed, these were attractive conditions for Octavia Williams Johnson. A resident of Destrahan, Octavia attended high school in Donaldsonville because there was no high school for Blacks in her hometown at that time. A classmate of Claudia's, she lived at our house during her junior and senior years at Lowery Training School.

When the opportunity came, our family subscribed to the Louisiana Power and Light Company for electrical services. We were the first in our immediate neighborhood to have radio, which made our house popular during broadcasts of championship boxing from Madison Square Garden. Joe Louis was the reigning champion in the heavyweight division from 1937 to 1949 and, as such, was the idol of every Black American. Those invited to hear the bouts included several White neighbors. It was difficult not to be jubilant as the loser was being counted out by the referee who announced that "the Brown Bomber has again successfully defended his heavy weight title." Somehow, we managed to show compassion for Primo Camera, Max Baer, Jimmy Braddock, and the others. We figured that no one would lose face this way. The approach was evidently effective, as the next fight would bring us all together again.

As children, we spent countless hours sitting around the radio listening to *Amos 'n' Andy*, *The Lone Ranger*, *Fibber McGee and Molly*, *The Inner Sanctum*, and *Let's Pretend*, our favorite program on Saturday mornings. A children's feature that started in 1934, *Let's Pretend*, allowed the young listener to pretend to be anyone or anywhere in the world, with yet more choices of being in the real world or the world of make-believe. It is amazing how malleable children's minds were and continue to be.

During winter nights, the fireplace was the nightly gathering place for the family after supper. After finishing homework, we gathered around the fire and talked about the day's happenings, and sometimes told stories before turning in. Occasionally, we roasted peanuts from Grampa Ogeese's garden. When someone happened to visit, they too would pull up a chair (politely vacated by one of the children) to the fire and get comfortable. Unlike the potbellied stove that would eventually heat the entire room, the fireplace did not provide that comfort—especially during the ebbing hours of the night when the embers provided less and less heat.

Summertime was our best season of the year. Most days of the year were enjoyable, mind you; but there were so many things offered by summer—crawfishing; playing on the levee; visiting Aunt Mable, Uncle Joe, and the Dorsey cousins who lived "down the bayou"; earning a few dollars grassing rice in the fields in Modeste or in the Evan Hall sugarcane fields grassing cane in McCall or picking Kentucky Wonders (pole green beans) on the Tubby Ewen's truck farm in Darrow; helping Grandpa in his gardens; or just playing in the yard.

The Cistern

Our main water source for drinking, bathing, cooking, watering the garden, and doing laundry was the cistern, a wooden vat for holding rainwater channeled from the roof gutters. The vat was made from cypress staves held together by metal bands. (A similar procedure was used to make wooden barrels.) The top of the vat was screened to keep out leaves and other foreign matter (balls, rocks, and anything else that fit in the hands of children!) and especially the insects. Unfortunately, the screens were not effective in preventing *wiggle tails* (mosquito larva) from the water. We swallowed thousands of these little creatures during our early years, I'm sure.

A spigot was attached to the cistern to facilitate drawing water. Since the vat was elevated on brick pillars, the height of the spigot averaged from two to three feet aboveground, a comfortable height for handling buckets of water. We used a galvanized bucket for transporting water. An occasional dry season made it necessary to haul water in steel barrels from the Mississippi River to refill the cistern. This was done using buckets to fill barrels that were delivered to our house on a horse-driven cart by "Pa Sam" Clark. Buckets were then used to transfer the water from the barrels into the cistern. While no waterway was pristine, even then, water from the Mississippi River in the 1930s and 1940s was indeed clean enough to drink.

A typical Saturday for us involved a series of routine events that were repeated during most of my elementary school years: listening to several radio programs (*Let's Pretend* and *The Lone Ranger),* doing household and yard chores, working in Grandpa August's flower and vegetable gardens, weekly tub baths, a matinee movie, and bingo at our grandparents' house. On most Saturdays, Walter and I collected scrap metal, brass, copper, and aluminum from behind the levee and by door-to-door canvassing and sold these items at Elray Kocke Service.

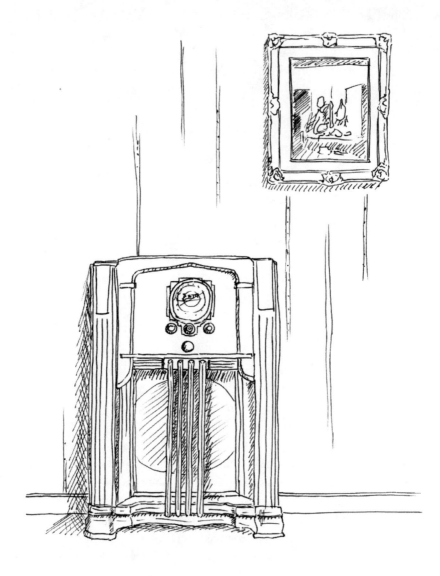

Floor Model Radio

Saturday Routines

Household chores for the children included sweeping, mopping and waxing floors, dust mopping, cleaning the bathroom, dusting furniture, sweeping and occasionally mopping porches and steps, cleaning the fireplaces during the winter, polishing the wood stove, and washing windows. Outdoor chores involved sweeping, scrubbing the outhouse, raking leaves and yard debris, feeding the chickens, collecting eggs and cleaning the hen house, feeding the ducks and geese, cutting grass with the manual lawn mower, and helping tend the flower beds and vegetable garden.

My maternal grandparents lived a block from our house. One of our aunts, Henrietta, lived with them and cared for them. We called her Ret, since she was not much older than Walter. You'll soon learn why she was our favorite.

Bath time in preparation for the movies was never an easy event. Walter and I filled the galvanized tin washtub for everyone, using pails of water drawn from the cistern. The girls would take their bath first, each one demanding freshwater. When our time came, Walter was always first in the tub. "Because I'm older," he would say when I questioned him. He and I always shared the same water. When I was eight, he promised that I could be the first to bathe when I became the older brother. That seemed fair to me.

The Saturday matinee movie at the Harlem Theater was a special treat for us. The theater's sweet popcorn or a popsicle or Baby Ruth candy bar or a small bag of scrap candy for five or ten cents from the Mistretta and Sotile's Candy Factory on Saint Patrick Street added to the enjoyment. Movie time started with several cartoons, an RKO Newsreel production, and a chapter in a fictional serial about mud men living in the walls of caves trying to capture people for a fat ransom, or some similar plot. The main feature was usually a story about the Old West and cowboys winning over Indians who were usually on the warpath. The hero was Tex Ritter or Roy Rogers and his horse, Trigger, or Gene Autry or Tom Mix or Zorro or some other cowboy star.

After the movie and dinner, our family walked up the street to our grandparents' to play bingo. For prizes, there were choices of homemade gingersnaps, chocolate fudge, pralines, and popcorn balls, with caramel holding the kernels together in the shape of a ball, all prepared by Ret. Additionally, there would be jelly beans and silver bells (Hershey's chocolate kisses). That's why she was our favorite aunt!

The Cistern

Sundays Were Special

Sundays allowed the family to experience togetherness that did not exist during the week. They were truly special days that centered on family rather than on individual schedules. On Sundays, everything seemed to settle into a mood of enjoyable excitement coupled with quietude.

We attended services at our family church, Mount Triumph Baptist, where we children walked to Sunday school. Afterward, we would join our parents for the main service. We all sat up front "where children are supposed to be." Our mother sang in the choir. We were so proud of her! Some of us sang along as the choir sang "Leaning on the Everlasting Arm" and "The Old Rugged Cross." When the time came, we all politely placed our pennies in the collection basket and smiled up at the usher. Seldom did they smile in return. Collecting offerings was a serious business at our church, I supposed.

The sanctuary was not air conditioned, but you could always count on a slight breeze to move in and out of the side windows, making the air more bearable. However, the air was made even more tolerable with the aid of cardboard fans donated to churches by insurance companies, Brazier Funeral Home, and other business establishments. Electric window fans were really appreciated when funds became available for such "conveniences."

Occasionally, adult friends would stop by our house after Sunday school to say hello and perhaps enjoy a cup of coffee. Once in a while, folks would drop in during breakfast and, of course, would be invited to share the meal. Most declined, but exceptions did occur from time to time. It was during these times that we (children) didn't think too favorably of the idea, as we knew that one additional plate would mean less breakfast for us.

Sundays allowed us to wear our "Sunday go to meeting" clothes. We didn't have much in that line but took pride in looking neat and being clean. During the summer, my sisters wore dresses that were made alike but in different colors of organdy, dotted swiss, voile, or gingham. Unlike the girls, my brother and I needed but one Sunday outfit, which usually consisted of a white dress shirt, navy trousers, a matching sports coat with a black or navy tie, and black shoes. In winter, gabardine and wool provided warm, attractive outfits for the girls. A heavy coat added to the warmth, and it was not unusual for a single winter coat to be worn by each of the three older sisters, as it was handed down as the older girl outgrew it. This was a routine arrangement with most of the girls' clothing and with the boys' clothing, especially during our teen years.

Paddle Wheel Pleasure Boat

CURTIS J. JOHNSON

Leisure time was observed during the afternoon. Grown-ups usually visited and shared coffee and conversation. Children played games but stayed dressed in their church clothes—which meant games and activities had to be selective and played with care. Grass had a special way of staining starched navy or white pants. Girls were held to the adage of being "sugar and spice." Even tomboys slowed down on this day and limited their activities to preserve their dresses.

The much-awaited event that took place each Sunday was the enjoyment of Sunday dinner. Typically, this feast would consist of flank steak or fried chicken, potato salad or macaroni and cheese, petit pois (small) green peas), green salad, and sweet potato bread or Jell-o with fruit cocktail and pound cake for desert.

After the dishes were washed, we spent most evenings on the front screened porch enjoying the summer breezes, talking about the week's activities and quietly listening to the church service two doors away at Saint Luke AME Church. Occasionally, an entertainment paddle boat (*show boat*) would pass heading downstream in the river. Its music and reveling crowd could be heard as the boat made its way to New Orleans.

People passing by in the graveled street would wish their "good evening," some following up with a spontaneous, "Another hot one!" assessment of the weather. We enjoyed the interchange, and occasionally were entertained by people who had partaken too much of "the social grape." On one such occasion, one memorable passerby turned to our mother Elzena and remarked cryptically, "Lordy, Miz Zena, the world turning green!"

Laundry Day

Every Monday was the traditional laundry day for most people throughout the region and beyond. Our mother used a number ten galvanized washtub for washing and another for rinsing. Washboards made of wood, and corrugated tin or corrugated glass were used to scrub soiled clothes. With the help of warm water and Octagon soap, the clothing items to be washed were submerged in the soapy water and rubbed repeatedly against the metal on the washboard in a downward and rotating motion until the item was "washed" clean. The item was then twisted using both hands to "wring out" as much of the soapy water as possible before placing the item into the rinse water tub. Heavily soiled clothes, such as our father's sometimes oily and grimy overalls and denim shirts resulting from his job, would be placed in

Laundry Day

CURTIS J. JOHNSON

boiling water using lye soap in a cracklin' pot over an open fire in the yard. The clothing would be stirred occasionally using a cracklin' paddle that resembled an oar.

After the washing and rinsing process, and using clothespins, the clothes were hung on clotheslines made of galvanized wire that was stretched between two metal poles that stood about six to seven feet tall. Both poles were anchored in concrete and had a metal crossbar with three to five holes for binding the clothesline at both ends (for three to five lines). Once the clothes were pinned onto the line, they were kept from touching the ground by using *props.* These oak poles, about seven or eight feet long with a branching Y at the top, lifted the clothesline and kept large or heavy items such as sheets from becoming soiled again, and from dragging on the ground.

White clothing was rinsed with *bluing* added to the water. Much like modern bleach, this liquid concentrate, blue in color as the name implies, was used to "bring out" the whiteness.

Clothing or any household items that required ironing after drying were saturated in a liquid starch solution in a small tub or basin and, again, "wrung out" before being pinned to the clothesline. The liquid starch solution was prepared by combining water and Argo brand dry starch and cooking until the starch was dissolved.

When dried, these items to be ironed would be set aside for a later day. When that designated time came, the clothes to be ironed that did not require starch along with the starched items were dampened with water from a bottle that had holes punched in the top with a nail. The "sprinkled" items would then be rolled separately and set aside for the dampness to penetrate the entire item.

A "flat iron" was used to iron clothes. This tool was shaped somewhat like the modern electric iron, except it was smaller in size and made of solid iron. The iron was heated by placing it on a bed of charcoals or on a hot stove, and tested for the right temperature by rubbing it over a separate cloth other than the one on the ironing board.

Sometime during the early 1940s, we bought an electric wringer washing machine that expedited the process tremendously. By then, our mother was using boxed *washing powder* detergent, such as Rinso and Duz. Some of the detergent companies included inside the box one item of dishes (plates, cups, saucers, and drinking glasses) or bath and dishtowels as giveaway marketing gimmicks.

Monday was also known for its dinner meal (served at noon) of red (kidney) beans and rice. Dried red beans required three to four hours to cook "down" and required no attention other than an occasional stir. Most times, the laundry required three to four hours to finish. For the usually busy mother, the washing and cooking complemented each other conveniently well. The red beans with smoked sausage were usually served over rice. The tradition of restaurants in South Louisiana offering red beans and rice as a featured menu item each Monday continues today.

Our yard, which to small children appeared to be large, was our playground and outside gym. Many dirty hands and dusty bottoms were the result of a miscalculated somersault. Bruises, cuts, and nosebleeds were expected trophies collected at boxing matches. The hen house was a frequent hideout in games of hide-and-seek, and under the house was a welcome retreat from the midday heat.

Eventually, a water main was installed on our street and into other areas of Port Barrow. (The survey to determine the number of new subscribers to the city water system was conducted by Claudia's senior high school class.) We immediately tapped into the system and installed bathroom fixtures and a cesspool in 1946. It was not long afterward that we realized how things had changed in our household. Walter, now discharged from the army, was working in New Orleans. Odile had completed college and was teaching the business curriculum at Lowery High School. Both Claudia and Edith were students at Southern University, and I was well into high school, with Carolyn just three years behind me. Looking back, it seems like only a few years ago we were all in the yard playing stickball . . . and having our usual grand time.

What We Did for a Living

At a time when the national hourly minimum wage was forty-five cents, and with the area economy still reeling from the Depression, it was not enough to have a minimum-wage job. To maintain an already-limited quality of life, families had to do other things to add to their income.

During the early years of development of our family, our mother worked in the El Trellis Cigar Factory in Donaldsonville that made El Trellis and, later, Tiparello cigars. Her job entailed stripping the tobacco leaves from the stalk in preparation for the leaves to be rolled and pressed into cigars. She did this for several years until caring for the several toddlers and baby grew into a full-time job.

The main source of our livelihood was our father's job with Elray Kocke Service. His job required him to help load and haul heavy equipment, timbers, and other building materials and packaged "mud" that was used in oil fields throughout the coastland of South Louisiana and parts of Mississippi and Texas. Kocke's trucks had the capacity to handle large loads at a time and were among the largest in the area. Eddie's assigned truck was Big Bertha, the largest in the fleet. Occasionally, he would take me on a trip to Pointe a la Hache in Plaquemines Parish east of New Orleans or Golden Meadow in Lafourche Parish. I truly enjoyed those excursions that allowed me to see different towns and villages while lunching on sandwiches my mother fixed for the two of us and sharing his coffee that was kept piping hot in his quart-sized thermos.

At this same time, he also held a part-time job at Bloch Brothers Clothing Store, located at the corner of Iberville Street and Railroad Avenue in Donaldsonville. There, he worked as a janitor and packaged merchandise for mail shipments.

Early Work Experiences

The male family members were responsible for catching logs from the river, sawing them into desired lengths, and chopping them into stove—and fireplace-sized pieces. Everyone worked in some capacity in the garden with the vegetable crops. Edith and I peddled vegetables from Grandpa Ogeese's garden from arm baskets. We also sold fresh river shrimp by the quart for Uncle Eddie Pinkins, who baited his shrimp cages each evening and collected the shrimp early the next morning. Our main area for sales was the more affluent Lemanville community.

We all picked blackberries, figs, and gathered pecans for home use as well as for selling. The older girls did light housework for families in the community. Walter and I picked green beans in Darrow for which we were paid thirty-five cents for each bushel. We grassed rice, hoed grass from corn and sugarcane rows, and gleaned white potatoes from fields in McCall for family use after the harvesters had done their job.

Fisherman

CURTIS J. JOHNSON

When I became twelve, I worked after school and on some Saturday mornings for a neighborhood gentleman (Samuel "Pa Sam" Clark) who had a woodcutting business. He kept about twenty families supplied year-round with custom-cut hardwood for cooking in the summer and for cooking and heating in winter. Along with two of his nephews (Warren "Rock" Joseph and Harold "Tootie" Williams), we performed a variety of chores, the main ones related to the sawing, chopping, stacking (for drying), and eventual delivery of a half cord or cord to his customers. Mr. Sam had two horse-cart dray teams that we used for the deliveries. We also cared for the horses (Prince and Long), including hitching the horses to the carts, making the deliveries, stacking the wood for the customer, and at the end of the work day, unhitching the horses and riding them two and a half blocks to a pond for watering, walking them back for feeding and rubdowns. And, of course, occasionally, we cleaned the stables.

En route to the pond, we walked the horses for the first block until we were out of Mr. Sam's sight and hearing range, then raced for the remaining one and a half blocks, up and then down the levee and a left turn to the pond. One day while riding Long, I made a rather sharp turn at the bottom of the levee and fell from the horse, landing on my neck. Stunned, I was able to remount with the help of Rock, who found the whole thing too hilarious for words. Until the fall, I was winning by at least two lengths. Of course, we never talked about the incident around Mr. Sam.

During the mid-1960s, I began having discomfort when turning my head or looking up to serve a tennis ball. Over the course of six to eight months, not only did the pain become intolerable but also a swelling in my lower neck caused me to seek medical relief. I had surgery that resulted in the removal of benign fibroid tissue from the area of the second vertebra. I asked the surgeon what could have caused the growth. He said I could have been hit in the neck or fallen on it while playing as a child. Immediately, my mind flashed back to the horse incident, and I had warm feelings about the incident that could have been fatal forty years earlier!

My next work experience was for Mrs. Mary Lowery, the widow of Dr. John Lowery, the owner of the Africa Plantation in Modeste. My job, which I loved, consisted of a variety of interesting tasks, several unusual in nature, especially for a boy of fourteen years. For example, inside the house, I waxed hardwood floors and cleaned windows. In the yards (she had three), the chores included mowing the lawn, weeding

Boy Mowing Lawn

CURTIS J. JOHNSON

flower beds, trimming hedges, and fertilizing, and cultivating a dozen or more poinsettia plants in the front and side yards. The middle yard, immediately at the back of the house, contained several shade trees, a smaller yard that housed up to eighteen adult turkeys that I fed and watered, several storage sheds, a clothesline, and a two-car garage that sheltered a seldom-used black 1936 Ford coupe (used in earlier years by Dr. Lowery for his medical house calls), and a black 1938 Ford sedan that I cleaned once each week and used to chauffeur Mrs. Lowery to the post office and on grocery shopping trips. The backyard accommodated about eight shade trees and several fruit trees: two fig, one wild cherry, and a Japanese (*Jiro*) persimmon, perhaps the only tree of its kind in the Donaldsonville area if not in the quad-parish region.

When almost ripened on the tree, the persimmons were literally given the *kid glove* treatment; that is, they were picked with carefully washed hands that could not touch anything before picking the fruit, and only one at a time. The picked fruit was then carefully wiped with a damp soft cloth and wrapped in tissue paper with the upper half uncovered and placed in a shallow wooden box to complete the ripening process. This procedure was continued until all the fruit had been removed from the tree, sometimes as many as 25 to 30 persimmons.

In addition to caring for the turkeys, my job was to prepare two of the heaviest toms, one for Thanksgiving and the other for Christmas, for the family. If you've ever butchered an adult tom turkey, you have firsthand knowledge that this can be an extremely challenging procedure.

I tied the turkey's legs together with thin rope. A wooden board was placed under the head, and a rag was placed over the head while stroking the tom into a state of calm. A washtub was placed over the bird with his head protruding outside the tub. The neck was then slowly stretched to allow space for the hatchet to fall to complete the job. The frantic wing flapping and kicking feet of a twenty-five-pound tom required the remainder of my energy to sit on the tub to hold him.

I worked at the Hotel Donaldson on Mississippi Street as a bellhop for about ten months during 1946 and '47. The hotel was a four-story red brick structure with forty-three to forty-four rooms that were used mostly by traveling salesmen who were called drummers. A lounge/restaurant located at the street level on the left side of the hotel was accessible from the lobby. Next door to the right side of the hotel was a restaurant co-owned and operated by "Li'l Ralph" Falsetta and Lawrence "Lala" Rageria.

A family friend, James "Cliff" Joseph, was assigned to help me transition into my bellhop duties. He worked at the hotel as the maintenance technician and supervisor of the laundry operations. He also worked as the part-time bellhop during the normal working hours. My working hours were from 6:00 p.m. to 6:00 a.m., with ample time in between for homework and sleep.

My job consisted of carrying guests' luggage and operating the elevator. Occasionally, I was asked by Mrs. Smith, the night manager, to go next door to Li'l Ralph's for a sandwich for her and me. I really enjoyed the job, as many of the clients were somewhat friendly and tips were great, especially on Saturday nights after guests returned from the bars. Saturday nights were also frightening at times, especially when I was asked to help ladies who had too much to drink to their rooms. I was fifteen at the time, and I reported to Dr. Lake, one of the owners of the hotel, that I was uncomfortable with that task and that I would leave the job if I had to do it again. He assured me I would no longer have to help anyone who was drunk.

Ms. LeBlanc (not her real name), a White woman, started working as a substitute night manager who covered for Smith occasionally to allow her time off. Before long, I became uneasy working under her direction. She engaged in conversations with White male guests who often talked about *niggers,* how stupid they were and how terrible they smelled. They spoke freely despite my presence in the back office, where my bed was placed. There was no door between us; I heard every word.

When she started touching me, on the arm or the hand or the shoulder, I decided I had had enough. I packed my books and other belongings, and told her I was leaving. She became anxious at my announcement; however, I left anyway. I stopped at Dr. Lake's house and explained the recent occurances and told him I could no longer work at the hotel. He apologized to me for Ms. LeBlanc's recent actions, assured me that he was aware that I was a good worker, and wished me well in school.

Texaco Service Station

My replacement for the job was Eddie Singer, a Black friend who was several years older than I was. After about six months on the job, LeBlanc, who was now the night manager, claimed Eddie tried to "attack" her. He was found guilty in a court of law and was sentenced to several years in Angola State Prison. He was later paroled and allowed to join the navy.

I worked as an attendant at Mike Marcello's Texaco Station pumping gas,checking and adding oil, wiping windshields and back windows, and fixing flats that included hot-patching the innertube and placing a "rubber boot" inside the tire when necessary.Washing the tops of cars required a small ladder, and the rubber padding on the running board was the devil to clean. Mike's was one of the few service stations in the area that used an electrical gasoline pump. His brother, Vic, was my supervisor, and more like a mentor when it came to teaching new service station skills. I thoroughly enjoyed this job. I was allowed to do my work with minimum supervision and at my pace. That measure of freedom caused me to work harder and more thoroughly, and I was often complimented by both brothers and sometimes customers for doing good work.

Several of the older service stations continued to use the manual-type pumps that required two steps: the first was to manually pump the gasoline from the underground tank into the glass container at the top of the pump, calibrated with lines that were numbered 1 to 30 indicating the number of gallons in the container. The "pumping" was done by pushing and pulling a lever connected to the tank until the gasoline level in the glass container reached the desired number of gallons requested by the customer. Step two involved transferring the gasoline via gravity flow from the glass tank to the automobile gas tank. An occasional nickel tip was rare but always appreciated.

Around that same time, I had a newspaper route delivering the *Louisiana Weekly* to households in Smoke Bend, Port Barrow, Donaldsonville, and Darrow. I had about seventy-five scattered customers that required most of a Saturday morning to complete deliveries using a bicycle given to me by my cousin, Lawrence "Germany" Dorsey, who had made the bike from scrap bicycle parts. He was my hero! And at a nickel profit on each paper, I was the envy of several of my peers and a few adults as well.

Holiday Celebrations

True Meaning of Holidays

Most of the traditional national holidays were celebrated in the region, some with more emphasis than others. Independence was not a reality for Black people during those years, and so Independence Day was not widely celebrated. The national anthem in the Black community was "Lift Every Voice and Sing." (The song originated from a poem written by James Weldon Johnson in 1900 and set to music by his brother, John Johnson, in 1905.) Labor Day held little meaning to us, as it was just another workday for most Black and poor White people. New Year's Day was only a one-day transition from *the old* to *the new*.

We did, however, celebrate several holidays—Mardi Gras, Easter Season, Halloween, All Saints' Day, and Christmas. The ones that held special meaning for us were Easter and Christmas.

Mardi Gras

New Orleans pre-Lenten festivities for Mardi Gras (Shrove or "Fat" Tuesday) may have been colorful, but the Donaldsonville "ma 'dee gra" activities were by far the most exciting. We certainly thought so. People came from miles around to Donaldsonville to enjoy a day of greeting, eating, fellowship, and fun, knowing that the next day, Ash Wednesday, would be the first in the forty-day atonement period before Easter Sunday. Mardi Gras, or "carnival" as it was mostly referred to in our community, was the time of year when people freely welcomed you into their homes to enjoy the last day of the merry-making season, which started in New Orleans two to three weeks before.

The festival was also celebrated in Lafourche. Rev. Wallace stated that there were two carnival clubs in Lafourche, both located in Thibodeaux: the Ghana and the Shaka. "Costumes were quite original, with elaborate masks and colorful accessories. And the floats were beautifully decorated, much like those seen in New Orleans. The *hit* of the carnival parade was usually the costumed mounted Black cowboys," he said.

In our family, preparation consisted of deciding on a suitable costume. We wore homemade costumes that were simple but effective, being made from some cast-off garments or other materials on hand. One or two months prior to carnival, the costume making began—choices were storybook characters, Indians, and animals. Usually, several household members would sew well enough to do a good job on the costumes, but each family member contributed in some way to the finished product. Grandma Antoinette, however, made most of the costumes. Masks were homemade also, but once in a while, they were purchased from local stores that stocked them. The more affluent people purchased or rented costumes that ranged from the very simple to the most elaborate.

Most children went to bed early on Monday night before carnival day. They wanted to be up early the next morning to be costumed and masked to "run Mardi Gras." This meant going throughout the immediate neighborhood greeting persons on the street and at their doors in a festive and friendly manner as people tried to guess their identity. Some used makeup to disguise their faces instead of wearing masks. Other families went to New Orleans to "make Mardi Gras" and see the extremely elaborate costumes, colorful floats, and people dancing in the streets and catching beads and candy thrown from the beautifully decorated floats.

CURTIS J. JOHNSON

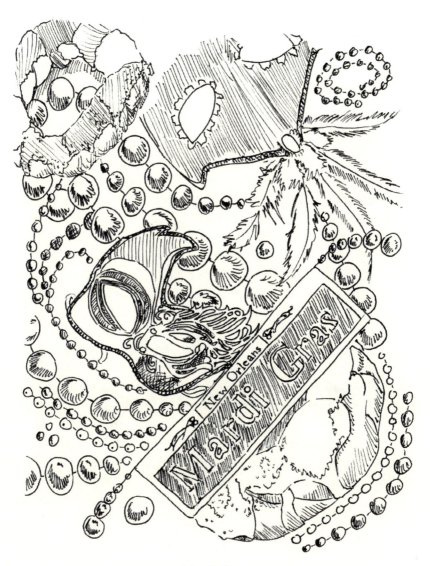

Mardi Gras

There was also unscheduled excitement caused by older boys and men who used the masquerading occasion for frightening and intimidating others under the guise of celebrating. Some masked horseback riders with cracking whips would keep most adults on their toes and *all* children off the streets. It was frightening—yet fascinating—to see a rider approach your direction although you were securely hidden behind bushes or buildings. Overcome by excitement, the power to resist would give way as we ran for the house to bolt the door. The mounted masked men were many times strangers to us, but some were familiar: Son Missouri, "Ice Cart" Joe, and John Edward Johnson, all folks we knew well.

In some Black communities, carnival clubs staged a parade in late morning and again in early evening on Shrove Tuesday, and a carnival ball that lasted from early evening until midnight. Such was the case in Donaldsonville. The parade floats were colorful, creatively crafted by area schools, church groups, and social clubs. Claiborne Williams Band led a parade of costumed groups and individuals on foot and on floats. Signaled by the ferryboat whistle, the procession began near Elray Kocke's on Mississippi Street and continued along a traditional route which included Railroad Avenue in the direction of Texas and Pacific Railroad Depot, turning left onto Williams Street and right two blocks later onto Saint Patrick Street, stopping at the True Friends Hall. Here was the site for an exciting and hilarious evening of fun and merrymaking: dancing, eating, and drinking. Dressed in royal regalia, the king and queen reigned over the ball, their identity secret.

Before midnight, when the unmasking took place and participants identified, many of the revelers were truly surprised to find their guesses about whose faces were behind the masks had been totally wrong. Of course, all who attended the ball were not in masquerade. But all had a good time. Promptly at midnight, the ball ended and everyone left the True Friends Hall to make their way homeward. Several could be heard making the familiar remark, "Wait 'til next year," promising a bigger and better carnival celebration. Catholics began their observance of the forty days of Lent. It was not uncommon for non-Catholics to also observe the Lenten Season.

As children, we were not allowed to attend the True Friends Hall Ball, but after the parade, we returned home to reminisce about who wore the best costume, who was the ugliest masker, who strutted the most in the parade, and the like. Most of us were exhausted from *running* Mardi Gras, but already we were making plans for the next year's celebration. Even that was exciting!

The Easter Season

Compared to Christmas, the Easter holiday season had more religious overtones, but fewer aspects. For children, the baskets of jellybean, candy eggs, chocolate bunnies, and dyed boiled eggs said it all. For adults, the secular nature of the holiday showed in clothing; people wore their finest suits, dresses, and hats and joining in the parade to and from Easter church services.

Holy Thursday started the four-day religious holiday season, and it was usually a quiet and solemn day. Good Friday was observed as a holiday in the area by most people, and although fishing was a favorite holiday pastime, few people fished on that day. It was generally "understood" that the fish did not bite on Good Friday.

Holy Saturday was regarded with nearly as much solemnity as Good Friday, but with more shopping activities for new clothing, buying, and dying eggs, in preparation for Sunday.

Sunrise service at Mount Triumph and churches through the region made early risers of us all. Members dressed in their Easter finest to witness the Resurrection and to hear Rev. Emile Johnson preach a spirited homily. His sermons followed a traditional format: scripture readings, followed by an enthusiastic and understandable explanation and translation of what actually took place "at the tomb on the third day," with his delivery becoming more and more emotional. His story was so vivid that it seemed a reality. Seldom did the high-pitched preaching end before at least one sister shouted and "fell out." To the average churchgoer, his message left a good feeling and renewed assurance that Jesus had followed through on his promise to his disciples and to the world.

An important part of the sunrise service was the calling of sinners to the mourners' bench to repent and be prayed over. The mourners' bench was the first pew at the front of the church. Of course, my siblings and I had to go sit on the bench when our mother "gave us the eye" from her perch in the choir. Many who came forward to receive prayers said they "felt the Holy Spirit" had descended upon them, and they were ready to commit their lives to God.

After church service, the children were more anxious than ever to get home to the Easter baskets and breakfast. It was the only breakfast of the year where sugary treats trumped actual food.

A common Easter myth was that if you looked at the sun at sunrise, you could see it moving or "shouting," a sign of rejoicing at Christ's Resurrection. And, of course, everyone looked at the sun to see the shouting. Some used a piece of colored glass to look at the sun. Most didn't. How some of us are able to see *at all* today remains a pure mystery!

Halloween: The Storm!

While children anticipated ghosts and goblins, many adults spent time sprucing up the graves of deceased family members for All Saints' Day that followed. Our family members placed cut flowers at family gravesites and helped Grandpa Ogeese with cutting and selling dahlias, mums, roses, and other cut flowers to the public from the many beds surrounding the house. It was easy to lose sight of the meaning of the day in preparing for it. The day was for the dead. Steeped in superstition in our town and very likely throughout the area, the air filled with electricity as the sunset gave way to early evening.

Normal conversations about witches, gris-gris, mojos, and spirits were enough to keep the average child and some adults on edge any night of the year. "True" stories about the mounted headless Confederate soldier, the eight-foot-tall grazing cow, and other phenomena "seen" in and around graveyards on previous Halloween nights were convincing enough to keep even adults indoors after sundown. Few children ventured out alone on Halloween night, which was not a trick-or-treat occasion. Instead, flour "bombs" (baking flour in small paper bags), soaped messages on windows, and overturned garbage cans were among the evidence that "tricks" had been pulled by someone or some*thing* the night before.

We made jack-o'-lanterns from shoeboxes. The "face" was cut out of the box top, with cellophane paper pasted over the face from the inside to prevent the wind from blowing cut the candle. This homemade version was carried by a handle made of string attached to the long end of the box.

CURTIS J. JOHNSON

"Treats" were provided for the children at home and, at our house, consisted of goodies prepared by Aunt Henrietta who was helped by the older girls in the family. Occasionally, Marguerite Ricardo would make ginger cookies and pralines for us. All of these would be enjoyed during the early-evening hours as the older Ricardo girls, Adele and Aileen, told stories of ghosts and extraordinary happenings on Halloween evening. Frequently, the older children added to the tales, extending their imaginations to further frighten the younger children.

As children, we ventured out occasionally to look for truth in any of the many Halloween tales we had heard over the years. None of us can say we actually saw anyone or anything unusual. One incident does stand out in my mind, however, as mysterious to everyone in our household except for my brother and me.

Our mother returned home one Halloween night after a visit with her parents and complained that something had cut her throat as she walked home. As the family gathered quickly in the living room, Edith shouted, "Zena's been hurt! Zena's been hurt!" as Dile ran for iodine and a bandage. Walter and I promised never again to stretch thin copper wire from a utility pole to a tree across the sidewalk as a Halloween trick!

All Saints' Day: The Lull

The activities of the day following Halloween were the opposite of the evening of fun on Halloween. All Saints' Day was observed with much dignity while attention was focused on paying respect to the dead. Most families placed flowers on gravesites.

The early-morning hours on All Saints' Day were very busy for our family. The day started with helping Grandpa Ogeese cut and deliver bouquets of dahlias, mums, and other cut flowers across town and in our general neighborhood. Buyers came until all of the flowers had been sold. After that, some shoppers were interested in buying some of the remaining flower buds. We set aside nice bouquets for our use when we visited our family gravesites later during the day, when things had settled down at grandpa's flower sale.

Halloween

CURTIS J. JOHNSON

Our family had deceased members in the Catholic, the Protestant, and Mount Triumph Baptist cemeteries. Several of us children would accompany an adult to each of these sites to place flowers on graves of family members, and by doing so, we learned where family members were buried. The remainder of the day was relatively quiet and solemn. It was not uncommon in Donaldsonville and nearby towns for out-of-towners to traveled great distances to visit and place fresh flowers on graves of relatives.

Christmas Celebrations

I love the Christmas-tide and yet:
I notice this each year I live;
I always like the gifts I get,
But how I love the gifts I give.

—Carolyn Wells

Without a doubt, the holiday most celebrated by our family was Christmas. It was a special time of year for everybody, and our parents always made it even more special for us. We were accustomed to the usual commercial trappings of the tree, colorful lights, gifts, toys, and the special dinner. Families acknowledged and honored the meaning of the special birth.

The day before the exciting day was just as memorable. Earlier in the afternoon, we cut and tied together with twine limbs from the Acosta's giant cedar tree across the street from our house. We shaped the limbs in a treelike fashion and planted them in a pail of garden dirt. The pail was covered with green paper to resemble grass. All family members chipped in to decorate the tree with the bell and ball cutouts from various colors of construction paper and attached to the tree by loops of number 8 sewing thread. The "snow" that covered the branches in strategic spots was made from Lux soap flakes with a little water added and using an eggbeater. Stringed popcorn was used to drape the limbs from top to bottom. Hot homemade eggnog and cookies were served on Christmas Eve, a ritual that became a family tradition.

Christmastime

CURTIS J. JOHNSON

Then came Christmas Day!

Starting with early-morning church service (some family members may have attended midnight Mass the night before), the day promised to be one filled with enjoyment. Neighbors and relatives stopped in to exchange greetings. Grandpa August, Grandma Antoinette, and Aunt Henrietta would spend the day with us, making the occasion even more special. Aunts, uncles, and cousins from the community and New Orleans dropped in to bid "Merry Christmas" and to share in a glass of homemade or Mogen David "cheer" and a slice of cake. Our father's annual gifts from Elray Kocke's included a large bag of hard candy, a half gallon of cane syrup, a half gallon of sweet wine, and a turkey or smoked ham that came in handy and were enjoyed each year. Hog killings were planned to coincide with the holiday season. The aroma of fresh pork roasts, hams, turkeys, geese, ducks, and chickens being cooked filled the neighborhood.

It was also traditional for children to use firecrackers and sparklers during Christmas Eve and on Christmas Day. For a nickel a pack, our best buys were at Ma'am Inzerella's vegetable market located at the east side of the footbridge that spanned Bayou Lafourche. You knew that you were big when you were allowed to shoot firecrackers. From then on, sparklers were strictly for "children."

Each youngster in the household got one toy from Santa. As we grew up, we received more practical gifts, usually clothing. The older children would chip in to buy small gifts for our mother and father and baby sister, Carolyn.

Christmas dinner was actually a feast with the preparation literally orchestrated by our mother. The chores began the day before with shopping at grocery stores, meat markets, and local supermarkets. The food preparation began with chopping green peppers, garlic, shallots, and other seasonings. This was a two-person job in itself. The cooking really began on Christmas Eve, and with minimum time for sleeping, it was not completed until dinner was served the next afternoon. Each child was allowed a small glass of wine at dinner. Edith traditionally gave her glass to Claudia in exchange for Claudia doing Edith's share of washing the dinner dishes.

The Christmas we remember most was in 1934. As the children gathered in the living room to see what Santa had left for them the night before, Grandma Annette brought in a small bundle wrapped in a blanket, announcing that Santa had brought us a live baby doll. It was Carolyn, born at one o'clock that morning. She was real and doll-like, and we believed she was our special toy from Santa. We still do many years later.

Old Schoolhouse

CURTIS J. JOHNSON

The Three Rs and Secondhand Books

School is a building that
Has four walls—
With tomorrow inside.
                            —Lon Watters

A unique design of earlier architecture that is seldom used in modern building construction is the *keystone*. Building arched bridges, arches over windows, doors, and porticos would be difficult without this important piece of masonry. In addition to being the main support element of the arch, this simply shaped stone also added to the attractiveness and value of the design.

The literature along with many years of personal experiences support the conclusion that *education* has been the *keystone* in the lives of successful people throughout our international society, and the mainstay of liberating persons of low income, especially people of color.

Today's low-income families are described by some authorities as victims of social and economic doings: inadequate health services, low-paying jobs and high unemployment, separation from mainstream society, substandard housing, and high crime rates. Experts remind us that 90 percent of a child's mental faculties are developed by age four. Therefore, if children from low-income backgrounds are continually exposed to these substandard conditions, chances are they will not easily advance.

With this backdrop, consider education in Ascension Parish before the twentieth century.

In 1871, as a result of his belief that everyone should know how to read, Louis L. Butler, Sr., a Black man, opened the Modeste School in Modeste (Ascension). The February 24, 1872, issue of the *CHIEF,* the Donaldsonville weekly newspaper, printed the minutes of the Ascension Parish School Board meeting held on February 19, 1872. At this meeting, the board approved several teachers who had already started teaching at their schools. Butler was named teacher and principal of one of the schools in the First Ward, Modeste.

The Rise and Fall of Leland College, a thesis, dated May 1974 by Lionel Lee that was presented to the faculty of the graduate school, Southern University, presents a history of another school for Blacks in Donaldsonville. The following are related excerpts.

Holbrook Chamberlain, a resident of Brooklyn, New York, came to New Orleans for the purpose of establishing an institution of higher learning for Blacks of Louisiana. Leland University was founded in 1870 by Holbrook in the basement of Tulane Avenue Baptist Church. Leland was named after the wife of Chamberlain, whose father was Elder John Leland of Cheshire, Massachusetts.

The aim and objectives of Leland University were for the purposes of "educating and training young men and women for preachers, teachers, irrespective of race, color or previous condition of servitude."

It was evident that Leland University was prepared to do its work in the field of education. A system of affiliated schools was inaugurated by which the faculty of the university could exercise control over the preparatory course of study in secondary institutions established at important centers outside of New Orleans.

The first one of these schools which became a part of Leland University was Howe Institute of New Iberia, founded in 1890 by "the son of Peter Howe of Wenona, Illinois." The institution was placed under the control of the president of Leland University. Another institution which became a part of Leland University was Leland Academy, which was located at Donaldsonville. In 1892, . . . the institution became an auxiliary of Leland [University] . . .

Between 1900 and 1901 . . . Leland Academy of Donaldsonville had an enrollment of 106 students.

In a paper entitled *Leland University* compiled by Angela V. Proctor, an archivist, she noted, in part:

Another institution, which became a part of Leland University, was: Leland Academy. In November, 1892, the Trustees of the Slater High School at Donaldsonville. La., made application for acceptance as an auxiliary school under the name Leland Academy, and was accepted by the Board. The Principal, Professor S. S. Gray, a graduate of the Normal department, in which the school gives promise of success and usefulness. The academy had the services of Miss Pauline Taylor as directress of instrumental music, and Dr. John H. Lowery as lecturer in Physiology and hygiene.

Donaldsonville Academy, located on Railroad Avenue, may have been the first public school for Blacks that was started in 1897. This was followed by Leland Academy which occupied the land that would eventually become the site for Lowery High. An article in the November 16, 1929, edition of the *Donaldsonville Chief* carried this story:

NEW SCHOOL FOR COLORED PUPILS IN PORT BARROW

> *Provision has been made by the Ascension Parish School Board for the erection of a new school building for the teaching of the colored children of this community. The new school will be a one story structure and will contain six class rooms and an auditorium. It will be located on the present site of the Leland colored school which occupies a ten-acre tract of land. The old Leland school building has been donated to the school board for the lumber from that building as well as the lumber from the old Donaldsonville colored school, situated in [sic] Railroad Avenue, will be used in constructing the new. It is also hoped to use the lumber from the old schoolhouse in Brusly Sacramento, which is no longer used for teaching purposes, in the new building. The ten-acre tract of land on which the new school will be erected will be purchased, with funds presently being raised for the purpose by the colored citizens of this community.*
>
> *The cost of the new building will be between $7000 and $8000 and it is hoped to have it ready for occupancy at the opening of the school session next fall. The building and grounds will belong to the parish school board.*
>
> *The school board will receive aid from the Rosenwald Fund in the sum of $1500, in defraying the cost of erecting the new school building, as evidenced from the following letter received a few days ago by L. J. Babin, parish superintendent:*
>
>

March 9, 1929

>
> *Superintendent L. J. Babin, Donaldsonville, Louisiana.*
> *Dear Mr. Babin:*
> *Beg to advise that your application for Rosenwald aid in the construction of the Donaldsonville School has been approved in the amount of $1500. You may proceed with the construction of this building with full assurance that the amount named above will be*

available whenever the building is completed and inspected according to the requirements of the Fund.

Yours very truly,
A. C. LEWIS

The Rosenwald Fund derives its name from Mr. Rosenwald, head of Sears, Roebuck and Company, who has created a fund to assist in building schools for colored children in the south. It is said that Mr. Rosenwald has already donated $50,000,000 to this fund.

This new school was named Lowery Training School, after the local Black medical doctor, Dr. John H. Lowery, whose financial contributions aided in the school's completion and whose widow employed me for household and yard work when I was fourteen.

Lowery Training School consisted of three buildings during the early 1930s. One building served as the elementary school for grades one through five. A second building served as classrooms for grades six through eight and for the high school grades as well. The industrial education shop occupied the third building.

Batiste-Rogers stated that there was only one private school for children of color that existed in Donaldsonville. It was owned by Vivian Sullivan (grades kindergarten to six). Several other area private schools operating during the same time included Edna Mae Ricardo's (kindergarten) in Port Barrow and Bessie Clark's (kindergarten) in Smoke Bend. All of these schools had closed by the end of the 1930s due to rising costs.

Initially, there were no public schools in Saint James for Blacks during the 1920s, according to Rev. Thomas. "Back then, Black churches and benevolent societies' facilities were used for classrooms for Black children. White children did have school buildings and attended school for nine months from September to June, while Black children started in October and ended in April," he stated.

"This time difference was created to have the Black children, who represented *cheap labor,* to work in the fields grassing corn and sugarcane or harvesting Irish potatoes for twenty-five cents a day," added Octave.

In an undated paper delivered by Mrs. Feliska Stewart Taylor at a Magnolia High School reunion, she shared the history of schools for

Blacks who lived on the west bank of Saint James Parish during the "early years." Parts of her paper are quoted as follows:

> In the beginning before I attended school, the Black Baptist Church was used as school buildings to teach Blacks. Parents paid teachers and bought school books. As time went by, and I was old enough (1927), the Benevolent Societies built halls for their meeting place and we were allowed to use those buildings.
>
> I knew the White children had schoolhouses, and I thought society halls were schoolhouses for us. (I was very young and naïve).
>
> As the White school buildings were condemned, we were allowed to use those buildings and new schools were built for the others (Whites). I did not know why until a news reporter (Meg Carter) found out in the research on education that the [Louisiana] legislature did not provide any funds for education of Blacks on the West Bank (St James Parish).
>
> I can only recall as far back as 1927. I attended school in the Silver Key Benevolent Hall on the New Vacherie Road and in the Friends of Hope Hall located in Magnolia.
>
> There was one teacher for all the grades (1 thru 7), Mrs. Philomena Hibert ("Miss Feelow"). In the hall was a heater that we furnished wood for and there was also coal. By the time I was in third grade, Mrs. Helen Sarparu joined Mrs. Hibert, giving us a total of two teachers.
>
> At that time, we did not have nine months of school. It was about six or seven months. I am not quite sure. But the White children received nine months. During our first year, we had ABC's and primer. We had to be seven years old to begin school. During our second year, we were in first grade; third year in second grade, and so on. But, we were required to be in the even grades two years to make up for the short terms.
>
> The old Magnolia Elementary School that was located on Church Lane was previously a White school located on Vacherie Road. It must have been condemned, so it was torn down and rebuilt in Magnolia. I can remember our parents giving donations to help purchase the land.
>
> Since there was no transportation for Negroes, every area had its own school. For instance, there was Baytree Elementary in Baytree Hall; Cedar Grove in Moonshine; Burton Lane in Burton Lane, and St. Louis in Welcome. All of them began with one teacher for all grades.
>
> We never knew what it was to receive new books. We were given the old books that the Whites had used for four or five years. We never had enough books. Those children who lived close together . . . had to

share the books. And, of course, the first two or three lessons were never in the books. The one book that had these lessons was for the teacher. The teacher would write them on the black board, and we had to copy them from the board.

There were no desks; only benches. We wrote with our papers on our laps or we knelt down and wrote on the benches.

Later on there were two teachers to a school and the number slowly increased, but so did the children. For the children living back of St. James, there were no schools for Negroes. But, the farmer or boss man contributed money to the bus line so the Whites could attend school.

I graduated from the seventh grade in 1936 from Magnolia Elementary School located on Church Lane. There were no high schools, but a few of us were able to live with a relative in New Orleans. Even though I came from a country school, I studied and stayed in the top 10% of my class. I came back to work at Magnolia Elementary in 1944 and was paid a salary of $60.00 per month. The teachers or parents had to buy little extra learning devices to help educate our children. By then, most of the time there was one teacher per grade. We had as many as 45 to 48 students in one grade.

I began teaching with only a high school education. Within a few years, we could take extension courses from Southern University. We also went to summer school at Southern [Baton Rouge], Xavier [New Orleans], and even Grambling [near Ruston in northern Louisiana].

After some years, they added eighth grade to Magnolia Elementary. Then the next year, ninth grade, and so on through 12th grade. So they added four more rooms on one side, and a lunchroom or cafeteria. Magnolia Elementary and Magnolia High School were combined.

Somewhere in the late 1940s or early 1950s, we received transportation. One driver, Mr. Ben Roussel, picked up children as far up as St. James [township]—back to Back Quarters or Ozone and St. Phillip and the Vacherie Road . . . He could not take the bus [to his] home. It had to stay at Cazenave. This meant the children from the St. Phillip area were the first to get to school in the morning and the last to leave in the afternoon.

Taylor goes on to say that after Magnolia High was built, children who lived the longest distances from the school were shuttled by two or three different buses to get to school. There were no shelters for the children during these exchanges to protect them from inclement weather. "But God was with us, and he protected us during those days of hardship," she wrote.

CURTIS J. JOHNSON

Even though they had graduated from college and had completed their practice teaching, they [teachers] still had to attend workshops every six weeks. All teachers did research and prepared additional information on all subject matter. "It was still good, and we produced quality students who were successful wherever they attended college," she wrote.

In Lafourche, very few Blacks lived in Golden Meadow, and practically none lived below that area, Reverend Wallace stated. "There were no public schools south of Raceland for Blacks. Public schools for Whites were located throughout the parish and were housed in dedicated buildings. School buses were provided for White students, but none were issued for Blacks. There were separate school facilities for the Houmas and Chitimacha Indian tribes living in the parish. However, there were no public school buildings for Blacks. Elementary schools for Blacks were established in Black-owned churches and other available facilities owned by Blacks." He gave as an example the Raceland Colored Elementary School, where he initially taught in 1941 and later.

During the mid-1930s through the mid-1940s, public schools for Blacks were built in Black communities throughout each parish. The exterior of these buildings was built with cypress clapboards, and some were painted. The interior was finished with gypsum board walls and ceilings and pine board floors. Classroom furnishings included one-person desks, a slate blackboard, a bulletin board, a pegboard for hats and coats, a teacher's desk and chair, and a potbellied stove for heat in the winter.

Students helped maintain order and cleanliness. Girls and boys took turns erasing the blackboard at the end of the school day. However, the boys washed the board several times a week. Girls helped the teacher "decorate" the bulletin board. During the winter, boys brought in kindling wood and a scuttle full of coal each morning to maintain the fire that was started earlier that morning by the janitor.

In the region prior to 1945, one high school for Blacks was located in Lafourche (C. M. Washington in Thibodeaux) and one in Ascension (Lowery). Students who graduated from outlying elementary schools in those two parishes had to be shuttled in cars and private buses to Thibodeaux and Donaldsonville. Students from Saint James were transported to high schools in surrounding parishes as well. Reed High School was constructed in Assumption (Napoleonville) in 1945. Although buses were appropriated to White elementary and high schools, there were no buses allocated to Black schools. Some students walked to and from school, a six-to ten-mile round trip. Several private buses brought high school students from Assumption, Saint James, and distant locations in Ascension to Lowery. Students who lived in East Ascension were transported to the ferry in Darrow where they walked to Lowery school in Port Barrow. Others came in private automobiles and carpools. The Thomas brothers would occasionally ride the family horses from Smoke Bend to school at Lowery. Sometimes their friends enjoyed the short horseback rides during recess, away from the playground and the eyes of the teachers, of course.

Eventually, public elementary schools for Blacks were scattered throughout each parish. On the west bank in Saint James, schools were located in Saint James Township (Fifth Ward Elementary), Brookstown (St. Louis Elementary), Chapman (Burton Elementary), Burton (Cedar Grove Elementary), Vacherie (Baytree Elementary and Sixth Ward Elementary), and South Vacherie (Shell Mound Elementary). Those schools situated in the east bank were in Lutcher (Cypress Grove Elementary) and Gramercy (Colonial Elementary).

In addition to Lowery Elementary School and Lowery Training (High) School, Modeste Elementary was the only other public school in West Ascension. On the east bank, schools were located in Gonzales (Smith Elementary, Gonzales Colored Elementary, George Washington Carver Elementary, Kennedy Junior/Senior High), Prairieville (Prairieville Elementary and Prairieville High), Sorrento Elementary (Sorrento), Galvez Colored Elementary (Galvez), and Hillaryville (Marchand Elementary).

In Assumption, elementary schools were built in Belle Alliance, (Belle Alliance Elementary), Bertranville (Woodlawn School), Clarktown, (Newbelle), Supreme (Hymalaya School), Paincourtville (Paincourtville Colored Elementary), and Napoleonville (Napoleonville Elementary and Canal Elementary).

Students in Lafourche attended Ken Hadley Elementary and Raceland Colored School, both in Raceland, and the Negro Corporation School, an elementary school in Thibodeaux. After classes for older children were added, the name was changed to C. M. Washington Training School, named after Cordelia Matthews Washington, a Black pioneer who canvassed for years for better educational opportunities for Blacks in Terrebonne and Assumption parishes as well as Lafourche. In December 1950, C. M. Washington High School was dedicated, with Professor Robert M. Harris serving as the principal. Washington's daughter-in-law, Leola Washington, was the principal of the elementary school.

Potbellied Stove

Some students brought their lunch from home, although the school served hot lunches. Many students received free lunches based on family income. Others who lived in close proximity to school walked to their houses for lunch. Periodically, one or two of us in my family would eat lunch at school; however, the cost—ten cents—was an expense few families could afford.

The regional school boards used a hand-me-down supply system for school equipment, furniture, books, and some supplies for Black schools. Only when White students had used an item, sometimes for many years, was it relegated to Black students. Some of the books I received in elementary school had torn or missing pages and contained homework assignments, love notes, as well as a note, "To the nigger who will use this book," and other such trivia written by previous users. Rev. Wallace recalled, "There was hardly enough space left for a student to write his or her name in the books because they had been used so many times before." Wooden desks came carved with names, hearts with initials, Cupid arrows, and other doodles, making it difficult to write without using a smooth surface such as a tablet to cover the ruts and holes. Many desks had to be repaired and refinished in the schools' woodwork shop before students could use them.

Our Teachers, Our Future

Teachers in elementary and high schools were mostly women, and seldom would a male teacher be found in an elementary school classroom. Few men were teachers at the high school level. Usually, the principal, the shop teacher, the agriculture teacher, and occasionally, the health and physical education teacher would be men.

Teachers maintained good order and discipline in their classrooms. Most students were orderly and respectful toward the teachers and their peers. Students knew that the teacher or other students would report their disorderly conduct at school to their parents. Considering the alternative, usually a good whipping, this factor was motivation enough for them to remain orderly, attentive, and cooperative with other students as well as the teacher. When called for, and depending on the severity of the infraction, violators were disciplined with five or more *whacks* with a ruler in the palm of the hand that was bent downward by the teacher holding the student's fingers, or across the knuckles. In more serious cases, the student was sent to the principal to explain what he or she did.

Under the leadership of Mr. E. C. Land and a cadre of excellent faculty and staff members, basic and advanced education for the students at Lowery was comprehensive and far-reaching. Our principal encouraged excellence in performance, courage, respect for all, helping others, independence, thrift, and other admirable qualities. His demonstrated leadership qualities and high standards set the example for the teachers, staff, students, and community as well. Our lives were enhanced for having had him as our principal.

Several teachers at the Lowery Elementary School were indispensable in making our educational experiences successful. They were well-respected as community leaders. They provided the love and care—and discipline—needed to motivate students to achieve. Two of our teachers, Mary Speight and Evelyn Pierce, were never short on discipline tactics. There was a well-understood, yet unwritten contract between these teachers and parents that the children would be taken to task when necessary. Mrs. Speight was an expert at using the ruler on bent-back palms of hands. Mrs. Pierce, on the other hand, was good at throwing a two-foot-long stick of wood in the direction of the perpetrator without hitting the innocent students. A lot of time was spent ducking in that first-grade class, though it was my "immaturity"—not dodging projectiles—that kept me in the first grade for two years. And such was the beginning of public school for me and life away from home for a substantial part of the day.

All of our teachers had received higher-education training, and most held college degrees. It was not uncommon for teachers to spend each summer in teacher-training programs at either Leland College in Baker, Southern University in Baton Rouge, or Grambling College in Grambling. Summer workshops were held to assist teachers in becoming more proficient in their teaching skills. Teachers from out of town held room-and-board relationships with families in the community. During these years, some of these instructors lived with our Pinkins grandparents, sometimes two or three teachers at one time.

My siblings and I were fortunate to be in close association with these college-trained instructors. We ran errands and performed small chores for them for which we were rewarded with a nickel or dime from time to time. Most times, however, our mother required us to perform the chores free of charge. She believed we were getting the better part of the relationship, since the impact of these instructors on our lives could not be measured in terms of money. It could be that such influence, along with that of our parents, can be credited with forming our love of education and preparation for a secure future.

Black teachers who desired to advance their education to the master's or doctoral degree level had to apply to the Louisiana State Board of Education for grants to fund tuition, travel, room and board, and related stipends to attend out-of-state universities where segregation was not enforced. Although Louisiana State University (LSU) was located in Baton Rouge and only thirty-six miles from our house, two of my sisters (Odile and Edith) had to apply out of state to pursue graduate studies at the University of Illinois in Urbana during the summer months between school years because of Jim Crow segregation. My third sister, Claudia, had to attend the University of Georgia for her initial semester for the advanced degree in counseling. When she started the second semester a year later, LSU had started accepting Black students; and consequently, her second semester was completed there. She completed the final phase of her counseling requirements at Southern University which, by then, began offering the master's degree in counseling.

When asked about teachers' salaries, Worley, who taught in New Orleans public schools as well as schools in Assumption and Ascension, explained, "Colored teachers were paid about $40 a month during the 1930s. After many years at that level, the salary was increased to $75 a month, making us [teachers] surprised and happy! It was not until the 1950s that salaries were increased to about $200 a month. Although the salary for colored teachers with college degrees was closer to $300 a month, this range remained far less when compared with salaries for White teachers with the same credentials and longevity."

On the subject of teachers' pay, Rev. Wallace said, "Salaries for White teachers were always appreciably more than for colored teachers. The gap was never closed because when raises were granted, both White and colored teachers received raises. But the *amount* of the raises continued to be more for the Whites who were already in a higher pay bracket."

Teacher

Parent-Teacher Associations

Historically, the Black parents supported their children's schools in many ways. In addition to buying raffle tickets, attending extracurricular programs, supporting bake sales, and other fund-raising activities, many were members of or volunteers for the schools' Parent-Teacher Association (PTA). Parents actively attended and participated in PTA meetings. Families bought and sold tickets to fund-raisers such as varsity basketball and baseball games and stage plays. Mothers made costumes for their children for dramas and other stage plays. Mothers baked cakes, cookies, and pies and made pralines and fudge for bake sales to support the PTA.

My siblings and my attendance at Mount Triumph Baptist Church and Saint Catherine Catholic Church laid an active spiritual foundation for each of the Johnson children. Lowery Training School provided our educational and social roots that, coupled with our spiritual training, became the basis for our civic, recreational, cultural, and professional growth and development. We credit our school and the PTA for our academic and extracurricular achievements during our elementary and high school years.

Our mother was president of the PTA for several terms and spent long hours with the committee planning and coordinating the association's activities. Most of the other parents were also quite active in supporting their children as well as the children of the neighborhoods.

My siblings and I received a lot of support and encouragement from our parents. Long before buying our first set of *Collier's Encyclopedia* (1941) to help with homework, both parents attended school activities and plays, tutored us in memorizing scripts for stage plays, and offered a shoulder to lean on when needed.

Extracurricular Activities

Lowery's recreation, cultural, and athletic programs featured extracurricular activities for both students and folks from the community as well, and camaraderie among students was usually high. Our competitive sports program was limited to baseball and basketball. My sisters, Claudia and Edith, played varsity basketball; and I played varsity basketball and baseball. As the school did not have a gymnasium, all team sports were played outside.

On game days, when games were scheduled, players were excused early from classes to prepare the basketball court or baseball field ("liming the lines") for the game that began as the school day ended. The school had a number of "cheers" ("Hey, hey; ho, ho; beat 'em Ole' Lowery and beat 'em some mo!") but no cheerleaders, per se. Members of the girls' teams performed as the pep squad during the boys' games. The boys reciprocated during the girls' events.

And after a rain, we'd set fire to the basketball court with gasoline to dry it off enough for us to play visiting teams. We envied Morgan City and New Iberia High Schools that had gymnasiums.

Various professional clubs that held our attention included Home Economics, Vocational Education, Science, Dramatics and Mixed Chorus. We raised funds to help build the lunchroom by acting, singing, and dancing in those fun-packed minstrel shows orchestrated by "Boss" Hiram Martin, our vocational education teacher.

The mixed chorus performed at almost all community-related programs held at Lowery, and won several Louisiana Interscholastic, Athletic, and Literary Association (LIALA) Best Mixed Chorus titles in our region. The Home Economics Club played host to community food-canning demonstrations that were held several times each year. Members of the Vocational Education Club worked during the summer months building and repairing houses in the community to gain practical experience and exposure while raising funds to purchase tools and needed equipment for the vocational shop programs.

Schools were also the social centers in Black communities. In addition to the sports activities, social events included school dramas using themes that focused on holidays, cultural programs, musical concerts, and showing of family health instructional films by the State Education Department. Families were invited to these activities regardless of whether or not children from these households attended the school. Families took advantage of invitations to these events, both those that charged a small fee as a fund-raiser as well as the free events. One such event was described in an article that appeared in the Friday, September 11, 1953, issue of the *Gonzales Weekly* newspaper "Prairieville Sets Negro Fair Dates," as follows:

> *A display of livestock, poultry, agricultural products, food conservation, clothing, flowers, plus an educational display from the parish Negro schools, will feature* [sic] *the Ascension Parish Negro Fair,*

Sept. 25-27, at Prairieville High School, L. C. Christy, fair manager has announced. The fair is sponsored by the Ascension Parish Negro Fair Assn., Inc., in conjunction with the Ascension Parish Teachers Organization, and the Women's Industrial Club of Prairieville.

In 1950 the Negroes of Ascension Parish submitted a charter which was approved by the Secretary of State. State appropriations have continued to aid the group annually, and in amounts equal to that given other fairs. Also, Southern University has rendered assistance through its Agricultural Department to improve the quality of the fair.

Prairieville, because of its central location, is the site for the fair each September. In the past two years, attendance and number of displays have more than doubled.

Association officials are: Dennis Dorville, president; John Cornish, first vice president, James Robinson, second vice president; William Tillotson, secretary; L. J. Dorville, assistant secretary; Leo Christy, treasurer; S.L. Christy, consultant; Lloyd Parms, chairman, board of directors, and L. C. Christy, consultant and manager of the fair.

All in all, the six Johnson children graduated from Lowery, although Walter attended high school for one year in New Orleans then returned to Lowery for graduation. He was drafted into World War II and, after being discharged in 1945, worked in New Orleans for the United States Postal Service at night while maintaining a full-time work schedule in building construction as a carpenter and brick layer. Odile and Edith were named salutatorian of their classes, and Claudia was named valedictorian of her class. After receiving degrees from Southern University, both Odile and Claudia returned to Lowery as teachers; and Edith began her teaching career in Saint Tammany Parish Training School in Slidell. Upon graduating from Southern, I was commissioned a second lieutenant in the U.S. Army Corps of Engineers, and began a twenty-year army career. Carolyn attended Southern for one semester but was unable to continue because of health problems.

It is apparent to us that attaining an education can make a major difference in one's quality of living. A good spiritual family foundation coupled with our educational experiences gave my siblings and me the edge we needed to succeed in life. Those educational experiences that gave us the formal knowledge, skills, and abilities to survive and achieve in life were started at Lowery by those wonderful, nurturing teachers of whom we continue to believe are, in part, responsible for our life's achievements.

Joe Lawson, a native of Donaldsonville who attended Lowery, became a successful business manager, musician and orchestra leader, publisher, and founder of the African American museum in Sacramento, California. Joe credited our teachers at Lowery for his achievements and success in life. He referred to those of us who attended Lowery as "engineers." In addition to the life skills we learned, "We were taught professional skills such as carpentry, furniture making and woodcraft, electrical wiring, food service, and a course in sewing and tailoring," he said, reminiscing about the quality education we received. He expressed my thinking and sentiments of other schoolmates as well.

Desegregation of Public Schools

Brown vs. Board of Education was, indeed, legislation that became law in 1954. However, desegregation of public schools in Louisiana and other Southern states did not begin until 1968 following almost two decades of protest marches and other acts of civil disobedience against segregation in public facilities by local law enforcement.

In a *Time* magazine article dated July 13, 1970, entitled "Education: The Bad Side of Integration," the article reads, in part, as follows:

> *According to the Justice Department, 97% of Southern black children will attend integrated school systems next fall. For many, the experience will not be pleasant. They will find that thousands of white children have fled to new private "segregated academies." In many cases white school officials have sent public school equipment along with them. Louisiana went a step further last month by approving state financial support for private schools.*
>
> *Less obvious—and more insidious—is what happens to black students and teachers in some school districts where the terms for desegregation have been determined unilaterally by local white school boards. In recent testimony before the Senate Select Committee on Equal Educational Opportunity, five young blacks and an official of the National Education Association described a bleak pattern of "internal segregation," which produces separate classrooms, separate lunch and*

gym periods and even separate bells so that blacks and whites will not use the halls at the same time. In DeSota Parish, busses pick up blacks at 5:30 a.m., so that white students can ride later separately. One white teacher herds all his black students into a corner of the classroom and turns his back on them while he teaches . . . .

Desegregation for many black students simply means schools run by hostile white instead of sympathetic blacks. One result: a crushing loss of status for middle-class black educators, who have provided the South with a sense of pride and leadership. A final "tragic consequence of desegregation," in the words of the N.E.A. report, "is the forfeiture of school spirit and group identity." Left behind to be stored, scattered or abandoned are trophies, pictures, plaques, and every symbol of black identity, of black students' achievements. For one black school in Louisiana, the wonders of integration were symbolized by the fate of a large mural depicting Booker T. Washington and George Washington Carver. When whites took control of the building, they wasted no time in painting over it.

Overall desegregation of public schools in the quad-parishes was completed with relatively little violence. The Lafourche School District, however, did experience an incident "of tragic consequence of desegregation." Also appearing in the above *Time* magazine article was the following:

James Noah, who was head coach at all-Black C. M. Washington High School in Thibodaux, La., had 16 years of successful football behind him when he was "integrated"—transferred to a formally all-white high school and made assistant coach on the "B" team. White officials explain that there are simply not enough comparable jobs to go around, and invariably find the whites better qualified. One favorite ploy is to assign a relocated black to teach a subject in which he has no certification. Then he is closely observed and fired for incompetence.

Ascension school district experienced several serious problems at the onset of desegregation. One case occurred in East Ascension and was recorded by the *Gonzales Weekly* on September 5, 1969. Here is the article verbatim:

Schools In East Ascension Closed For Lack Of Pupils

Pickets appeared at all East Ascension Schools on opening day protesting a court order which will prohibit a "Freedom of Choice" plan similar to other school districts in this and neighboring parishes.

The boycott of the schools has closed most of them. The school board in a meeting with the citizens last night had nothing new to report on the situation according to a school board member.

Mr. W. C. Brunson in a question and answer program on a TV station stated that some phone calls of a threatening nature had been received by some employees of the school system and that four schools were closed: Galvez, Dutchtown, E. A. Elementary and St. Amant for lack of pupils.

A suit filed by East Ascension Group for School Freedom in the local court was removed by the U.S. District Court from the state court to the federal court. The case will be tried in October.

Padlocks were put on Galvez and St. Amant elementary schools some time before school was to open Tuesday morning. They were still on Wednesday morning.

Mayor Pasqua called for a limited curfew Friday night after a negro [sic] youth received minor wounds in Gunplay at the Hancock station on Burnside St. after a day of tension.

About 3:00 p.m. Friday a Negro was killed when he ran his car in front of a freight train. According to Sheriff Waguespack the negro [sic] and one of the white pickets had exchanged words down town and the negro [sic] left saying he was going to get a gun. A gun was found in the car.

Sheriff Wagespack put into effect a ban on the sale of Beer and Liquor in the Parish, which is still in effect and an 8:00 P.M. to 6:00 A.M. curfew is still in effect in Gonzales.

During the transition of integrating Lowery High School (LHS) students with Donaldsonville High School (DHS) students, Claudia became the assistant principal at DHS.

Under the Freedom of Choice integration ruling, parents had to write letters stating that their children chose to attend their school of choice and why. As Lowery's high school counselor, Claudia was asked by the superintendent to conduct a survey of Lowery's high school students who would be attending the all-White DHS. After reading the questions, she was not in favor of conducting the survey because of the way the questions were written, such as:

> "Why do you want to attend (name of school)?"
> "Why do you believe white schools are better than colored schools?"
> "Do you like white people?"
> "Have you had any interactions with white people?"
> "How do white people treat you?"

After being asked by Mr. Land to conduct the survey, she reluctantly agreed. She was later subpoenaed by the court to answer questions about the survey; however, she was never called to testify during the hearings.

When integration was being enforced, it became apparent by the actions of the White teachers and students that Black students were not welcome. In Ascension, continuing instances of blatant segregation were evident. For example, White teachers would not call on Black students who raised their hands to respond to questions. And when Black students were eventually called on to respond and gave the correct answer, there was hardly an acknowledgement by the teachers.

At first, there was some apprehension on the part of Black students to participate in competition with Whites. However, they were soon able to prove themselves as capable as their White counterparts. The band director at DHS, who was White, assigned very capable Black music students to second—and third-chair positions, but never to first chair.

This same band director had consistently refused to address Claudia as "Mrs." when reporting Black students to her office. The principal had to insist repeatedly that the director respect her position and follow established protocol.

Fights among White and Black boys were reported to the principal, especially after athletic competitions. Eventually, these altercations subsided and relations between the two groups improved after repeated counseling.

Drivers had to stop school busses to quell fights between Black and White students. These episodes were stopped with the help of monitors stationed on all school busses provided by the school board.

Claudia learned from the survey that many Black parents and students in Donaldsonville assumed that White schools were better than Black schools in every respect. What they didn't realize was that the long delay in providing Black students with decent schooling meant that Lowery had been actually constructed more recently than were many White schools. Only as Black students were being transferred to formally all-White Donaldsonville High did Black parents and students realize that the building was old and needed repair. In comparison, Lowery's facilities were more modern with tile floors and up-to-date restroom accommodations.

An even more critical difference between the two teaching staffs was the disparity between the educational level of Black and White teachers. In her role in working with a team at DHS on the development of the annual report to the state, Claudia had access to all school records. What she learned was that, compared to LHS teachers, those at DHS were trailing substantially in teaching qualifications. Black principals ensured that their teachers were professionals and had received at least a basic degree and encouraged them to seek higher levels of education. While all LHS teachers held at least a bachelor's degree in their teaching area, some teachers at DHS did not hold degrees at the bachelor level; and those without the requisite degree had been certified to teach by the state, usually at the elementary level. Educators from Saint James and Assumption reported similar shortcomings.

Based on the many stories I was told and read about public school integration, I believe that discrimination by some White administrators, teachers, and students caused harm to Blacks during those times. Yet enough determined Blacks and Whites from both school systems fostered a "can do" spirit that allowed school integration to unfold but not without challenges for the Blacks.

In Donaldsonville, the integration efforts resulted in these major physical changes:

- The name *Lowery High School* was replaced with *Lowery Junior High School*, leaving the name *Donaldsonville High School* intact, where all high school students attended, intact;
- The two elementary schools integrated grades one through six in both locations; and
- Seventh—and eighth-graders from both schools attended the newly established Lowery Junior High School.

It was not widely known, but an attempt was made by several White administrators to rid the system of the name *Lowery* from the school. For a short time, the junior high school was known as Donaldsonville Junior High School. It was learned that influential Blacks rallied to retain the name *Lowery* in the system because of the influence Dr. J. S. Lowery had in the formation of educational opportunities for Blacks. The name was restored.

Heretofore, there had been no Blacks holding supervisory positions with the local school board. Because of the many problems that arose in the educational system due to integration, it seemed wise for the board to include Blacks to supervisory positions. Ironically, when Claudia decided to retire as the assistant principal at DHS in 1971, she was offered a board supervisory position as an incentive to keep her in the system. She turned down the offer because of her decision to retire. Her sister, Odile, replaced her as assistant principal.

At the beginning of the integration of schools, Ralph E. Ricardo served the parish as the principal of Lowery High School. An article in the *Record in Educational Administration and Supervision, Vol. 3, No. 2, Spring, 1983,* by Dr. Jo Ann Cangemi, gave this brief yet comprehensive professional biography of the positive impact Ricardo made on the education system in Ascension:

> *Ralph Ricardo has served the cause of public education in Ascension Parish since 1957. His modes of service have been varied and successful. Throughout the nine year period (1957-1966) of his teaching career, Mr. Ricardo displayed an unwavering interest in the fields of mathematics and science; this interest was matched only by his enthusiastic devotion to the act of teaching. For him, there was little else that could compare to the pleasure derived from leading students into a deeper interest and wiser understanding of mathematics and science. Many students, not interested at the onset, became devoted students of these subjects through the example and challenging instruction of their teacher.*
>
> *In 1966, Ricardo serves as assistant principal of Lowery High School in Donaldsonville, Louisiana. The next year, he was made principal of Lowery High, a position he held for three years. This was followed by another principalship assignment, that of Donaldsonville Junior High from 1970-73. Using his "scientific" as well as his experience in research, he began to display those qualities which have come to characterize his professional demeanor. With a fine command of academic content coupled with a clear mastery of pedagogical*

principles, Ricardo became a principal of unusual ability. His personal trait of clear decisiveness won the respect of those who noted that his decisions were usually wise and fair. Personal integrity and professional leadership were of such high order that neither was ever questioned. These traits were necessary to the success of any administrator struggling with the effects of court-ordered integration, but for a black man they were even more paramount.

In 1973, Ricardo entered the central school board office as Project Director and Supervisor. In 1975, he was promoted to Assistant Superintendent and in August he became the first to serve as superintendent of a Louisiana public school system. Ricardo viewed the significance of his appointment by giving credit to the School Board and to the freedoms we enjoy as Americans. He said:

> *I thought very little of it at the beginning. I'm so interwoven into the "American Way" that it did not have a substantial impact on me at all. It was only after so many people began to react to it that I began to think that it was something noteworthy. I don't mean to minimize it. I think that it speaks well of the people who appointed me. They stood up for what they thought was right and that's very important. And for the community to react the way they did is also important. I couldn't have received more cooperation under any set of circumstances. I trust that what has happened to me will serve as an inspiration to others. I hope it says to people who have become despondent, that if you really work hard to develop some degree of excellence and adequacy, then there is no barrier against you—and that's one of the great aspects of this country.*

The appointment has spoken well for the school system because in just one and one-half years important changes and realistic benefits have been accomplished under Ricardo's leadership. Among those accomplishments are:

1) *the attainment of a $2,500,000.00 surplus of funds; this is most significant since the system was wallowing in a $40,000.00 deficit when Ricardo came to the helm;*
2) *the introduction of management by objectives;*
3) *the involvement of principals and teachers in the educational decision-making process;*

4) *the implementation of competitive salaries to attract highly qualified teachers;*

5) *the launching of a needs assessment program which is designed to evaluate and determine the status of some courses and areas of instructions . . .*

Ralph Ricardo, the man who has risen to these educational heights, was born and reared in the area he serves. He attended Lowery Elementary School and was graduated in 1951 from Lowery High School. He received his B.A. Degree from Southern University in 1954. During his tenure as a teacher, he was recipient of a National Science Fellowship which provided the impetus for graduate study and studies in mathematics. He received a Master's Degree from Southern University in 1962 and engaged in graduate work in Educational Administration and Supervision from Louisiana State University. Some of his leadership abilities he credits his military training which was highlighted by his service as Commanding Officer of Research and Development, Missile Battery at Fort Bliss, Texas and White Sands Proving Grounds in New Mexico.

Ricardo is married to the former Doris Richard, who works as a paraprofessional at the Donaldsonville Elementary School. They are the parents of two children, Ralph, Jr. and Iris. When asked to provide some perspectives about public education in Louisiana, Mr. Ricardo offered the following:

It is my belief that programs such as personnel evaluation, pupil assessment and basic skills that were mandated by the State Department of Education and implemented by the local school systems have contributed greatly to improved confidence in public education in Louisiana.

In the best of times the public schools are very vulnerable to criticism because of their visibility. In my opinion, the public school has been the victim of rising expectations without a corresponding rise in performance. We must communicate to people what we can and what we cannot accomplish. Because of the rapid changes in the supply-demand relationship for various kinds of work, no school can guarantee that every graduate will find the kind of job for which he has been prepared. His area of specialization may not exist a decade after leaving school.

No school can safely promise parents that their children will become productive citizens who are socially and psychologically well-adjusted. All it can promise is an opportunity to learn in a favorable environment with the help of a competent teacher and a variety of multi-sensory materials and equipment necessary to provide enriching experiences.

No matter how excellent the program, however competent the teacher, it must be remembered that learning is a highly personal endeavor. It is the child who must do the learning. If this fact can be made clear to parents, their demands of the school will change and they will accept a greater responsibility for the role in their child's education.

In the opinion of this writer, these remarks are characteristic of Mr. Ricardo. He is a person of fine moral character. He has great vision as to the possibilities of educational development. He has tremendous energy and enthusiasm coupled with considerable administrative ability. Mr. Ricardo has become a notable promoter of all that pertains to the betterment of educational organization and operation. He has accomplished much in a short of time. Louisiana is better for his having served and worked as one of its most effective leaders. In a brief time, he has brought metamorphosis to the attitude of the people of this area. The change has been so positive and so pronounced that the "danger" of its spreading statewide is a real and viable possibility. For that many of us are grateful.

Willis Octave, a former principal in the Saint James Public School System, provided the following additional insight about school integration in that school district:

Prior to 1944, Blacks had to seek a high-school diploma outside the parish, since no high school for Blacks existed. Some students attended high school in Ascension Parish (Lowery Training School) and some had to go to seek a high-school diploma in other surrounding parishes.

When the parish was pressed for total integration, it chose the "Freedom of Choice" model. A limited number of Blacks attended St. James High and Lutcher High Schools, a limited number because St. James was not totally integrated.

As time passed, the Court declared a unitary system which was the beginning of total integration.

Presently, St. James has two high schools, St. James and Lutcher High Schools, both totally integrated.

Referring again to Feliska Stewart Taylor's reunion paper, her ending remarks included these:

Then, along came integration and all of the Black high schools became junior highs and the White schools became the high schools for the parish and state. We learned enough to know we needed to know more. We went on to receive Master's degrees—plus additional credits. Students from Magnolia High School are gainfully employed all over these United States . . . Young people need to know—that we came through the storms and the rain. But we made it!

Within five years after the integration of public schools, Edith became a member of the Calcasieu Parish School Board as Department Supervisor for Child Welfare and Attendance. I retired from the army as a lieutenant colonel after twenty years of service in 1974. A year later, I became the program planner and manager of the job training branch for the Office of Human Affairs, the Newport News, Virginia, community action agency serving the poor and the underserved.

The Music of Our Life

Our appreciation for music went deeper than one or two isolated songs or musical experiences during childhood years. Our association with music really began in our maternal grandparents' home where the old upright piano was the center of attraction.

Both of our aunts, Williana and Henrietta, played the piano. It was not unusual to find the entire family seated on the floor near the piano or standing around singing and harmonizing tunes such as "The Little Brown Church in the Vale," "Annie Laurie," and "Juanita" among others.

Actually, family ties with music began long before the 1930s when Grandpa Ogeese was an amateur flutist who entertained the family once in a while, but only after ample coaxing. Uncle Paul Rodrique was a jazz trombonist and leader of a small band that played at social gatherings in nearby communities. In New Orleans tradition, local bands in our area offered "first line" and "second line" music at funerals of musicians, Uncle Paul Rodrigue's jazz band occasionally led the procession of mourners to and from area churches to the cemetery for the funeral of local musicians and others.

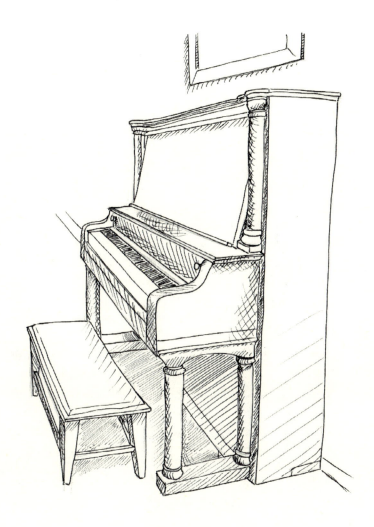

Upright Piano

There were several musicians in our immediate family too. Odile and Claudia were piano students who studied with Mrs. Ethel Turner and Mrs. Bella Williams Sullivan, sister of the famous Claiborne Williams whose band had great national and international popularity. I played the piano by ear. None of us was a standout by any stretch of the imagination, although I was told that I did save the day as a stand-in at a particular high-school program.

At the end of the school year in 1945, the music teacher at Lowery Training School, Ms. Susie Robinson, resigned suddenly and did not appear for the baccalaureate program. With a crowd of several hundred waiting in the auditorium, Mr. Land realized no one was available to play the processional march. No one, that is, until Edith announced to Mr. Land, "Curtis can play that march." With a whole lot of prompting, I reluctantly (but *flawlessly*) played the "War March of the Priests" to the amazement of the audience and myself!

The Johnsons were given Aunt Henrietta's old upright player piano and a number of rolls of songs that were the center of family entertainment for a number of years. The player piano required only the pumping of foot pedals to operate the mechanical music maker. With no imagination and constant pedaling, one could "play" the piano with beautiful music resulting without touching the keys. Odile and Claudia played familiar songs that entertained family and friends.

As children, we made and played musical "instruments." We used Grandpa's flute as a model and made a piccolo-like device from a joint of cane reed that sounded much like a flute. It contained five or six notes, depending on the number of holes put in the reed, a bit fewer than needed in most songs. The kazoo was another favorite with children (small kazoos were given as prizes in Cracker Jack boxes), as was the Jew's harp. And everyone tried to mimic the Mills Brothers by mouthing instrumental sounds.

The blues, pop, swing, spirituals, gospel, Creole, Cajun, and mainstream music were all enjoyed in our household. From our front porch during the early-evening Sunday service, we often added our voices to the choir at the Saint Luke AME Church located a half block away. WPA workers who were building a new levee one and a half blocks from our house also entertained our part of the neighborhood. We enjoyed listening to them in a session of guitar-playing, harmonica-blowing, and blues-singing after a hard day's work.

CURTIS J. JOHNSON

Some of the blues numbers that we still appreciate today were sung by guitarists who told about hard times, romance problems, and prison life. Some of the Black nightspots in Thibodeaux, Napoleonville, Belle Alliance, Modeste, Gonzales, Vacherie, and other locations featured several musicians and singing entertainers every Saturday night. "Guitar Slim started out in Thibodeaux," Rev. Wallace said.

The region celebrated a host of talented music professionals, some of whose prominence propelled them to international stardom. Records maintained at the River Road African American Museum in Donaldsonville provide an eye-opening history of Black musical greats. For example, Donaldsonville's native son, Claiborne McLellam Williams, was born in 1885 on the Valenzuela Plantation four miles south of Donaldsonville on Bayou Lafourche. He was a composer, arranger, and music teacher who mastered the violin, cornet, and various other instruments. During his lifetime, he was the leader of several bands: the Claiborne Williams Orchestra, the Claiborne Williams String Band, the Peerless Brass Band, and the Saint Joseph Brass Band. In the 1890s and early 1900s, he directed the famous Billy Kersand Minstrel Troupe Orchestra and toured the United States, Canada, and Europe. He organized the first Mardi Gras parade in Donaldsonville in 1907. He played locally at the True Friends Hall, the Grand Theatre, and the Harlem Theater. The "Professor," as he was sometimes called, and his bands were well known throughout the river parishes and South Louisiana. He died in 1952.

Some of the other area musicians include the following:

Joseph "King" Oliver (1885-1938; cornet, trumpet, trombone) was born on the Saulsburg Plantation near Abend, Louisiana. He was one of the most popular jazz musicians in New Orleans before he left for Chicago. He played with the Melrose Brass Band and the Olympia Brass Band of New Orleans before forming King Oliver's Creole Jazz Band. He mentored fifteen-year-old Louis "Satchmo" Armstrong, who called him Papa Joe.

George "Pops" Foster (1892-1969; cello, string bass, tuba) was born at McCall, Louisiana, and grew up in Donaldsonville where he played cello in a string trio with his brother, guitarist Willie, and his sister Elizabeth on mandolin. Pops played in the bands of such music greats as Kid Ory and King Oliver. In the 1940s, he was featured on the Mutual Radio Network in the program, *This Is Jazz*. He worked with pianist Earl "Fatha" Hines and toured Europe in 1966.

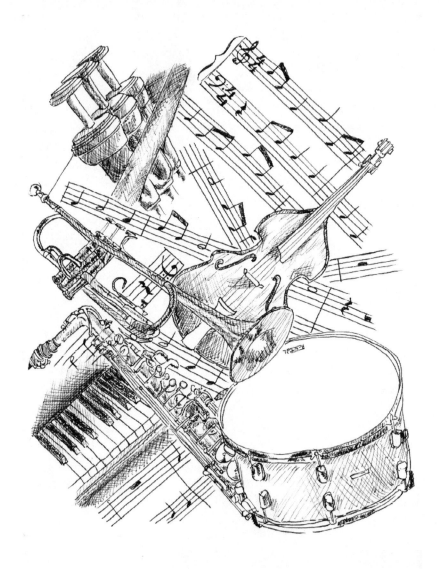

Musical Collage

CURTIS J. JOHNSON

Willie Foster (1888-unknown; violin, banjo, guitar) was born four years earlier than his brother George in McCall. He worked with guitarist Louis Keppard's band and traveled in the Midwest with Joe Oliver's Band. He recorded with Fate Morable's Society Syncopators on the Okeh label in 1927.

Richard Myknee Jones (1889-1945; piano) was born in Donaldsonville, where he started playing the alto sax on the streets as early as 1902. He came from a musical family and by 1908 was playing the piano. He played with the Olympia Orchestra and later led his own quartet. He joined Okeh Records in 1925 and worked mostly as an arranger and became most famous for his composition, *Trouble in Mind.*

Davidson C. Nelson (1906-1946; trumpet and other instruments) was born in Donaldsonville and was said to be the nephew of cornet player and bandleader Joe "King" Oliver. He recorded with Ma Rainey and toured with jazz pianist Jelly Roll Morton before leading his own ensemble in 1927. In 1929, he moved to New York to play with King Oliver. He recorded on the Victor label as Dave Nelson and the King's Men. In 1930, he toured with the Mae West show, *The Constant Sinner.*

Emmanuel Sayles (1905-ca. 1980s; banjo, guitar) was born in Donaldsonville and began playing in bands while still very young. He played with Mack Thomas's Pensacola Jazzers and Jones-Collins Hot Eight Band in the 1920s and 1930s. He led his own band in Chicago from 1939 to 1949. He recorded extensively on Atlantic, Riverside, and other labels. *This Cat Can Play Anything*, his bio-documentary, was aired on PBS in 1980.

Plas Johnson (1931—; saxophone) was born in Donaldsonville, where he and brother, Ray, began their musical careers as a combo, the Johnson Brothers, in the late 1940s. His first big gig with his brother was at the True Friends Hall. Plas joined the Charles Brown Band and recorded on the Regal label in New Orleans. His saxophone solos can be heard in the introduction to Henry Mancini's *Pink Panther Theme,* the bird call in Bobby Day's hit, *Rockin' Robin,* and the theme to the TV series *The Odd Couple.* He was a fixture of the orchestral recordings by Nat King Cole, Peggy Lee and Frank Sinatra. Some of the most familiar saxophone notes of the twentieth century have been played by this Donaldsonville native.

Renald Richard (1925—; trumpet, lyricist) has a musical background that is deeply rooted in Donaldsonville, Louisiana. In 1954, he became the first bandleader of the Ray Charles Band. He wrote the lyrics to Ray's first number one hit, "I Got a Woman." He became administrator at Atlantic Records, a music teacher, side man on Little Richard's "Long Tall Sally," and lyricist for Big Joe Turner, Jerry Lee Lewis, Guitar Slim, Louis Prima, David "Fat Head" Newman, and numerous other Ray Charles records.

Antoine "Fats" Domino (1928—; piano, lyricist, singer) was born in New Orleans according to the literature; however, Rev. Thomas and Edwin Octave stated that Fats was born and spent his early years in South Vacharie in Saint James Parish. His first language was French; he first performed in public at age ten. By age fourteen, he was playing in New Orleans nightclubs. During the mid-1940s, he joined the Dave Bartholomew Band where Bartholomew became his co-writer on many of his hit songs. He signed a contract with Imperial Records in 1949 and made his first recording, "The Fat Man," to hit the R & B chart in 1950. His music was reportedly influenced by Joe Turner and Lloyd Price. His most memorable songs include "Ain't That a Shame," "Blue Berry Hill," "Blue Monday," "I'm Walking, Walking to New Orleans," and "Lady Madonna."

Bill Summers (1948—; exotic percussion instruments) grew up in Donaldsonville and Darrow, Louisiana. As a percussionist and ethnomusicologist, he worked with Miles Davis, Quincy Jones, Stevie Wonder, Kenny Loggins, and Herbie Hancock. He formed the New Orleans-based band, Los Hombres Calientes, with trumpeter Irvin Mayfield. Summers is internationally recognized for his work on television series *Roots* (Emmy Award), *The Wiz*, and *The Color Purple*.

Leonard Julien, Sr. (1910-1994; trumpet, trombone, piano), a native of Modeste, Louisiana, is most recognized for his invention, the sugarcane planter. He was a self-taught piano player, wrote music, and performed with the Leonard Julien Orchestra throughout South Louisiana in the 1940s, '50s, and '60s. Julien taught each of his children to play an instrument and was the bandleader of an album, *In Search of My Heart*, and wrote and performed a crowd favorite, "Broken Hearted Boogie Woogie Blues."

Bands from New Orleans offered special talents as well, and included such famous personalities as the Johnson Brothers, among others. During the late 1940s, Ray Johnson, trumpeter for the band, along with his saxophonist brother, Plas, formed the foundation for the group. Their sister, Gwen, sang songs written by her brothers. I can attest that they were an instant hit with their first appearance in concert at the True Friends Hall in Donaldsonville during mid-1940s. I was there.

Some of the talented musicians and musical groups who entertained in and around the region included these:

- Homer Richard, piano, Donaldsonville
- Lee Dorsey, singer, Thibodaux
- Leonard Julien III, saxophone and clarinet, Modeste
- Cher Levi, percussion, Donaldsonville
- Worthia Thomas, trombone, Napoleonville
- Stanley Francis, singer, Donaldsonville
- Ernie K-Doe, singer, Thibodeaux
- Tony Hudson, piano, Donaldsonville
- Ernest Claverie, bass fiddle, Donaldsonville
- Elmo Claverie, saxophone, Donaldsonville
- Lloyd Bell, percussion, Donaldsonville
- Oscar "Papa" Celestine, Napoleonville
- Bella Williams Sullivan, piano, Donaldsonville
- Earnest Hines, Ernest Hine's Band, Napoleonville
- George Williams, Sr., saxophone, Donaldsonville

Our musical experiences in high school and college added significantly to our music appreciation and development. Several of the Johnson children sang in high-school groups and in stage plays. Several were awarded medals for performances at district and state-level LIALA competition.

One of our proudest moments came when Claudia was in the eighth grade at Lowery. The music teacher, Mrs. Chatters, well known for staging high school operettas, chose *HMS Pinafore* as a year-end production. As an eighth-grade student, Claudia auditioned for and was given the lead role in the play. Her role as lead sailor was demanding and required her to be the narrator and lead dancer as well. Because she would be appearing on stage with upperclassmen who were more experienced in drama performances, some amount of apprehension remained with her and the family as she practiced endlessly with marked determination. The whole family helped her in perfecting the dance steps and learning and rehearsing her lines.

Then came *showtime.*

The hard work and tiring rehearsal efforts had paid off. A sell-out crowd from the school and community was thoroughly entertained by a super, flawless performance by Claudia and her cohorts on the night of the operetta. We were so proud of her!

"The *Revenooers* Are Coming!"

Some households in the area made sweet wine from one or more of several available local fruits. Blackberries were most used; and wild cherries, white and concord grapes, muscadine grapes, and raisins were used in various recipes for wines and brandies. The more "seasoned" folks also made *homebrew.*

Before prohibition was repealed in December 1933, people everywhere made wine and beer at home. Because of this, Internal Revenue Service inspectors would visit the communities every few years to destroy illegally prepared whiskey, wines, and homebrew. Their targets were not people who made several gallons of wine and beer, but the bootleggers who operated stills and the tavern managers who sold the unlawful products. When word that "the revenooers are coming" spread, regardless of the targets for the lawmen, everyone who had any amount of homemade wine and beer on hand went about destroying their supply by smashing jugs or throwing them out into the outdoor toilets to destroy the evidence.

One day as the raiding inspectors approached our area, Grandpa and several of his sons quickly hauled a number of wine containers from the barn and dropped their home supply into an open well that was used for watering the garden and farm animals.

It wasn't until several years later that the well, which had been partially filled with silt and trash, was reopened. We were told that the wine was chilled and had aged to perfection.

Bottle of Wine

How We Were Disciplined

Recall that I grew up in a household of eight: four sisters and a brother in addition to our parents. Three of the sisters and the brother were older than I was. We were all active children; however, for reasons unknown, I chose to partner with the most active sister, Edith. She was also the most talkative of all, a "talent" that landed her in trouble almost every day. Of course, when she got into trouble, I was automatically swept into the action. It was a given that when she was disciplined, so was I. Unfortunately for the two of us, neither time out nor the Child Protective Service had yet been established.

Methods of punishment varied from family to family. In our household, our mother was the disciplinarian for routine day-to-day infractions. When the situation deserved more than a hard slap on the butt, our father's dress belt—an imposing two inches wide—was her "weapon" of choice. Our dad handled the more difficult cases. He used the same belt but would hit much harder. But it was our mother who would torture us by talking to us as she held on to an arm while wielding the strap that always found its target. The monologue went something like this:

"I told you [*Pow!*] never to go [*Pow!*] behind the levee by yourself! [*Pow!*] Haven't I told you this [*Pow!*] a thousand times?! [*Pow!*]" Now you [*Pow!*] wait 'til your daddy [*Pow!*] gets home from work! [*Pow!*]"

This familiar scenario occurred at our house three to five times each week. Edith and I were usually the reason. She and I still laugh about this whenever we get together. She remembers the details of what we did. I remember the whippings.

Engineering the Outhouse

Several homesteads in various communities chose to duplicate the design of their house in the design of the outhouse. Some outhouses were well-designed and adorned with features (shutters, moldings, decorative designs) that resembled those that could be seen on the main house.

The Outhouse

The outhouse played an obviously important role in family life. Looking back, it is a wonder that we were able to enjoy relatively good health. We did pay attention to possible contamination, however, by relocating the outhouse about once every eight to ten months. This required digging a hole approximately three feet wide, four feet long, and four or five feet deep. Once dug, the outhouse frame was moved to the new site using wooden rollers and two-by-six planks and placed over the new hole.

Dirt from the new hole was used to cover the old one, but only after a generous application of powdered lime was spread thoroughly before and after the dirt layer to neutralize the residual smell. It was a pleasure to do business in the new facility, which would be stocked with sales catalogs from Sears, Montgomery Ward, and Lane Bryant and discarded newspapers, made softer by crinkling and used for toilet paper. Our family budget did not allow toilet paper to be a priority in our households at the time.

One of the less-favored chores at my house on Saturdays was "deodorizing" the facility. This involved sprinkling lime through the holes to cover the contents. Other chores involving the outhouse included removing all scrap paper, sweeping the floor and the area outside surrounding the door, removing cobwebs and spiders, scrubbing the seat and floor with soapy water and an old broom, and replenishing the catalogs when needed.

Some families scrubbed the toilet seats and floor with powdered red brick to ward off any would-be hex. One could never be too careful in an area where voodoo was widely practiced . . . and feared by many.

Coping with Roaches, Chinches, and Mosquitoes

Summer also brought special challenges for us. For example, no matter how hard we worked at it, we found it impossible to get completely rid of the roaches. These were large flying roaches that scattered and flew around the room whenever a light was switched on after being off for a while at night. Temporary control was about the best we could achieve.

In spite of screens on windows and doors, seemingly well-trained mosquitoes would slip by the Flit insect spray to nip and hound you during the night.

Chinches were as plentiful as the mosquitoes. These little bedbugs hid themselves in crevices of the bedspring and mattress during daylight hours. But they came out *en masse* at nighttime for their "meal." Our mother used to sit on the side of the bed, pick them out of the mattress, and squish

The Flit

them in old newspapers. These bugs had a peculiar mell that resembled that of the pungent June bug. Although I haven't smelled a bedbug in over sixty-five years, I'm sure I can immediately identify one by its smell.

The summer was also the season that moss-filled mattresses were ripped open, the moss aired or washed and dried or replaced with fresh moss collected by *pickers* from live oak trees. Mattress ticking was washed or replaced also.

Family Humor

There were humorous incidents that surrounded our family members' daily activities, too many, in fact, for them to be recorded here. But several, because of their particular slant, stand out as being among the top of our family ladder, and are shared to tweak the reader's memory of similar kinds of humorous incidents that may have occurred in their families.

This incident started out as funny but soon changed to one where family members were pleading for mercy for the "victim."

It seemed that our cousin, Manuel Rodrique, Jr., was extremely fond of white (navy) beans. As a boy, he boasted of his unusual capacity for them and begged his mother practically every day to cook them for dinner. His father became increasingly annoyed by this daily routine and decided to put a stop to it. Uncle Manuel "Cocoa" Rodrigue, Sr., cooked a "cracklin' pot" half full of navy beans, as Manuel, Jr., drooled and talked about how he could eat that pot of beans all by himself. When the cooking was done, Manual, Sr., called his son over, handed him a tablespoon, and ordered him to eat the entire pot of beans!

Junior is said to have smiled and joked his way through four or five bowls of the *musical fruit*, until he became stuffed. Ignoring his discomfort, Uncle "Cocoa" persisted on having Manual eat the whole thing, in spite of family members begging the father to stop the ordeal. After several more bowls full, the father relented. We are told those were Junior's last white beans for some time to come!

A favorite social outing for our aunts, Vickie and Williana Pinkins, was attending dances down Bayou Lafourche at Belle Rose on Saturday nights. Grandpa Ogeese would take them in the horse-drawn wagon. On one occasion, Vickie was being punished for a month and forbidden to go anywhere other than to church and to work. During that period when a dance was scheduled, Vickie and Mrs. Landry, the lady for whom she worked, plotted a scheme that would backfire on Vickie.

Landry lured Grandma Annette outside to admire the flower garden while Vickie collected her evening gown and other clothing without Grandma seeing her, and sneaked into Mrs. Landry's car to hide. That night, Henrietta and Williana went to the drugstore and met Leslie Isreal, a neighbor. He told Williana that he had just seen Vickie at a dance in Belle Rose with two of Claiborne Williams's bandsmen. Williana quickly reported this to Grandpa Ogeese upon their return home.

With the aid of Uncle Paul, who drove the horse-drawn wagon, Grandpa Ogeese set out for the dance hall. When they arrived, someone told Vickie that a man was at the door to see her. Thinking it was a young man to flirt with her, she went to see who it was. She nearly fainted when she saw her father! Grandpa told her, "Get your hat and come on!" Vickie was so frightened she went back into the hall to look for her hat, not realizing that she hadn't worn one!

For punishment, she could not leave the house after working hours for another month!

~ ~

All of the Johnson children were required to sit on the right side and near the front of the church so that our mother, Zena, who sang in the choir (which was also on the right side of the church), could keep an eye on us. On a particular Easter Sunday morning service at Mount Triumph Baptist Church, twelve-year-old Claudia was seated next to Aunt Elizabeth Pinkins. As the sermon became more and more rousing and emotional, several of the church sisters "shouted" and "fell out." Aunt Elizabeth had to be restrained by several ushers who took pride in their ability to calm a shouting sister. In attempting to get out of the reach of Aunt Elizabeth's flailing arms, Claudia's new straw bonnet was crushed beyond repair. Seeing her hat destroyed, Claudia's howling and frenzied demonstration caused the ushers to think she had gotten happy too and was also shouting.

Distraught over her crushed hat, bruised from the blow from Aunt Elizabeth's hand, and literally frightened out of her wits, Claudia raced from the church, haunted by sounds of "Catch her!" Churchgoers also thought she had been seized by the Holy Spirit.

Imagine the embarrassment of her parents who knew of Claudia's fear of a "shouting" person. Someone finally "caught" her, but her Easter had been ruined—only until the children were given their Easter baskets after breakfast later that morning.

Annual revival service in the Baptist churches in the area was as much a part of the church calendar as was regular church services. The services provided an opportunity for members who had strayed during the year to return and profess their faith and become renewed in their commitment to the church community. It offered a chance for non-Christians to become more exposed to a church's offerings, a marketing drive for new souls, so to speak. The services also gave young people the chance to be called to the *mourners' bench* to be prayed over. This tradition was embarrassing to many children, and some parents discovered themselves distressed over the resulting conduct of their children, as witness this case.

It was during a particular revival service at the Mount Triumph Baptist Church that prayers were being offered by Bobby Freeman, who continued for perhaps too long trying to invoke the Holy Spirit to descend upon the young children who were kneeling and fidgeting at the mourners' bench. Our sister Edith and Berthal Tilman were among the dozen or so children being prayed over. Time went on and as Mr. Bobby continued his prayer, "Help them, Lord. They're trying to come through." Reverend Emile Johnson asked one of the ushers to "go wake 'em up." Edith and Berthal had fallen asleep! Another embarrassing moment for our parents!!

When I was younger,
I could remember anything,
Whether it happened or not.
—Mark Twain

CURTIS J. JOHNSON

PART THREE

Hometown Heroes

INTRODUCTION

T HE RECORDED HISTORY of the United States military shows that Black men and women have traditionally played significant roles in the success of the country against hostile forces. Starting with the Revolutionary War in 1775, Blacks also served on both sides during the War of 1812 and the Civil War that began in 1861. From the end of the Spanish American War in 1898 to the end of the Vietnam War, Blacks were united in their allegiance to the United States of America. Each of these wars, including World War I (WWI), World War II (WWII), the Korean and the Vietnam wars will be summarily addressed below.

Emphasis in this part is given to WWII, the Korean War, and the Vietnam War due to their overall impact on Blacks in the military during my lifetime.

Immediately after the start of WWII, the federal government began sending fathers, sons, uncles, and nephews off to the military system. In urban areas, mothers, daughters, and sisters replaced the men in factories manufacturing military supplies and equipment to support the war and goods to support the domestic economy. In rural areas, more women took on jobs in family and commercial farming, as attendants and mechanics at service stations and as managers of small businesses. Older men left retirement to support a workforce that lacked workers in certain skill areas. In time, women would be allowed to participate directly in this war and in those that followed.

Practically everyone in communities of all sizes took an active role in supporting our military efforts nationally and overseas. Some families maintained *victory gardens* in their backyards as a voluntary effort to supplement the commercial food supply line. Feeding the troops became a priority. Certain foods and materials were rationed by the federal government (the Office of Price Administration) and could only be purchased with special stamps allocated to each family member in each household. Items rationed included butter, sugar, gasoline, shoes, household appliances, and nylon stockings, to name several. The rationing initiative became mandatory to ensure that our fighting forces would have first priority for the rations, supplies, and equipment needed to sustain the fighting men and women. Able-bodied civilians took part in civil defense air raid alert drills and occasional *black-out* exercises. Few people complained.

On the national scene, the Lucky Strike cigarette company, which until now packaged its cigarettes in a dark green pack, introduced a new white pack with the slogan, "Lucky Strike Green Has Gone to War!" The green pigment used previously in the cigarette packaging process was now being dedicated to manufacturing the olive drab color used for war equipment, military uniforms, camouflage netting, and other items used in war zones. Reminders of the need for security during a time of war were posted on billboards and utility posts ("A Slip of the Lip Can Sink a Ship").

This part provides insight into the participation of men and women of minority cultures from the quad-parish area as well as those of communities throughout America in the defense of our country. Condensed information is recorded about the slaves who participated in the development and defense of Fort Butler (in Donaldsonville) during the Civil War; the *buffalo soldiers* who, immediately following the Civil War, established the first line of defense for America in the Western Plains; the brave U.S. Coast Guard Life Savers of Pea Island, North Carolina; the courageous American Indian code talkers of WW I and WWII; the unparalleled success of the Tuskegee Airmen during WWII; the men (and the women who supported them) who made up the unique Cajun Coast Guard; and the hundreds of thousands of Blacks who served between 1775 and 1975 during the Revolutionary War, the War of 1812, the Civil War, the Spanish-American War, WWI, WWII, the Korean War, and the Vietnam War.

Military Trailblazers

If you see a turtle sitting upon a fence post,
You know it didn't get there by itself.
—Anonymous

The old saying above holds true for the men and women of color who stood on the shoulders of other people of color who were successful in military service from the Revolutionary War in 1775 through the end of the Vietnam Conflict in 1975 and beyond. The intervening wars included the War of 1812, Mexican War, Civil War, Spanish-American War, Philippines War, and the Mexican Punitive Expedition, World War I, and World War II. Although history books are replete with recordings of exemplary military service by Whites, comparatively little is included about people of color. The summaries listed below are examples of patriotism, dedication, volunteerism, and heroism demonstrated by Blacks and American Indians who served successfully during the Civil War and beyond and World War II.

Fort Butler

As children growing up in Port Barrow, I, along with several of my friends (Warren Joseph and his cousin, Harold Williams, brothers Charles and A. G. Augusta and Ralph Ricardo), spent many hours playing on the levee four blocks from our house. In a particular part of the levee was a cave that measured about six feet high, eight feet wide, and extended twelve or so feet deep into the levee. War artifacts were found in the cave and in the graveled streets after the road grader driven by Mr. Gilleaux Morris made several sweeps to smooth out potholes. Lead musket cartridges used during the Civil War could be found everywhere. It was not generally known by local people at the time that Port Barrow, later annexed to Donaldsonville in 1958, was the site of Fort Butler, complete with redoubts overlooking the Mississippi River.

During the Civil War, Black slaves as well as Black freedmen of the South fought bravely alongside their White owners against the Union Army and Navy. Likewise, free Blacks living in northern locations actively participated in battles as members of the Union Army and Navy against the Confederates. The history of Fort Butler in Donaldsonville serves as an example of the courageous roles played by Black slaves during the development and defense of that Union Army bastion.

The building of the fort was completed in February 1863. This encampment became a stronghold for the federal troops. And realizing its strategic location and geographical value, the Confederates believed that the fort would have to be destroyed before their mission to capture Donaldsonville could be achieved. An attempt by Confederate Army troops to overthrow the fort in June of that year failed terribly. Casualties for the invading rebels numbered nearly three hundred, compared to twenty-three for the Union side.

A Slip of the Lip

CURTIS J. JOHNSON

An inscription on a monument that marks the site of Fort Butler summarizes the beliefs of a Union Army officer during the preparatory stage for the defense of the Fort against invading Confederate troops. Captain James B. Ingraham, First Regiment of the Louisiana Native Guards, wrote:

> We are still anxious, as we have ever been, to show the world that the latent courage of the African is aroused, and that, while fighting under the American flag, we can and will be a wall of fire and death to the enemies of this country, our birthplace.

Another inscription on the monument quotes Donald S. Frazier, assistant professor, McMurry University, Abilene, Texas, as follows:

> This fortification is a symbol of the African American contribution to their own freedom. Not only did black hands construct this citadel, but African American soldiers helped in its defense.

The Buffalo Soldiers

Soon after the Civil War, two groups of freed Black slaves were formed by the U.S. Army into two regiments. The first, the Ninth Cavalry, was formed in New Orleans, Louisiana, during 1866 and ordered to Texas in 1867. The Tenth Cavalry was also formed in 1866 in Fort Leavenworth, Kansas, and deployed in 1867 to the Western Frontier and locations west of what is now Oklahoma. Both units were given the mission of protecting towns, stagecoaches, mail routes, and settlements from being attacked by hostile Indian tribes, bandits, and Mexican revolutionaries. The soldiers also built forts and roads.

These Black troops were called buffalo soldiers by the Western Plains Indians because of their skin color, the texture of their hair, their courage, their bravery, and their fighting ability, which, to the Indians, all resembled those attributes of the highly esteemed buffalo.

Before the end of 1869, the Twenty-fourth and Twenty-fifth Infantry Regiments were formed and sent to the Western Frontier to join the cavalry. Together, these four regiments made up 40 percent of the troop strength on the Western Frontier. As testimony to their courage, commitment, and valor, twenty of these brave soldiers were awarded the Congressional Medal of Honor.

Lifesavers at Pea Island

The first Blacks to serve in United States Coast Guard provided lifesaving services to ship crews in the Outer Banks area of North Carolina during the 1880s. A historical marker that is located at the Pea Island National Wildlife Refuge and entitled the Pea Island Life-Saving Station provides this summary:

> You are near the site of the Pea Island Life Saving Station. The United States Life Saving Service built the station in 1878, and when a crew was chosen in 1880, men were selected not only for discipline and dedication, but also for color—they were black. Until then the life saving service generally hired blacks only as stable hands and boat tenders.
>
> Between 1880 and 1947 all Pea Island crews were black. They comprised the only black crews in the history of the Life Saving Service or its successor, the U.S. Coast Guard. The Pea Island surfmen saved more than 600 lives, and earned a reputation as the "tautest" crew on the Carolina coast.

Tuskegee Airmen

Years before the approach of WWII, Blacks desiring to serve in the military were rejected for reasons such as "ineptitude," "lack of desired skills," and "illiteracy."

Nevertheless, they continued to press for induction in the three major branches of the military service: army, navy, and Army Air Corps.

About a year before the start of WWII, the U.S. Congress passed a law that began the drafting of men for mandatory service. The draft presented the first major opportunity for Blacks to enter the army and navy, but not the Air Corps, the forerunner of the U.S. Air Force. This branch of service was resolute in its tradition of banning Blacks from induction. That is, until 1941 when the U.S. Congress passed another law that allowed for the training of Black airmen at Tuskegee Institute in Alabama to participate in flying and maintaining fighter planes in support of the Air Corps' mission.

CURTIS J. JOHNSON

Buy War Bonds

With this new law was born the Tuskegee Airmen, a name that identified the men assigned to the famed Ninety-ninth Fighter (Pursuit) Squadron. Their support record spoke loudly for itself: while flying more than fifteen thousand sorties escorting bomber aircraft over Europe (Germany, Italy, France), they destroyed over four hundred enemy aircraft in the air and on the ground. Their accomplishment of losing few Army Air Corps bombers to enemy fire is said to have set a record never broken by any other similar fighting team. Eighty-five of these pilots were awarded the Distinguished Flying Cross.

Dr. Harold Brown, one of the original Tuskegee Airmen and a member of the Advisory Board for the Commemorative Air Force Red Tail Squadron and retired Air Force Colonel, provided the following summary of their military experiences:

"Because of our skin color, we were not allowed to train or fight alongside our White fellow countrymen in the same units. However, we proudly identified ourselves by painting the tails of our aircraft red, earning the nickname Red Tails. Denied salutes by many White enlisted men—and given the cold shoulder by many of the White pilots at first—we Red Tail pilots were determined to prove our worth. Before long, we became the *requested* fighter escort for many bomber pilots.

"The commander of the Strategic Fifteenth Air Force acknowledged our 332nd Fighter Group's exceptional record by awarding us the Presidential Unit Citation for our performance during the longest bomber escort mission to Berlin on March 24, 1945.

"After the war, many bomber crewmembers remarked in interviews how they had a sense of relief being escorted by our unit. But we paid the price. Sadly, sixty-six airmen lost their lives and thirty-two of us were captured as prisoners of war. Ironically, for the first time that I did not face racial segregation in the military was in that Nazi prison camp. When we returned home, there were no ticker tape parades for our units. In fact, Tuskegee Airmen on the troop train after the war were told to give up their seats to White Nazi POWs. And it was several years before we could comfortably enter some Officers' Clubs.

"I bring up this history not to dwell on the sins of the past. Like most airmen, I feel blessed to be an American and am proud of what the Tuskegee Airmen accomplished in World War II and later in life. Yes, we Tuskegee Airmen felt the ugliness of racial discrimination. But we weren't defeated by it. We rose above it."

American Indian Code Talkers

Military records contain episodes of the American Indian serving heroically during the Great War. Even before they were recognized as American citizens in 1924, their contributions were significant as a result of their voluntary service during WWI. They represented several tribes: Cherokee, Choctaw, Comanche, Creek, Navajo, Osage, Pawnee, and Pima and perhaps others.

They served in all branches of service and distinguished themselves in both the European and Pacific Theaters. However, the calling for which they were best known was their role as the code talkers.

The American Indian code talkers were seldom-talked-about minority heroes. Their history began in 1917 during WWI when a group of Choctaw Indians requested to join the army. These volunteers were asked by army authorities to use their language in coded messages throughout the European Theater because it had been proven to be indecipherable by the enemy.

During WWII, a group of young Comanche code talkers was given the mission of sending and receiving military intelligence information to U.S. and Allied forces that confused the enemy in the European Theater. These soldiers were soon followed by a group of Navajo volunteers who were deployed to the Pacific Theater with the identical mission given their European counterparts. Together, these soldiers were credited with saving countless numbers of U.S. and allied soldiers and civilians. Their heroic efforts resulted in six Indian soldiers being awarded the Medal of Honor.

The Cajun Coast Guard

Although little known and not people of color per se, the men of a South Louisiana special Coast Guard unit is yet another example of exemplary performance of service in a mission only they could achieve. The need for the organization grew out of the presence and destruction of U.S. military ships by German U-boats during WWII off the Louisiana Gulf of Mexico coastline. Made up of volunteers, this organization was not a part of the U.S. Coast Guard (USCG) but was officially named the U.S. Coast Guard Beach Patrol Unit that, unofficially, became known as the Cajun Coast Guard. Their mission was to patrol the coastline and report sightings of German ships and boats to the USCG.

The uniqueness of their mission was not in the mission itself, but the conditions under which it was performed. Except for a blue uniform and a $21 monthly stipend provided by the U.S. War Department, these volunteers were said to have carried their own shotguns, provided their own meals (prepared mainly by the mothers and wives of the sailors), and used their own horses and boats in conducting their duties. They received a small "feed allowance" for the horses, referred to as Creole horses because they had wide hooves that kept them from sinking in the marshes. Their other *real* challenge came from the mosquitoes that were said to be so thick, at times they could clog the nasal passages of cattle and suffocate them. It was reported that on one occasion, the mosquitoes were so dense that the horses just lay down and refused to go out on patrol.

The unit also became known as Swamp Angels after rescuing thirty-five airmen who were downed while target-practicing over the swamps and marshes, and saving them from exhaustion and possible death that came from fighting the elements and the mosquitoes.

The Revolutionary War

There is no one event that singularly led to the revolution. The American people were strongly independent and believed that they were entitled to the full democratic rights of Englishmen. The British believed that the American colonies were just colonies, to be used and exploited in whatever way best suited Great Britain. These two conflicting views made war inevitable.

The American Revolution may have been a blessing in disguise for many Blacks, as it paved the way toward freedom from slavery and helped them to embark on their journey toward equality and civil rights. Blacks joined the war because the principles underlying the revolution implied the end of slavery and granting of rights for them. American historian, Benjamin Quarles, understood the Black community's need for equality and freedom when he summed it up by saying, "Realizing that loyalty was not to a place or a people, but to a principle."

Approximately five thousand Blacks served as soldiers in the Continental Army and about twenty thousand in the British Army. More Blacks supported the British because they promised freedom to those who fled rebel slaveholders. In 1775, Lord Dunmore issued a proclamation in Virginia with such a promise and formed a Black

CURTIS J. JOHNSON

regiment of British soldiers. For these soldiers, the Revolutionary War was as much a war of liberation as it was for the American colonists rebelling against England.

Blacks served as soldiers, guides, orderlies, mechanics, scouts, laborers, messengers, and spies for both armies. They proved to be honest and brave soldiers, despite many misgivings on the part of the White Southern Americans, especially about arming them with weapons. Some of the soldiers considered to be heroes by commanders, including George Washington, were Crispus Attucks, Peter Salem, "Colonel" Louis Cook, Salem Poor, Colonel Titus "Tye" Cornelius, Jack Sisson, and Thomas Peters.

The War of 1812

The United States declared war against the British Empire in 1812 for several reasons, including trade restrictions brought about by Britain's ongoing war with France, the impressment of American merchant sailors into the Royal Navy, British support of the American Indian tribes against American expansion, outrage over insults to national honor after humiliations on the high seas, and possible American desire to annex Canada. The British victory at the Battle of Bladensburg in August allowed them to capture and burn Washington, D.C. America victories in September 1814 and January 1815 repulsed all three British invasions in New York, Baltimore, and New Orleans. The Battle of Baltimore inspired the lyrics of the United States national anthem, "The Star-Spangled Banner."

No legal restrictions regarding the enlistment of Blacks were placed on the navy because of its shortage of manpower. The law of 1792, which generally prohibited enlistment of Blacks in the army, became the United States Army's official policy until 1862. The only exception to this army policy was Louisiana, which permitted the existence of separate Black militia units that drew its enlistees from freed Blacks. A militia unit, the Battalion of Free Men of Color, and a unit of Black soldiers from Santo Domingo offered their services and were accepted by General Andrew Jackson in the Battle of New Orleans, a victory that was achieved after the war was officially over.

Although official U.S. policy at the start of the war forbade the recruitment of Black sailors, a chronic shortage of manpower compelled the navy to accept any able-bodied man. In 1813, Blacks made up at least 15 percent of the United States naval corps. These Black sailors had a reputation for fearlessness in battle. When Captain Oliver Hazard Perry complained about having Blacks on his ship, Commodore Isaac Chauncey replied, "I have nearly fifty Blacks on this boat, and many of them are among the best of men." Perry soon had the chance to test Chauncey's statement. At the battle of Lake Erie, where Perry's fleet thwarted the British, his Black sailors performed so well that he wrote the Secretary of the Navy, praising their courage.

The Civil War

On April 12, 1861, at 4:30 a.m., the first shot hurtled over Fort Sumter, at the entrance of the harbor of Charleston, South Carolina. This marked the beginning of the Civil War between the North (Union states) and the South (Confederates states). Union troops were forced to leave the fort the following day. Thus, America began the conflict that would take the lives of more than 620,000 of its citizens and injure more than 375,000. The U.S. flag was not raised again at Fort Sumter until February 18, 1865.

The U.S. Congress passed the Second Confiscation Act in July 1862. It freed slaves of owners in rebellion against the United States, and a militia act empowered the president to use freed slaves in any capacity in the army. President Abraham Lincoln opposed early efforts to recruit Black soldiers, although he accepted the army's using them as paid workers.

Union Army setbacks over the summer of 1862 led Lincoln to emancipating all slaves in states at the war with the Union. In September 1862, Lincoln issued his preliminary Emancipation Proclamation, announcing that all slaves in rebellious states would be free as of January 1. Recruitment of Black regiments began in full force following the proclamation of January 1863.

The United States War Department issued General Orders Number 143 on May 22, 1863, establishing a Bureau of Colored Troops to facilitate the recruitment of Black soldiers to fight for the Union Army. Regiments, including infantry, cavalry, engineers, light artillery, and heavy artillery units, were recruited from all states of the Union and became known as the United States Colored Troops (USCT). Approximately 175 regiments composed of more than 178,000 free Blacks and freedmen served during the last two years of the war. Their service bolstered the Union war effort at a critical time.

CURTIS J. JOHNSON

Union Soldier Guard

By the end of the war, the men of the USCT composed nearly one-tenth of all Union Troops. The USCT suffered 2,751 combat casualties during the war and 68,178 losses from all causes. Disease caused the most fatalities for the troops.

The Corps d'Afrique was formed in New Orleans after it was taken by Union forces. It was formed around the Louisiana Native Guards which were militia units raised in New Orleans and were formed from property-owning free people of color, who had developed as a third class in New Orleans since the colonial years. Although they wanted to prove their bravery and loyalty like other Southern property owners, the Confederates did not allow them to serve and confiscated their arms. The Confederates said that enlisting Black soldiers would hurt agriculture. Since the units were composed of freeborn Creoles and Black freemen, it was clear that the underlying objection was to having Black men serve at all.

Despite class differences between freeborn and freedmen, the Corps served with distinction at the Battle of Port Hudson. Its troops served throughout the South.

Research revealed two Black men from Donaldsonville had active roles in the Civil War. Records maintained by the Appomattox Court House National Historical Park Cemetery, Appomattox, Virginia, includes one who was a soldier. A plaque at the grave site provided the following information:

> **DEMESME, OSCAR F. (FREDERICK).** *Enlisted at Donaldsonville on 9/13/1861, 1st Corporal, promoted to 3rd Sergeant, March 1863. Born ca. 1837 in St Jermain, France. Laborer in New River, 4th Ward of Ascension Parish, living with his mother, the widow G. Demesme, and another older woman (both were born in France) along with an older brother Charles Paul Demesme. Brother was an overseer on the Laferiere Levesque Plantation in Assumption Parish that had a real estate value of $100,000 along with 77 slaves, two of them being a one and two year old mulatto. The Demesme's after Levesque's death in 1850 moved to Ascension Parish. Sophia Demesme (colored) in The New Orleans Directives of 1890-1891 identified herself as the widow of Charles Demesme, Oscar's older brother, and it seems they were the parents of three mulatto sons born ca. 1850, 1851, and 1858. The oldest they named Oscar, the middle Paul, and the youngest Leon. The mulatto named Oscar Demesme (listed by the census taker as Mesme, Mesmate, and Masino) was the Cannoneer's*

nephew who later had seven children with the oldest named after his grandfather, Charles. His next son was names Lord Byron, and the next son, the fifth child, named Oscar Junior. Charles' mulatto son Leon also named a son of his Frederick Oscar Demesme.

In a related document by Vera Smith Stanley, *A History of Appomattox County* (Appomattox, Virginia, 1965), information about Oscar F. Demesme's death is provided as noted below:

Levy Diary *noted the Canonnier Oscar Demesme, a younger brother of Charles, was killed "in the course of a melee" at the battle of Appomattox Station 4/8/1865.* The Donaldsonville Le Drapeau, 1/26/1867 *reported he was "killed and buried in the uniform of the Northern Army, in which, while acting as a spy, he is supposed to have been shot through mistake by his own friends." Buried near where he was killed until the Ladies Memorial Association of Appomattox Court House met to provide suitable interment of Confederate soldiers whose bodies had not been deposited in some regular burying ground. After coffins for the bodies were made with donated lumber, the re-interment with religious services took place on December 1, 1866 on top of a beautiful knoll deeded to the Association about a half mile west of the Court House. Grave No. 2 reads: "Sergt. O. F. Demesme, Donaldsonville Art. [Artillery] La." Today, the Appomattox Court House National Historical Park administers the cemetery that contains nineteen veterans' graves.*

An historic story that appeared in the November 2, 1902, issue of the New Orleans *Times-Picayune* newspaper briefly described the life of a Donaldsonville Negro man as that of a hero. The man, Louis Lefort, was not a member of a military unit during the Civil War; however, his accomplishments speak well for a man with many talents during the time of slavery in the United States. The article reads as follows:

NEGROLOGY

[Special to the Picayune]

Donaldsonville, La., Nov. 2. [1902]—Louis Lefort, a respectable and popular negro [sic], aged 72, died this morning of apoplexy. The death of a negro [sic], as a rule, would hardly attract notice, but the deceased was a man of reputation. He served throughout the war between the States as valet to the late Major Victor Maurin, commander of the Donaldsonville Artillery of the Army of Northern Virginia, and was with that officer until his capture with Jefferson Davis, near Washington, Ga., when he returned to Donaldsonville. Lefort left here with Major Maurin when the Donaldsonville Artillery left for the war, and besides acting in the capacity of valet, cook and body servant to the Major, often participated in battle. He was a noted chef, and could prepare the best of Creole dishes. After the war, he participated in politics and held many offices, among them Town Assessor, Tax Collector, Jailer, Postmaster, Constable and in all of these he performed his duties faithfully and honestly. While corruption and dishonesty were epidemic around him in those days, Lefort was honest and reliable. His bravery and courage was well known also, and a single incident will suffice. Under the Wormoth Administration opposing factions brought on a crisis, which resulted in the assassination of Judge Lawes, a brother of Judge Righter, of New Orleans, and Major Schonberg, by the negro [sic] militia, commanded by "General" Hunsaker and the negroes [sic]Olivers. The Olivers and Hunsaker sought to capture boxes in Donaldsonville for the purpose of returning Hunsaker elected as a State Senator. It was feared that if the negro [sic] militia was permitted to enter Donaldsonville rapine [sic] and murder would ensue. Lefort opposed their entrance in Donaldsonville, and sought by every means to deter them from marching in. This action on his part exited the animosity of the "Wormoth crowd," and to apprehend Lefort. The militia after marched into the town, and Louis Lefort with other courageous negroes [sic] sought to prevent them from indulging in excesses. The Olivers had him "arrested," tried by a drumhead court-martial and sentenced to be shot on the public green. Here it was that Lefort showed his heroism. He stood unbalanced in the middle of the public square, opened his shirt front and dared the negro [sic] militia to fire. The armed satellites were awed by the bravery of the man and refused to fire. He made his escape from the clutches of the assassins and lived to see their leaders retired from public life and consigned by history to well-merited obloquy. After a long public service he retired and operated a lunch stand in the public market, and he died enjoying the respect and good will of everybody. He had an extensive acquaintance with veterans of the Army of Northern Virginia. His funeral will take place to-morrow [sic] at the Catholic Church, of which he was a member. Veterans and sons of the late Major Victor Manrin [sic] will attend his funeral.

CURTIS J. JOHNSON

In another undated article by the *Times-Picayune*, Lefort was elected as an Ascension Parish school director.

The Spanish-American War

The sinking of the U.S. Navy battleship *Maine* on February 15, 1898, in the Havana, Cuba, harbor by Spain was the onset of the Spanish-American War. The Spanish presence in Cuba and Puerto Rico had been disturbing Americans for many years due to the proximity of these two colonies to the United States. The causes for the war related to the suppression of the Cuban people by Spain coupled with the loss of many American lives when the battleship was sunk.

The U.S. Army battle contingency, consisting of seventeen thousand soldiers, arrived by flotilla near Santiago on June 22, 1898. Included in that number were the all-Black Ninth and Tenth Cavalries and the Twenty-fourth and Twenty-fifth Infantry Regiments (about three thousand strong). The Spanish forces were engaged on June 22; and on July 3, the Spanish fleet was destroyed by American ships in the Caribbean, causing Spain's surrender on July 16, in less than one month of warfare. As a result, Spain relinquished sovereignty over Cuba and ceded the Philippine Islands, Puerto Rico, and Guam to the United States for the sum of $20 million.

World War I: The Great War

World War I started in Europe in 1914 with what began as a seemingly distant European conflict that became an event that would impact the social, economic, and political future of Americans.

The causes of the war are said to be many, with the major ones being conflicts, hostility, diplomatic clashes, imperialism, militarism, and alliances among the Great Powers of Central Europe. At the onset of the war, the main Allied Powers consisted of Great Britain, Russia, and France, followed by Italy, Japan, Canada, Australia, New Zealand, and South Africa. The Central Powers included Germany, Austria-Hungary, Bulgaria, the Ottoman Empire (Turkey), and Italy, which did not participate directly in the war and switched sides during the middle of the war.

The United States joined the Allied countries after a telegram written by the foreign secretary of the German Empire to Mexico was intercepted by Great Britain. The message was clear: if the United States was to declare war on Germany, then Mexico was to declare war on the United States as a move to stop the United States from joining in WWI. In addition, Germany's submarines sank several ships carrying American passengers during early 1917.

On April 1, 1917, President Woodrow Wilson issued a declaration of war against Germany, saying, "The world must be made safe for democracy." With those words, the United States had entered a pact with the Allied nations to support the allied nations in their conflict that had continued since 1914.

Segregation and racism remained rampant in the United States during these years, and treatment to Blacks by the country's military system was no exception to these government-enforced conditions. In spite of the racial restriction imposed by the government, Blacks were eager to enlist to fight in the war to show their patriotism and allegiance to our country. Some thought their voluntary willingness to serve their country would help to improve their opportunities and treatment they would receive at home after the war. Others believed that volunteering would prove their loyalty and commitment to serve and win the respect of their White neighbors and associates.

Soon after the declaration of war, the War Department realized that the current strength of the army of 126,000 men would have to be increased. So the Congress passed the Selective Service Act that required all male citizens between the ages of twenty-one and thirty-one to register for the draft. Now with the help of the draft, draft boards were doing everything they could to bring the Blacks into service. Although they comprised only 10 percent of the entire U.S. population, Blacks became 13 percent of all inductees. The army, although still discriminatory, was far more progressive than the other branches of service. Blacks could not serve in the marines and could serve in limited and menial positions in the navy and Coast Guard.

The war most directly impacted those Black Americans called to fight and labor in the military overseas. Over twenty thousand men served in France. The majority worked in service units, broadly characterized as the Service of Supply (SOS). They dug ditches, cleaned latrines, transported supplies, cleared debris, and buried rotting corpses. The largest number of Black SOS troops served as stevedores, working in the docks of Brest, Saint Nazaire, Bordeaux, and other French port cities to load and unload critical supplies.

Although technically eligible for many positions in the army, few Blacks got the opportunity to serve in combat units. The combat elements of the army were kept completely segregated. The four established all-Black regular army regiments (Twenty-fourth Infantry, Twenty-fifth Infantry, Ninth Cavalry, and Tenth Cavalry) were not used in overseas combat roles but instead were diffused throughout American-held territory. There was such a backlash from the Black community, however, that the War Department created the Ninety-second and Ninety-third Infantry Divisions. These two divisions, manned by approximately 40,000 Black soldiers, did experience battle in France. The Ninety-third Division was assigned to assist the French army, the only American division to serve exclusively under French command. Despite having to acclimate to French methods of combat, the division's four regiments were said to have performed exceptionally well.

W. E. B. DuBois, a Black American intellectual, whose call for racial equality marked him as a radical thinker in his era, strongly supported the war effort; but the patriotism of Black soldiers was not recognized or rewarded by White military commanders. For example, the public and private remarks of General John Pershing, commander of the American Expeditionary Force in Europe, exposed the often-hypocritical attitudes toward Black American among many White Americans in the early twentieth century. In a secret communiqué concerning Black American troops sent to the French military stationed with the American army, August 7, 1918, General Pershing stated, "We must not eat with them, must not shake hands with them, seek to talk to them or meet with them outside the requirements of military service. We must not commend them too highly these troops, especially in front of White Americans." At a later time, in Scott's *Official History of the American Negro in the World War,* General Pershing is said to have made this remark: "I cannot commend too highly the spirit shown among the colored combat troops, who exhibit fine capacity for quick training and eagerness for the most dangerous work."

The 369th Infantry was the first regiment of the Ninety-third Division to reach France. They arrived in the port city of Brest in December in 1917. After three months duty with SOS, the 369th received orders to join the French Sixteenth Division in Givry-en-Argonne for additional training. After three weeks, the regiment was sent to the front lines in a region just west of the Argonne Forest. For nearly a month, they held their own against German assaults, and after only a brief break from the front, the 369th was placed once again in the middle of the German offensive, this time in Minacourt, France. From July 18 until August 6, 1918, the 369th Infantry, now proudly nicknamed the Harlem Hellfighters, proved their tenacity once again by helping the French 161st Division drive the Germans from their trenches during the Aisne-Marne counteroffensive.

During this three-week period, the Germans were making small night raids into Allied territory. During one of these raids, a member of the 367th, Corporal Henry Johnson, fought off an entire German raiding party using only a pistol and a knife. Killing four of the Germans and wounding more, his actions allowed a wounded comrade to escape capture and led to the seizure of a stockpile of German arms. Johnson and his comrade were wounded, and both received the French Croix de Guerre for their gallantry. Johnson was also promoted to sergeant.

The Ninety-second Division, in comparison to the Ninety-third, had a much more harrowing experience. White Army officials characterized Black soldiers of the division as rapist and spread vicious lies among French civilians. Black officers were particularly singled out for racist treatment because of their status. Viewed as a threat to White authority, many were unjustly transferred out of the division and others were court-martialed on bogus charges. Despite inadequate training and racial discrimination, the division as a whole fought well. However, one regiment, the 368th Infantry, performed poorly during the Allied Meuse-Argonne Offensive in September 1918 and was used by the military to characterize all Black soldiers and officers as complete failures. Black soldiers would contest these slanderous charges well into the postwar period.

World War II

Every village, town, city, and parish (county) in the United States of America was affected in some manner when the Japanese bombed Pearl Harbor on December 7, 1941. This was one of the most traumatic days in my childhood and, for many reasons, one that I would remember for a lifetime. World War II had begun when Germany attacked Poland in 1939, and France and Great Britain declared war on Germany. On December 8, 1941, our country declared war against Japan and, in doing so, was now officially engaged in World War II.

I was ten years old when the war began. I remember vividly many of the incidents and related history recorded in this part. However, some of the stories herein were offered by oral history volunteers who either served directly in the military or who related stories from family members who served, and information found in the public domain.

Military Conscription: The Draft

Starting with the Civil War in 1862 and continuing through the major wars involving the United States (WWI, WWII, Korea, and Vietnam), men and women were sent off to the military establishment as draftees or as volunteers. Draftees were inducted into military units through the draft or military conscription process.

The federal law mandated all men between the ages of eighteen and forty-five to register with their draft board, often referred to as local boards. Once registered, these men became candidates for military service. For a brief period, the maximum age for registration was extended to sixty-five; however, it later reverted back to forty-five.

With the Selective Service System that became law on September 30, 1940, came mandatory military service for those men found to be physically and mentally capable.

In Ascension Parish, the draft board was located in the courthouse in Donaldsonville. Similarly, draft board offices were located in Saint James (St. James), Assumption (Napoleonville), and Lafourche (Thibodaux) parishes and other locations described by the draft policies.

Depending on the circumstances, draft boards were empowered to defer enlistment of potential draftees. Draft candidates could be deferred if they had dependent families that required the presence of the draftee at home to prevent "hardship," if the candidate's duties at the workplace were considered by the board to be *indispensable* to employers, or if they had temporary physical or mental disabilities. Candidates who were members of pacifist religious organizations were classified as *Conscientious Objectors*. This meant that these candidates were exempt from the draft but were required to perform services in other federal government agencies for the same amount of time they would have spent in military service.

"In one Black family in Saint James, two sons worked for Sidney Woods, a White farmer," Herman Nicholas stated. The mother arranged to have both sons deferred by their employer. Ironically, both sons decided not to accept the deferment because they wanted to serve, he said. In several other cases, White farmers were able to get their "good workers, both Black and White" deferments for the duration of the war.

The draft board issued cards to each registrant that notified the candidates of their induction date, giving them instructions as to the location, the date, and the time they were to report for induction. The card also warned that the candidate could be contacted at any time. In addition to the candidate's name, place of residence, mailing address, and telephone number, these cards noted the date and place of birth, the name and address of a person who would always know the candidate's address and the candidate's employer's name and address, and the place of employment or business. The back of the card required a description of the cardholder (race, height, weight, color of eyes and hair, and complexion). The card was signed by the candidate on the front, attesting to the accuracy of the information given. The registrar of the draft board who witnessed the cardholder's signature signed the back.

The draft became a topic of daily conversation among families, speculating as to which of the community men would be drafted next.

The draft card was regarded as "a badge of honor" by many of the area's Black candidates.

The Great Send-Off

Each community began preparing for a send-off as early as their young men began receiving their "intention of induction" notices from the president. The U.S. Custom House in New Orleans and Camp Livingston, located on the borderline of Rapides and Grant parishes north of Pineville, were two of the induction sites for Louisiana. The military was a segregated organization, and Black and White candidates were processed and inducted separately. The *Gonzales Weekly*, dated April 25, 1942, published the following article about the induction of men living in Ascension:

COLORED MEN OF ASCENSION LEAVE FOR ARMY

The following named colored men of the parish of Ascension have been selected for induction by the Parish board at Donaldsonville, La. at 8:30 a.m. on May 1st, whereupon they shall be sent to an induction station of the United States Army at Camp Livingston, La.:

Herbert Etienne, Joseph Forcell, Irwin Leon Gomez, John Holly, Moses Sam Jenkins, Gus Johnson, Eurine Maurice LeBlanc, Charlie Scott, Jr., Claud Sims, George Washington, Jr., Onell Williams, Andrew Johnson, Albert Zeno, Earl Joseph Rosemond, Joseph Butler,

Percy Dixon, Christ Harris, Joe Walton, Samson Earl, Alblon Ford, Henry Morris Levy, Roosevelt Joseph Reed, Fred Arthur Landry, Herbert Brunswick, Paris Harris Stephens, Lloyd Dupard.

On induction day for Ascension Parish, Black candidates who received notices assembled at the Harlem Theater for a modest reception with refreshments. There was a brief ceremony of speeches by community leaders, blessing of the candidates and their families by the clergy, and a parade (complete with a band and cheerleaders) to the Texas and Pacific train station where the candidates offered final good-byes to their families and friends. My sister Claudia was one of the cheerleaders.

Arriving at the induction center, the candidates were all given tests for aptitude, dexterity, and intelligence and physical examinations. Some who passed the physical exam were classified 1-A and immediately inducted into the army or navy and shipped out to a basic training camp. Others who had temporary physical problems were sent home to heal and report back on a given date. Still others diagnosed with serious physical problems or abnormalities or test scores below accepted standards were classified 4-F and were declined induction and sent home, much to the delight of some and the disappointment of others.

Community Reaction

People throughout the communities demonstrated a heightened sense of urgency, patriotism, and concern for others during the war years. Neighbors, both Black and White, appeared friendlier and were more eager to share homegrown vegetables, eggs, chickens, and other food items and to help one another during times of need.

Letter-writing campaigns to send mail to service members became family projects. Family members took turns keeping their soldier-relative informed about news on the home front—who got married, which child lost a tooth and was rewarded with a nickel by the Tooth Fairy, the eight-pound catfish caught by a neighbor yesterday, and other such tidbits thought to be interesting to the service members. In return, the soldier or sailor wrote about the weather, the barracks inspection, the terrible mess hall chow and promised to send money home on payday. K-rations, the U.S. Army pocket can opener (a.k.a. the P-38 that came with the K-rations), and later, C-Rations became an appreciated war souvenir to veterans and teens.

Service Star

Songs served as national morale boosters for our troops, especially the men who were serving in overseas campaigns. Compositions such as," I'll Be Seeing You (In All the Old Familiar Places)," "Ain't Misbehavin'," "Don't Sit under the Apple Tree (With Anyone Else but Me)," "I'll Get By (As Long As I Have You)," "Is You Is Or Is You Ain't My Baby," "Coming in on a Wing and a Prayer," and "Stardust" could be heard on radio programs and whistled by men at work and boys walking to and from school.

Some communities established a method of recognizing those men who were serving in military service. In our town, recognition featured an honor roll, an encased display with the names of its soldiers, sailors, and airmen, Black and White, listed alphabetically. The U.S. War Department issued a service flag to each family that had at least one member serving in the military. Families with sons and fathers and, later, mothers and daughters serving in the military proudly posted in front windows the red, white, and blue banners, an award, of sorts, for having their family members serve their country. The vertical flag measured approximately ten inches wide by twelve inches high with a blue star for each family member serving. Those who gave their lives while serving were remembered with a gold star. Families displayed the flag with pride and dignity . . . and with good reason.

Selected everyday items were determined to be vital to the war effort. Early on during the conflict, the White House made a call to the public to recycle steel, rubber, tin, paper, and waste kitchen fats (an ingredient for making explosives and some pharmaceuticals) to be used to manufacture the ships, tanks, planes, trucks, and other equipment and supplies needed to support the defense effort. Several of my friends and I began collecting any kind of metal we could find. Our Saturday scrap metal hunt became a ritual for us. Using homemade carts, we made our rounds through the streets looking through trash piles for the metal treasures they often brought. We knocked on doors asking residents for any scrap metal they may have had in their yard. Some people dumped trash illegally behind the levee. Arriving there before other scroungers often brought enough metal to quickly fill a wagon. A discarded iron bed was too big for a single cart, but two carts rigged in tandem usually solved the problem.

Several places in our town bought the scrap medal for recycling. At the Elray Kocke Service, Inc., the recycling operation was managed by Herbert Loton, a Black employee. He weighed the metal, by type, and recorded the results in a log. Then he wrote the type metal and weight on an invoice that we took to the office where it was redeemed for cash.

Heroes on Furlough

The service members who were issued overseas orders were allowed furloughs of several weeks to visit with families and friends before shipping out. These visits were often highlights for the entire community, with parties and other celebrations held in honor of these homegrown soldiers.

When our cousin, Eddie Pinkins, Jr., who lived three blocks from our house, came home on leave, he resembled the Pied Piper as he walked along the street that fronted our house. By the time he arrived home from the Greyhound bus station, there were twenty or so excited boys and girls, including me, following him and cheering him on.

Not long afterward, our brother Walter (sergeant, United States Army, Serial Number 38620348) came home on leave before being shipped overseas to the Aleutian Islands in the Asia-Pacific Theater. I was fourteen by then; and my only brother, at age nineteen, dressed in his winter olive drab (OD) uniform, looked like a general to me. The uniform, adorned with an assortment of medals, ribbons, decals, shining brass and gold stripes, was breathtaking! In less than one year, he had changed completely from the fun-loving yet serious teenager I had known much of my life to the handsome, mature man he had now become.

Service members on leave wore their uniforms occasionally and were easily recognized everywhere they went. Soldiers stood tall in their OD trousers, service cap, and Eisenhower jacket with tan shirt and OD tie during winter. They wore their assigned khaki uniform during the summer months, and regardless of the uniform, their brown shoes were usually spit-shined. Sailors dressed in their summer bell-bottom white trousers and over-blouse with spotless white shoes. During the cold months, the navy bell-bottom trousers and navy over-blouse with shining black shoes and navy pea coat combined to make each sailor stand out, even among their army counterparts. Sailors wore the white Popeye cap that every boy and girl wished for. It was amazing how the uniform had changed some of the servicemen. Those who were shoddy dressers before joining the service were now reformed models who even walked differently, now with their heads held high, chests out, and with pride in their steps, just as they had been instructed by their drill sergeants.

Added attractions to their uniforms were the chevrons (stripes) indicating the service members' rank along with the service medals and ribbons and other identifying pins and medals earned, such as weapons qualification, name tag, unit designation patches, branch of service patches, and other appropriate insignia. The service members made sure their *gig line* (alignment of the leading edge of shirt's facing, belt buckle, and trouser placket) on their uniform was aligned to ensure the properly worn military dress.

The community responded in kind, demonstrating pride in these hometown heroes and, in general, making a fuss over them at every opportunity.

Challenging Tours of Duty

Military authorities for all branches of service enforced racial segregation of on-base facilities including housing, mess halls and galleys, and recreation facilities and activities. When Black military units were formed, White commissioned officers made up the leadership of these units that were mostly service and combat support oriented. A cadre of Black noncommissioned officers (NCOs) served in these units as well. As the war continued, combat units for Black troops were activated, with the addition of one or two Black officers serving as members of the unit cadre. Eventually, all Black officers and NCOs were assigned as leaders in Black units.

Black servicemen who were home on leave reported that, as in civilian life, they were held to different standards than their White counterparts. Blacks had to work harder and sometimes longer; *any* infraction of rules and regulations, regardless of mitigating circumstances, brought them extra kitchen police or guard or area clean-up duties. Certainly, the Uniformed Code of Military Justice (UCMJ) rules and regulations were equally applicable to Blacks and Whites for more serious infractions; however, the resulting punishment was usually far less for Whites than that applied to colored troops. Job advancement opportunities were dismal in all branches of the military establishment for people of color.

The army offered little encouragement to minority service personnel to make career commitments. The navy and marines offered even less. The Army Air Corps remained steadfast in its tradition of "no Blacks" until 1941 when the Tuskegee Airmen program was introduced by the Congress.

Black service members were restricted to menial jobs. In the army, they dug ditches, built fences, constructed and maintained airstrips, and operated mess facilities. In the navy and Marine Corps, Blacks were cooks and bakers, laborers and stewards.

Weekend liberty passes issued to Blacks were few compared to Whites, according to some soldiers and sailors. White officers apparently feared that too many Blacks on pass would cause trouble in local communities. This meant that those few who were allowed off base on pass would have to demonstrate their ability to "walk the line" and stay out of trouble in order for others to be able to get liberty passes the next time they were issued.

The welcome sign for Blacks in the off-base communities in the South by White storeowners, restaurants, and other businesses simply did not exist. The same kind of treatment was experienced in many northern locations as well.

Servicemen on furlough told stories about how poorly they were being treated by White service members, both officer and enlisted. For Blacks, there were unwritten policies that would govern their relationships with their White counterparts working at the same posts, camps, and stations. Several stories related by Blacks included these:

❖ Blacks lived in barracks that were a distance away from White soldiers. During duty hours, comingling of the troops was avoided as much as possible or certainly held to a minimum.

❖ Rewards for work accomplishments were few in the Black units. However, monthly announcements for the same post, camps, and stations were published about the large number of White soldiers receiving citations for their "superior" work.

❖ A similar disparity related to Blacks serving overseas, where Whites were said to receive medals, commendations, and other performance citations "ten times more than blacks."

❖ Promotions were extremely slow to come to the Black troops. Because of this, their counterparts would ridicule them, calling them "dummies," and using the N-word as freely as they dared to.

❖ Altercations usually ended with Blacks getting the most punishment for the confrontation.

❖ White military police and shore patrol could arrest any soldier or sailor. However, Black military police or shore patrol could stop or arrest only minority servicemen.

- One Black soldier who had served in France told of Black troops having to sit behind German POWs at a USO show.
- Carroll Nicholas of Saint James was reportedly walking on the sidewalk in Fort Gordon, Georgia, as a White lieutenant approached him. The officer told him to get off the sidewalk when he (the lieutenant) was walking there. Nicholas refused, stating that he had the right to walk there too. The officer had him court-martialed for disobeying an order. Nicholas was sentenced to time in the stockade.

Black soldiers serving in the South Pacific were often reminded of their second-class citizenship status by Ikuko Toguri. This young woman was known for her broadcasts of Japanese propaganda over Radio Tokyo and was best known as Tokyo Rose. In her nightly broadcasts, she would chide Black troops for defending a country that treated them like "dirt" and a country that would never accept them as equal to Whites. She encouraged them at every opportunity to go AWOL (absent without leave) to save their lives "from the superior weapons of the Nippon army, navy, and air force." In spite of her daily chatter, there is no indication that her psychological attacks lessened Black GIs' patriotism.

Several families in the region sent two or more sons off to one or more of the three wars mentioned above as shown below:

- In Saint James, the Carroll Nicholas, Sr., family of Welcome sent four of their seven sons off to wars in WWII, Korea, and Vietnam. Earl, a sailor with twenty-one years, was a veteran of WWII, Korea, and Vietnam. Carroll, Jr., a soldier with almost thirty years, served in the Philippines during WWII and Vietnam. Russell was a soldier for twenty-four years, spent most of his years in California. Lastly, Warren was a soldier with twenty-three years and served in the Philippines during WWII.
- The Walter Ricardo, Sr., family of Donaldsonville sent a son to WWII (Walter, Jr.), one to Korea (Charles Ray), and a third (Ralph) to army service for two years after the Korean War ended. Walter Jr. was killed in action.
- Another Donaldsonville family, the Clifford LeBlanc, Sr.'s, sent one son to WWII (Clifford, Jr.), another to the Korean War (Reginald), and a third (Gerald) to army service for two years. Reginald was killed in action.

Difficult Returns

The majority of the men returning from the war had difficulty finding jobs that were commensurate with saleable skills they developed before and during their tours of duty. The lack of jobs affected some White returnees and most of the Black military veterans. This condition was echoed throughout the state and country. The government's response to this unemployment problem was the Servicemen's Readjustment Act of 1944 (also known as the GI Bill of Rights) that provided funds for veterans' education and trade skills training exclusively for returning military veterans.

The program offered returning veterans training in carpentry, brick masonry, auto mechanics, electrical application, and upholstery in the Bayou Lafourche Region. Training centers were located at the South Louisiana State Fair grounds facilities in Donaldsonville and Gonzales in Ascension, Belle Alliance Junior High, Napoleonville Junior High in Assumption, and C. M. Washington High School in Thibodaux. Saint James veterans attended the training facilities in Assumption and Ascension. Each course was taught by journeyman craftsmen or teachers for the crafts being offered. Participants were each given a set of tools for their particular trade while training and were retained for their use upon successful completion of the training. Walter attended a carpentry course at the Belle Alliance Training Center, developing skills he later used successfully for many years in a daytime "second" job.

Veterans who persevered and completed training courses were guaranteed jobs, and some were rewarded with substantial paychecks for their skills. For example, two Donaldsonville veterans, Clarence Joseph and Charles Ricardo, became so skilled at laying cinder blocks that, on a good day, both would earn about $100 each. This amounted to more money than many salaried workers with families made in a week, including my father. I can attest to their expertise because I worked as one of two mortar boys for them for about a week on one particular building project at Lowery High School. Keeping them supplied with mortar was the most difficult job of my life. A week was about all the time I could endure working for them, and ditto for my partner.

Unfortunately, few men attained such levels of proficiency as demonstrated by Joseph and Ricardo. Some Black veterans were lucky to gain minimum-wage jobs that paid fifty-five cents an hour.

Man Laying Bricks

The skills training programs were considered successful by government standards, although as many as 35 percent of the participants dropped out of the courses before completing the training. Some sold their tools for a few dollars; still others were unwilling to escape from lounging on the street corner.

While many of our postwar experiences for Blacks were disappointing, there were bright spots. Rev. Wallace shared one noteworthy example that occurred in Thibodeaux. "After so many years of Black people being denied their rightful privilege of voting, I returned home right after the war ended, pumped up and ready to vote. I went to the voter registration office in my army uniform and found the receptionist and other voter registration officials to be exceptionally nice! The voter registration clerk, a White man, encouraged me to get other Blacks in the parish to come in to register, a fact that, heretofore, was unheard of. I voted for the first time in December 1945," he reported.

Veterans' Stories

Black WWII veterans served their country at a time when segregation was enforced in all aspects of life. In spite of differing levels of support provided by the federal government, these veterans shared a high level of camaraderie and morale. Although the numbers of these veterans are diminishing, we were able to locate several whose stories appear below.

Carrol Joseph Cayette, Sr., Jamestown (St. James), Army, WWII, Korean War and Vietnam War

Carrol J. Cayette, Sr., completed the seventh grade in 1937; however, there was no high school for Creoles and Blacks in the parish at the time. Several teachers volunteered to continue teaching the recently graduated students for a small fee, and Cayette continued through the eighth grade before dropping out of school in favor of working in his first paying job, stripping tobacco for his father to make and sell cigars.

Later, realizing a chance to return to school and receive a salary in the process, he joined the Civilian Conservation Corps (CCC) in Keithville, Louisiana, and was assigned to the CCC Camp in Lake Charles. There, he was selected as a member of the camp cadre and became the recreational area supervisor. As a part of their training, the youth learned army terminology and formations, how to give commands, leadership skills, and close-order drill using wooden rifles. There were two active duty army officers assigned to the camp.

He continued to work in the CCC Camp system as a tutor in the education center and in the woodworking shop before he was drafted by the army in Baton Rouge in 1943.

Cayette, a Creole who was classified as Negro, was assigned to Camp Walters, Texas, for eighteen weeks of basic training where he quickly learned that the army was highly segregated and quite different from the way folks lived in Saint James with Creoles and Whites getting along with little racial tension. "In Texas, Blacks trained in the front portion of the camp while Whites trained in the far back area, quite a distance apart," he said. He also stated that it was recorded in army doctrine that Blacks could not lead Whites.

During late 1943, there were two Black army divisions, the Ninety-second Infantry deployed in the Far East and the Ninety-third Infantry deployed to Italy. Following their basic training, some of the Black soldiers at Camp Walters were trained as infantry replacements for the two deployed divisions. Others, including Cayette, were reassigned to the Quartermaster Corps at Camp Maxie near Austin, Texas, to train as railroad operators, truck drivers, and graves registration specialists. Cayette was trained as a truck driver and assigned to the 3399th Quartermaster Company (truck) that was soon deployed to England in early 1944. Their equipment was shipped ahead of them and had arrived in the port of Lynnbrook by the time the troops arrived after nine days aboard a British passenger ship that carried them from the Brooklyn, New York, port of debarkation.

The main equipment and personnel of the 3399th QM Co. included forty-eight two-and-a-half-ton cargo trucks and seventy-two drivers (one and a half drivers per truck) divided into three platoons. The company was commanded by a White captain, with three White lieutenants as platoon leaders. The noncommissioned officer cadre was all-Black.

The company was assigned the temporary job of transporting American and British troops along the English Channel corridor in preparation for the D-Day invasion in France. Cayette stated that his company was placed on alert to participate in the invasion; however, his commander reported that he had no knowledge of when this would occur.

For the next four months, the 3399th continued its interim mission successfully. Because of his extensive army training and leadership qualities gained while in the CCC, Cayette was "skipped over" becoming a corporal (E-4) and promoted to buck sergeant (E-4), making him a noncommissioned officer with more rank and privileges. The next day, he was promoted to staff sergeant (E-6) and appointed platoon sergeant. Within a week, he was given the additional position of field first sergeant. These types of promotions were made only to those who demonstrated excellence in leadership qualities and abilities.

D-Day began on June 6, 1944, by sea across the English Channel and from British and Allied Air Force bases by air. Their destination was not disclosed to the troops until they were well underway. Operating under the code name Operation Overlord, 179,000 Allied troops invaded the Normandy Province of France where the German military forces were well dug in and held the high ground.

During the early days of the invasion, the 3399th continued its temporary mission. On the eighth day following D-Day, the company loaded medical supplies onto the trucks and drove the trucks onto U.S. Navy landing crafts in preparation for their deployment. The company was deployed the following day.

In describing the activities of the 3399th's duration of the war against Germany, Cayette gave the following summary:

> "The company landed on the Normandy Beach Area in northern France and was attached to the 29th Infantry Division and assigned to the Communication Zone (COMZ, or the rear area). The trip to shore was not uneventful, as the company lost several trucks due to flooding during off-loading.
>
> "Immediately upon our arrival, the "word" was out that General Dwight D. Eisenhower, Commander of Allied forces, wanted to be certain that no Blacks were killed, because he did not want Blacks to be held as "heroes." He was said to hold little, if any, respect for support troops, especially those in Black units. We ignored the "word" because we knew we had a job to do.
>
> "The company's initial mission was in support of armor units in the advance section, and included delivering tank shells and ammunition, POL (petroleum, oil and lubricants) and all other supplies and equipment from the beach area to units within the advance section behind the combat zone. Gasoline was transported in 5-gallon Jerry cans. When 12 or more loaded trucks were dispatched, the platoon leader would travel with the convoy. As

platoon sergeant, I would travel with the convoy when eight or more trucks were involved. Loaded convoys were sometimes led by combat Military Police to destinations and on return trips. At all other times, the MPs were posted at critical junctions to give directions. The off-loading of gasoline and ammunition was done by soldiers assigned to the receiving units. However, for off-loading most other supplies, the trucks were allowed to back-up at a high rate of speed and slam on the brakes, dumping the boxes in the process. Trucks were considered extremely valuable equipment because every unit needed transportation for a myriad of reasons. And while in the advance area, trucks were subject to confiscation by senior officers for short periods of time. Return trips from the advance section usually included carrying dead soldiers to Graves Registration units and the less-seriously wounded to medical units in the COMZ for recuperation.

"Our mission was changed to supporting combat engineer units. For my company, the only significant change was the type cargo that we now hauled in our mission. Our main cargo consisted of collapsible bridges and other engineering equipment; and we ran convoys day and night delivering this equipment to units in the advance section. As platoon sergeant, I rode as passenger in the lead truck, and the platoon leader rode in the jeep at the end of the convoy. Our farthest destination into the advance section was marked by the longest range of German artillery.

"Allied forces were successful in the Battle of the Bulge, the final defensive stand taken by the Germans, to end the war in Europe. Our company camp was located in Czechoslovakia at that time."

Cayette grew up in a household where French was spoken fluently and English was a second language. He stated that during the war, he was often used as an interpreter in his unit's dealings with the French people. Although there were other Creoles assigned to his company, their level of fluency was below that which was required to be an interpreter.

The 3399th was awarded four battle stars for its courageous support provided during the war efforts.

Cayette returned to the United States via troop ship, landing in Boston on December 20, 1945. He received an honorable discharge from the army with the rank of staff sergeant at Camp Shelby, Mississippi, on December 27, 1945.

Hardly one to ponder over decisions, Cayette renewed his desire to go to Hollywood to work in crafts or trades as a prop specialist. He realized he needed to increase his educational level and sought someone's advice. "Ms. Alice was the principal of Saint Louis School in Brookstown (St. James Parish). For a small fee, she tutored me and my friend, Caroll Nicholas, Jr., for a few weeks," he said.

In 1947, while speculating what specific skills he would need to succeed in the industry, he heard about Southern University's industrial education program and thought that may be the answer to his needs. Armed with a strong desire, he traveled to Southern in Scotlandville, Louisiana, and met with Mr. Nickolas Harrison, an instructor in the Industrial Education Department. Along with Dr. Elton Harrison, the department head, they worked out a special two-year certificate curriculum that included the courses he would take to achieve the skills needed to build practically any type of prop used in the movie-making business. The schedule for study entailed eight hours a day, five days a week, and all related expenses would be paid by the federal government under the GI Bill.

In 1948, Cayette needed one point to complete his high school requirements to enroll as a student at Southern. Encouraged by Dr. Harrison, Cayette took the General Educational Development (GED) test and passed the requirements for completion. Upon his enrollment, he was given credit for the industrial education courses he had completed and started his college curriculum in industrial education as an advanced sophomore.

He joined the Reserve Officer Training Corps (ROTC) in the second class of the Corps history at Southern. He was appointed to the position of sergeant major of the ROTC Regiment by the professor of military science and tactics and as a cadet on the precision drill team.

Cayette earned the bachelor of science degree in industrial education from Southern University during May 1951. At the same time, he was commissioned a second lieutenant in the U.S. Army Transportation Corps.

Eighteen months later, he entered the U.S. Army again, this time as an officer. He was assigned initially to temporary duty at the U.S. Army Transportation School, Fort Eustis, Virginia, to attend the three-month transportation officer's basic course. His next assignment would take him to the Republic of South Korea in late January 1953.

Although the war was continuing to the north near the 38th parallel line, the unit to which he was assigned was located in Haeundae, several miles east of Pusan, the southernmost port city in the country. He was assigned as a platoon leader in a light truck company in a truck battalion involved in hauling supplies and equipment from the military port to storage depots. The war ended six months later in July 1953.

After returning to the United States in 1954, he had a brief assignment at Camp Chaffee, Arkansas. His follow-on assignments included the following:

- Fort Sill, Oklahoma, where he served as the Transportation Battalion motor officer for two and a half years.
- Stuttgart, Germany, in 1957 serving first as commander of a light truck company in support of Headquarters, Seventh Army Corps, U.S. Forces, then as a commander of a car company that supported the same Headquarters.
- Erie, Pennsylvania, in a civilian component advisory position with the Headquarters, West Pennsylvania Sector Command, Twenty-first Army Corps unit in 1960. (When Cayette decided to bring his family to Erie, he was told he could not move into a White neighborhood. The next day, he drove his wife and three children to the Pentagon. As he entered the facility, he was approached by a general officer who asked him if he needed assistance. After hearing Cayette's story, the general told him that he could be assigned to any post of his choice in the United States.)
- Port of New Orleans, Louisiana, for several months, then to Camp Leroy Johnson, New Orleans, serving as the assistant operations officer in a terminal service battalion.
- Fort Eustis, Virginia, in 1962 to attend the Transportation Officers' advance course.
- U.S. Army ASCOM, Sixty-Ninth Transportation Battalion (truck) as the operations officer (S-3). In addition to providing transportation services to the ASCOM depot and units in the greater Seoul area, the battalion also trained Korean troops in logistics operations.
- Yakima, Washington, assigned as advisor to an Army Reserve light truck company.

- Fort Meade, Maryland, Headquarters, Second Army (Logistics, G-4), served as a technical service inspector for transportation equipment.
- Fort Eustis for two months in 1965, then on to Naha, Okinawa, assigned to the Twenty-seventh Transportation Battalion (terminal service) as the director of operations and the director of the Naha Port, including White Beach where all ammunitions and POL (petroleum, oil, and lubricants) were off-loaded.

In March 1967, Cayette received orders for Vietnam that assigned him to the Fourth Transportation Group (terminal service) that provided water and highway transportation services to military units in the greater Saigon area. His experiences in Vietnam included his involvement in the construction of New Port, a dedicated water port of operations for the U.S. forces located several miles south of Saigon. His job as the port commander involved discharging and moving of all United States military and state department cargoes to designated depots in areas surrounding Saigon, including Long Binh.

Upon returning to the United States in March 1968, he was assigned for a short period to Fort Chaffee, Arkansas. His final assignment began in August 1968 with the Military Ocean Terminal, Bayonne, New Jersey, where he served as the chief of Cargo Operations Division until his retirement in 1972 after twenty-four years of service, including his enlisted time. His decorations for commendable service included these:

➢ Bronze Star Medal
➢ Meritorious Service Medal
➢ Army Commendation Ribbon with Medal Pendant
➢ Good Conduct Medal
➢ National Defense Service Medal
➢ United Nations Service Medal
➢ Korean Service Medal
➢ European/African/Middle Eastern Campaign Medal
➢ WWII Victory Medal
➢ American Occupational Medal (Germany)
➢ Armed Forces Reserve Medal
➢ Vietnam Service Medal
➢ Republic of Vietnam Campaign Medal

Cayette stated that the most valued documents from his military service are the two telegrams he received from the president of the United States (Lyndon B. Johnson) requesting that he remain in the army for two additional years. Cayette indeed extended his army stay for the first two years.

Lieutenant Colonel Carrol Joseph Cayette, Sr., Serial Number 38494861, was one of the select military personnel who participated directly in three major wars while serving his country.

Larry Dorsey, Napoleonville (Assumption), Army

Larry Dorsey lives in the house where he was born eighty-nine years ago. The house is clean, comfortable, and well maintained. He claimed, "I was raised and not *driven* up by caring parents who taught me to respect others, to value life, and to be spiritual." To talk with him, one will agree that he learned his parental lessons well.

Dorsey left his home in 1938 and relocated to Peoria, Illinois, to escape the grueling fieldwork that was the only available employment in his hometown area. In Peoria, he was able to find a rooming house and a job as an elevator operator in an office building. On one occasion while passing a military recruiting office, he stopped in to inquire about enlisting in the navy. He was told there were no jobs available in the navy for him. He also learned that he had to be at least eighteen years old to enlist in any service. Additionally, he would need a letter of consent from his parents since he was only seventeen. He also knew his parents would never approve of him joining the military system.

In the same building housing the recruiting office was a Civilian Conservation Corps (CCC) office. He volunteered to join and was soon off to Annandale, Illinois, where he worked with a gang of recruits clearing wooded areas, building levees and other conservation projects. Before long, he was invited to be the assistant to the project supervisor. When he informed the supervisor he didn't know what the job entailed, he was told to "just do what I tell you to do." Dorsey agreed and was elated to learn that his pay would be $36 per month. His boss's salary was $54 per month.

In early 1941, President Franklin D. Roosevelt sent out invitations giving CCC workers priority in volunteering for the army. Dorsey no longer needed his parents' approval to join, so he volunteered for and was accepted by the army. He was assigned to the Seventy-sixth Coast

Artillery with a mission of defending water ports. At the onset of WWII, he was sent to Camp Lee, Virginia, where he was promoted to corporal (E-4) in the infantry and given the job of a six-man squad leader. By July 1942, he was promoted to buck sergeant (E-4) and given the status of a noncommissioned officer before being shipped off to Fort Jackson, South Carolina, by bus and then by train to Camp Kilmer, New Jersey. In two days, he would board a troop ship carrying Black soldiers to an unknown destination.

His ship stopped overnight in Halifax, Nova Scotia, where it joined a convoy ("ships as far as one could see behind and ahead") headed for what most of the troops on board thought was Europe. The convoy was threatened by what was believed to be a German submarine as they watched torpedo boats drop depth charges for over an hour. Nearing Glasgow, Scotland, a heavy storm interrupted their travel, driving the September temperatures down to the low forties.

Most of the ships in the convoy docked in Liverpool, England. Dorsey's unit was told they would be there for an undetermined length of time. In the meantime, the men were given liberty passes to visit the local surroundings. They learned that White soldiers had spread the word in the area that Blacks had tails, a rumor that nearly started a riot in Liverpool. The U.S. Army top echelon then distributed brochures throughout the city that informed the public that Black soldiers did not have tails and what was more important was that their presence would help England in its struggle against Germany. The fights were quelled.

The U.S. soldiers, segregated along color lines, passed the time away by helping British farmers harvest their crops before the cold, wet season set in. Dorsey's unit remained in Liverpool until the end of October when they received orders to leave for another unknown destination. They boarded the ship at night and departed. The men later learned that they had traveled down the west coast of France and Spain, passed through the Gibraltar Straights, and headed for North Africa.

The ship landed near a village near Oran, North Africa, at night, where the temperature was quite hot during the day and cold at night. Several times the men had to take cover in foxholes to escape the snow. A few days later, the unit received orders to pack up and reboard. The ship crossed the Mediterranean and arrived off the coast of Italy. With the use of landing crafts, the shipload of soldiers was deployed to the beach with orders to occupy the beachhead. The Italians held the high ground and "rained down fire on us," he said. Dorsey figured, however, that his unit, along with the other units in the army contingency, could have easily overrun the enemy positions; but he also realized that was not a part of their orders. The contingency remained at the beachhead for five months, replaced by more American troops.

In June of 1945, Dorsey's troop ship joined with other troop ships in invading France from the Gulf of Lyon in the Mediterranean Sea. The Germans offered little resistance as allied troops landed on the beach. As the soldiers moved forward, they found many Germans dead or appearing to be dead. To be sure, Dorsey and his comrades shot the Germans in the head as the American troops moved forward. Once well inland, they boarded trucks guided by Military Police escorts for several miles, boarded a train, and headed for an area near the Battle of the Bulge. They dismounted for an overnight halt during a snowfall and settled into their sleeping sacks for the night. At daybreak, they packed their sacks and loaded onto a convoy of trucks that would take them to the Belgium sector of the Battle of the Bulge. En route, they learned that the Germans had been defeated by the Allied forces. When they approached the battle area, dead Germans were everywhere, as were stragglers who tried to conceal their identity by wearing civilian clothing.

Dorsey's unit was sent to the Nuremberg area via Frankfurt. Their convoy periodically took on fire as they approached Frankfurt. When the firing became heavier, General Patton had all convoys withdraw and called in artillery fire on the German positions. Additionally, Patton had several tanks move through the area, firing on suspected sniper hideouts. The sniping soon stopped.

The convoy continued on to the Nurnberg area, camping near a concentration camp "where bodies were stacked up like firewood," he reported. "The stench was unbelievable," he added. The next day, Dorsey's unit received the news that the Germans had surrendered. Dorsey added, "From then on, the stench didn't matter. Everyone was cheering and just glad that the war was over. To celebrate, the mess sergeants got fresh milk from the local stores to go with the pancakes they served for breakfast. Some of the troops could not drink the milk because of the stench. "So I invited them to give me theirs. I was glad to get fresh milk for the first time in ages," he stated.

In May 1945, Dorsey received orders to return to the States. He boarded a troop ship at Antwerp, Belgium, arriving ten days later in Newport News, Virginia. He said, "As the soldiers disembarked, many of them fell to their knees giving thanks for being home again. People everywhere were cheering, even on rooftops, welcoming us back as the soldiers formed in ranks. Families invited us to stay with them until we left the next day. Sleeping between clean white sheets again was a treat indeed."

Dorsey was discharged from the army in June 1945. After returning home for a while and not being able to find a suitable job, he moved to Des Moines, Iowa, where he worked for over thirty-eight years on teams making tractors, earth graders, and other equipment for Caterpillar. He married, had three children, bought a house, and paid off the mortgage. When he decided to return to Napoleonville to live, he said, "I sold the house and other property to my son for one dollar."

He still lives at the family homestead where he enjoys gardening, caring for his orange trees, reading practically everything he comes in contact with, attending services at Saint Benedict Catholic Church, and watching mass services on television.

Robert Dorsey, Belle Terre (Ascension), WWII and Korean War

Robert "Son" Dorsey was born on August 26, 1920, in Belle Terre, Louisiana, a small community about five miles south of Donaldsonville. The oldest of four siblings, he was highly mechanically talented. He left school after completing the eighth grade and worked to help support the family. He spent his early teen years working as a mechanic at the Belle Terre Plantation and at garages in the surrounding areas. While the work of many Blacks of the area related mostly to the sugarcane, rice, and farming industries, his auto mechanic skills elevated him to more prestigious jobs, held predominantly by Whites.

During July 1941, Dorsey volunteered for the army and was sent to Camp Livingston, Louisiana, an infantry replacement training center located in Grant Parish, for induction. After the physical and other exams, he was sent to the Infantry Replacement Training Center (IRTC) at Camp Wheeler near Macon, Georgia. Established just before WWII as a temporary training camp for National Guard units, the camp was later used as an IRTC where new recruits received basic and advanced training to replace combat casualties. This is where Dorsey completed his basic and advanced infantry training, ending with his military occupational specialty being a rifleman. He also completed an eight-week cooking course at the Quartermaster School at Camp Lee, near Petersburg, Virginia. That cooking course set the stage for his successful military career.

Before his career as a cook would begin, however, Dorsey served as a rifleman in the Twenty-fourth Infantry Regiment during WWII. Although his available service records do not indicated where he served, a War Department letter order dated September 2, 1949, contained the following information:

1. *By direction of the President, under the provisions of Executive Order 9419, 4 February 1944 (Sec. II, WD Bul. 3, 1944), a Bronze Star Medal is awarded for exemplary conduct in ground combat against the armed enemy during the Western Pacific Campaign in the Pacific Theater of Operations to Sergeant (then Private First Class) Robert Dorsey, RA 43079594, 24th Infantry Regiment.*

2. *Authority for this award is contained in Par.15.le AR 600-45 and is based upon General Orders 33, Headquarters 24th Infantry Regiment, 25 August 1945.*

BY ORDER OF THE SECRETARY OF THE ARMY

[Signed] W. A. Leary
Adjutant General

Research showed that the Twenty-fourth Infantry Regiment departed San Francisco on April 13, 1942, and arrived on the island of Efate east of Australia on May 4, 1942. The mission of the Twenty-fourth was to defend a major portion of the perimeter of this large and mountainous strategic island against a possible Japanese attack coming from the Solomon Islands in the north. In addition to their combat mission, the Twenty-fourth was also used in service and supply functions to include road building, unloading ships, and installation maintenance. After the U.S. forces had liberated Guadalcanal and the danger of New Hebrides had passed, from March through August 1943, the Twenty-fourth departed Efate for the Solomon Islands.

It is not known if Dorsey participated in these Twenty-fourth Infantry Regiment's missions; however, the periods of these assignments coincides with the recorded time of his rank (private first class) and his next assignment to Camp Breckinridge, Kentucky, in October 1944, where he worked as a cook for ten months. From there, he was sent to Fort Sam Houston, Texas, where he worked as a cook and assistant mess sergeant.

Soon after the Korean War began, Dorsey was promoted to sergeant first class (E-6) in August 1950 and reassigned to Headquarters Company, Seventy-sixth Army Artillery Automatic Weapons Battalion, Camp Kimpo (near Seoul), Korea, as the mess sergeant. He reenlisted in December of that same year to remain in Korea for another eight months. This assignment was followed by a transfer to another mess sergeant position in Sasebo, Japan, where he remained for four years.

Dorsey also served in Fort Benning, Georgia (1956), Fort Richardson, Alaska (April 1962), and Fort Knox, Kentucky (December 1962).

In addition to the Bronze Star Medal, he was awarded the following medals, citations, and military decorations during his twenty-two years of honorable service:

American Defense Service Medal
WWII Victory Medal (Japan)
Army Occupation Medal
National Defense Medal
Korean Service Medal with two Bronze Stars
American Theater Campaign Medal
European/African/Middle Eastern Campaign Medal with two Bronze Stars
Asiatic Pacific Campaign Medal with Battle Star
Good Conduct Medal (3) with Clasp
Combat Infantry Badge
Meritorious Service Plaque
Service Stripes (7)
Overseas Service Bars (2)
Rifle M-1 Sharpshooter Badge
Carbine Rifle M-2 Badge

His overall military character and efficiency ratings as a soldier were noted as "excellent" and were supported by three Good Conduct Medals with three Loops, one for each award. He also received a Certificate of Commendation from the Secretary of War upon his retirement from the army on February 28, 1963.

When asked to comment on his overall service experiences, he stated, "It taught me discipline and the importance of being organized. I think all young men and women should spend some time in the military. It teaches you discipline and respect for people who have authority over you. If the young people of today would show more respect for those in authority, they would be better citizens."

Dorsey was married to Irene McNeal (deceased) on May 7, 1943, and is the father of Gretchen Marie Dorsey Wilson, Marion Dorsey Crawford, and JoAnne Dorsey Brown (deceased). Now deceased, he lived by himself in the house in which he was born ninety years earlier with the help of a daytime health assistant.

Black servicemen and women throughout the quad-parish area served honorably in all branches of military service during the five years following WWII and before the Korean War, during that war, and during the time between that war and the war in Vietnam. However, unlike many of their WWII comrades, some of them fared better at getting jobs after being discharged.

Prisoner of War Camp

Donaldsonville was the site of a World War II camp for German prisoners of war. Several hundred prisoners were encamped in barbed-wire-enclosed facilities at the South Louisiana State Fair Ground in 1943 and 1944. The prisoners, dressed in blue denim garb, worked in public service projects, and spent many days working at the mouth of Bayou Lafourche filling and stacking sandbags to prevent erosion of the bayou bank during the high-water season. When prisoners took rest breaks, bewildered onlookers often voiced the opinion that the prisoners were not being worked hard enough. Frequently, rumors spread that several POWs had escaped. Infrequently, one or two prisoners wandered off from their work assignment but were quickly returned by the guards.

The rationing of certain foods and household items was in effect to support the war effort. Coupons, stamps, and tokens were issued for purchasing certain items, such as refined meats, sugar, coffee, and butter. Syrup, brown sugar, and condensed milk were used by many families as a granulated sugar substitute.

Oleomargarine was introduced to the area for the first time as a butter substitute, and it became popular overnight. *Margarine*, as it was called, was purchased as a lard-like product which came with a small capsule of yellow food coloring. When mixed together, a butter-looking spread resulted. It is perhaps more than coincidental that oleo was first produced in France in 1869, as a butter substitute during wartime shortages.

Prisoner of War Camp

CURTIS J. JOHNSON

Horse meat began appearing in meat markets during this time. Complaints from area residents were raised because the menus for the prisoners included sugar, butter, and choice beef, items that were rationed to residents.

Several of the American soldiers who served as guards for the prisoners remained in the Donaldsonville area after the prisoners were repatriated. The GIs had dated local girls during their tour of duty, with some of them being discharged, marrying and settling in the local area.

Shortly after WWII ended, deactivation of certain army cavalry units began. According to Nicholas, "The federal government announced that it had no use for many of the horses and mules assigned to these units. Therefore, they gave some of the animals to families in the area, including Saint James Parish, to help them start or expand sharecropping or truck-farming businesses for retailing and wholesaling vegetables."

Korea: The Forgotten War

When the war started on the South Korean Peninsula in June 1950, I had graduated two weeks earlier from Lowery High School and had been accepted to attend Southern University in September. With that acceptance came a deferment from the war. Once at Southern, my participation in the senior ROTC program reinforced my deferment, allowing me to continue studies throughout the war years and obtain a bachelor of science degree in industrial education and building construction in August 1954. With the degree came my commission as a second lieutenant in the U.S. Army Corps of Engineers in the summer of 1954.

The war in Korea, although never "officially" ended, was over without my having to participate. However, many of my high school friends and friends at Southern who were not in the ROTC program were drafted and spent time in Korea and other locations during the three years and one month duration of the war. It would be ten years later when I would serve the first of two tours of duty in that country.

An order announcing a major change in the way the American military establishment would be expected to operate in the future was passed during the five-year break between WWII and the onset of the Korean War. In 1948, President Truman signed Executive Order 9981 that provided for equal treatment and equal opportunity for African Americans in all branches of military service. The U.S. Navy and Air Force came close to implementing this change within several years after passage. The army finally implemented Executive Order 9981 but not until about the time of the Korean War truce in 1953.

Korean Temple

CURTIS J. JOHNSON

Veterans' Stories

Davelin Wilson, Smoke Bend (Ascension), Korean War, Army

Davelin Wilson, a.k.a. David Moore, volunteered for the army three months after graduating from Lowery High School in 1950. He completed basic training and only two weeks of advance infantry training at Fort Riley, Kansas, before being shipped off to Korea to join the front line defense operation of the Second Infantry Division. There, he would receive "foxhole pay" for nine months while engaging the enemy in off-and-on combat tactics.

Although the executive order to integrate the military services was signed during 1948, it was not until October 1, 1951, that integration in Korea actually started. Black soldiers from Wilson's unit were taken to a specific area to be integrated into all-White units in the First Cavalry Division. However, on the next day before he was reassigned, he was wounded in the Battle of Bloody Ridge, a costly ground battle in the summer of 1951. Wilson was shot in his left arm and hit by shrapnel in the chest and right leg. "I was wounded seven days before I would accumulate enough points to return to the states," he said.

As he was being taken to an aid station, the station received a direct enemy hit and was destroyed completely. The ambulance medic gave him a morphine shot, and he woke up in a hospital in Japan a day later. He was evacuated to a hospital in Hawaii, remaining there for two months, then transferred to a hospital in San Francisco for several months and finally to the Fort Smith, Arkansas, army hospital. Together, he spent thirteen months in hospitals and received a medical discharge on September 5, 1953, at Fort Lewis, Washington. Among the medals he received was the Purple Heart.

Wilson started working for the Lockheed Aircraft Company as a paint chemist eighteen days after his discharge and continued for thirty-six years until he retired. "It was the only civilian job I ever had," he said.

He continues to maintain membership with the local Los Angeles Korean War Veterans Chapter and attends national conventions each year. He receives 100 percent disability benefits. His final interview statement was, "I'm looking forward to being buried at Arlington Cemetery."

Lloyd Edwards, College Point (Assumption) Post-Korean War, Army

Another positive experience outcome was shared by Lloyd Edwards, a resident of Saint James. Soon after graduating from Saint Catherine High School in Donaldsonville in 1953, Edwards entered Southern University in the school of education. Four years later after graduating with a bachelor of arts degree in education and with a teaching certificate, he returned home to find no teaching jobs available in Assumption or any of the surrounding parishes. However, he was aware of his deferment from the army during his college years and his two-year obligation to serve upon his graduation. He worked with his father on the family farm in College Point until receiving his notice of induction in December to report for duty in February 1958.

Although the United States was not at war, communism posed the greatest challenge to nations of the free world. The war in Lebanon was ongoing and growing, and world tension caused by the Cold War mounted.

After completing basic training at Fort Hood, Texas, he was sent to Fort Dix, New Jersey, where he traveled by troop ship to the port of Bremerhaven, Germany. From there, he traveled by train to Hanau just east of Frankfurt where his unit, the Twenty-third Engineer Battalion (Floating Bridge), was located. For the next eighteen months, half of his service would be in training at Hanau building aluminum pontoon floating bridges and half would be spent in field training as a machine gunner on an M-48 tank in Grafenwoehr near the Czechoslovakia border.

The mission of Edwards' battalion was twofold: the first related to constructing bridges over short gaps and water spans and rough terrain too difficult to accommodate heavy trucks and track-laying vehicles, including tanks. "The second was to train and fight as infantry to secure and defend the bridges during construction, while being used by combat troops, and during the recovery of bridges—dismantling them for future use," he said. Fortunately, their training mission was highly successful. Edwards assured, "We were 100 percent ready to build and protect and fight during these times—guaranteed!"

Edwards was discharged in February 1960 at Fort Benning and returned to his Assumption homestead. He taught French and Spanish at Capitol High School in Baton Rouge for three years, commuting daily. During this time, he and Maryann Braud, an elementary school

U.S. Army Ambulance

teacher from Welcome, were married and moved to Saint James Parish. When asked what caused him to return to his home area after his military service, he cited family, friends, and the high regard he held for the change predicted in his father's wisdom. He recalled his father telling him years before that "the day is coming when the South will become a place where a Negro man can make a decent living." This realization sparked a major change in his career path.

In 1960, Kaiser Aluminum Company began operations in Gramercy in Saint James Parish. A number of Blacks left the Saint James plantations to work for Kaiser in a labor pool consisting of skilled tradesmen (carpenters, welders, electricians, and plumbers), as well as laborers. By the end of 1963, DuPont Manufacturing Company had built its manufacturing plant in Reserve, also in Saint John Parish, and was recruiting heavily in adjacent parishes. Edwards recognized this as a rare opportunity considering that Kaiser had hired only a few Blacks for operational management positions. He applied and was hired by DuPont as a management trainee in 1964. He was assigned the job of machine operator and "was responsible for manufacturing nylon intermediate."

He was later promoted to the position of mechanic; several years later, he was promoted to maintenance foreman. He enjoyed five years as area supervisor of maintenance before retiring.

Willie Williams, Donaldsonville (Ascension), Korean War Era, Army

Willie "Bro" Williams felt secure in believing that his newly acquired high school diploma was his ticket to a good-paying job. He graduated from Lowery High School in June 1950 in Donaldsonville and immediately began his job search. He soon realized, however, that the only jobs available to him were low-paying, menial tasks that did not measure up to his expectations. A resident of Donaldsonville, he knew that the job market in his native Melville, Louisiana, would have even fewer career opportunities. He remembered several relatives who lived in Houston, Texas, and decided to search there for a job.

After three weeks of searching and applying for work in Houston and not being successful, he reluctantly accepted a job as a drying machine operator at a laundry shop. Cleaning dirty clothes wasn't what he wanted to do, but it paid the bills. Little did he know that his time in the laundry would be shortened by a letter from the War Department.

Williams was inducted into the army at the Custom House in New Orleans. He was sent to Fort Hood, Texas, for basic training and on to Fort Devens, Massachusetts, to attend an administrative clerical course. Following his completion, he was assigned to the Quartermaster Corps and served on the general staff for operations and training (G-3) as an administrative clerk-typist at First Army Headquarters, Fort Devens. In addition to general office duties, he was responsible for preparing and maintaining training schedules for G-3 personnel and annual field training exercises for post-wide units. Williams also handled incoming and outgoing mail for the staff. Williams remained in this position for eighteen months where he was often commended and was promoted to Corporal E-4 for his excellent work.

His final duty station was at Camp Drum, in Jefferson County, New York, where he was again assigned as an administrative clerk at Post Headquarters. He served as assistant to the pay officer for all Headquarters personnel, remaining at this job until he was discharged from the army in 1953.

Williams realized the need to improve his office skills to be able to better compete for a job as a civilian. He enrolled in the Cortez Peters Business College in Washington, D.C., under the GI Bill. His curriculum included accounting, business law, real estate, English, spelling, and advanced typing.

He completed the two-year program and immediately mailed job applications to the Federal Bureau of Investigations, the Department of Justice, the Internal Revenue Service (IRS), and the National Archives. His military experience and the additional college training combined to give him the competitive edge he needed.

Within two weeks, he was hired by the IRS, starting as a messenger, GS-1 (general service). This job involved delivering and picking up mail to and from IRS attorneys, tax code judges, and commissioners. He was later promoted to the position of librarian, where he assisted attorneys and paralegals in finding filed IRS court cases. Additionally, he worked concurrently as a plainclothes security officer in Washington department stores for nine years before retiring after thirty-seven and a half years with the IRS.

Emmit Lawson, Donaldsonville (Ascension), Korean War Era, Air Force

As a youngster, Emmit Lawson dreamed of becoming a builder. His ambition was reinforced by his classes in industrial arts and building construction at Lowery High School in the late 1940s. During the summer months of his junior and senior years, Emmit's shop teacher, Hiram Martin, engaged students in practical learning experiences, including building and restoring houses.

After graduating, he became a presser at Louis Picou Dry Cleaners in Donaldsonville and worked with his uncle in brick masonry on the side. However, the Korean War erupted, putting his building career on hold as he volunteered to join the air force.

In August 1951, Lawson was sent to Lakeland Air Force Base, San Antonio, Texas, for basic training and completed advance training in special services with a concentration in training aids and administrative duties. He was then transferred to the 782nd Air Control and Warning Squadron, Rockville Air Force Station in Rockville, Indiana, where he became the orderly room clerk. He also performed collateral duties as movie projector operator, showing movies two to three times weekly as well as showing training films at all weekly classroom training sessions.

During the second week in July 1953, Lawson boarded a troop ship headed for Japan. A week later while still en route, the ship received word that a cease-fire had been reached in Korea. He arrived in Japan at the Yokota AFB and became the orderly room clerk just as at his previous station performing a myriad of administrative duties: typing routine and special letters and reports, maintaining the duty roster and records, and handling, processing, and storing classified materials in the safe. His special responsibility in reconnaissance operations was developing film from recon fly-over missions in North Korea to identify potential bombing targets.

In August 1955, he returned to the States and was discharged. Immediately upon his return home, Lawson began his career as a brick mason, having learned the trade from his uncle. He joined a bricklayers union in New Orleans and worked mostly in Lafourche and Terrebonne parishes. His career lasted forty years.

Felton C. Ceasar, Vacherie (St. James), Post-Korean War, Army

As a youngster, Felton C. Ceasar had visions of a career as a U.S. Air Force fighter pilot. By the time he reached his senior year in high school, that vision became his career plan. Prior to his graduation from Lowery High School in Donaldsonville on May 29, 1955, he passed the air force entrance test and volunteered for the air force. Five days later, he signed in at Lackland Air Force Base, Texas, for basic training. He soon learned that his cumulative score in mathematics was below the requirement for pilot training, "by no fault of the teachers," he said. Given the option of several career paths, he chose parachute testing and was assigned to Chanute Air Force Base, Illinois, for training.

Upon completion of specialty training, Ceasar was reassigned to the 6511th Test Group (parachute) at El Centro Air Station, California, where he was engaged in "some of the most thrilling episodes of a lifetime," he recalled. Here, he would be involved in testing not only parachutes to be used by pilots and crew members but also parachutes for cargo drops, high-speed tactical aircraft, and the National Aeronautics and Space Administration (NASA) space program.

"As a basic procedure, all parachutes and life preservers purchased by the Air Force were tested by the 6511th," he said. Bailing out of aircraft at various altitudes, under varying weather and climate conditions, testing parachutes became routine for him. However, these assignments were not without challenges. For example, one bailout test involved testing a timer that automatically opened the parachute after a predetermined number of seconds had elapsed. These timers were used if a disabled airman had to evacuate a damaged aircraft. During one such test, Caesar's timer, set for twenty seconds, failed. In this instance, Ceasar was able to pull his rip cord. What if, however, he had been wounded and unable to use the cord? He was disturbed by the possibility. During another test, Ceasar almost drowned in the Salton Sea in Southern California as his team was testing life preservers to be used by pilots in the event of bailing out over water. Using two vests during the test, he discovered that both vests were faulty and had to remain afloat for an extended period of time. When the rescue boat arrived, he was completely exhausted and sinking.

During a night test jump, "I was with several other jumpers who were dragged approximately one-half mile across the desert by high surface winds," he reported. Luckily, no one was seriously hurt.

A unit under the Air Force Research and Development Command, the 6511th also tested parachutes to be used for retrieving NASA's first space capsule. Ceasar stated that for testing, they used a cluster of three WWII parachutes on three WWII four-thousand-pound dud bombs to simulate the twelve-thousand-pound weight of the capsule that was being built by NASA at the time.

Ceasar served as an observer while testing modified parachutes on some bust dummies. "My position was in the bombardier seat to observe what would happen when the pilot opened the bomb bay door and released the bust dummy rigged with a parachute," he stated. On this day at approximately 1100 hours, the airplane took off and everything appeared normal as they gained altitude on the way to the drop zone. Ceasar was looking out of the window. It was a clear, sunny day. As the plane gained altitude, the skies seemed to be darkening. But when the pilot opened the bomb bay and a burst of fresh air entered the compartment, he would become "revived." As soon as the bomb bay was closed, he would fall off asleep again. This occurred several times during the flight. As the airplane descended to a level that did not require oxygen, he woke up and, in doing so, noticed that an electrical connection that controlled the oxygen and the intercom system had become disconnected. He reinstalled the plug and immediately heard the pilot saying, "Airman Ceasar, Airman Caesar, do you read me?" Caesar responded, "No, sir, I did not." It was then that Ceasar realized he had accidently unplugged the oxygen and intercom systems with his feet, evidently when he was settling in for the flight. He said that upon landing, the captain pilot told him when he returned to his unit to tell his chief "to get some damn good equipment installed on that plane" [before future flights].

When he returned to his section, he asked one of the lieutenants how long one could expect to survive without oxygen. The lieutenant replied, "In fifteen to twenty minutes, you'll be unconscious. After that, you're dead." Ceasar suffered severe headaches for years. But the inconvenience of having to take Anacin every day pales in comparison to what could have happened in the sky. "I shall never forget that I survived an incident at fifteen thousand feet that should have taken me out!"

He tested parachutes for our first astronaut and was one of the few Blacks to serve in this capacity. He also tested undergarments for astronauts. After three and a half years of experimental and dangerous duties, Ceasar was discharged from the air force in 1958.

He immediately enrolled at Southern University, Baton Rouge, Louisiana. He spent two and a half years studying biology and geosciences before becoming married and joining the labor force. His first job was that of a labor foreman for a carpenters' union in Saint James. During the same year, he was hired by the Freeport Chemical Company located in Freeport, Louisiana, where he remained for twenty-two years. During this time, Ceasar attended Union Theological Seminary in New Orleans, spending six years on a part-time basis, and was awarded the master of theology degree.

Ceasar was elected the first Black Justice of the Peace for Fifth Ward, Saint James Parish, since Reconstruction.

Larry Christy, Prairieville (East Ascension), Korean War Era, Army

Larry Christy was a teacher at the Prairieville Elementary School when he was drafted in June 1950 for two years of U.S. Army duty. Following basic training at Camp Edward, Falmouth, Massachusetts, he was sent to advance individual training at the home of the Artillery Training Center at Fort Bliss, El Paso, Texas. There, he completed a nine-month electronics course, graduating as a radar technician.

His first and only military assignment was with the 446th Artillery Battalion at Camp Cooke in Lompax, California. This camp was initially established to detect incoming foreign aircraft during WWII, and was the forerunner to Vandenberg Air Force Base.

Although his job was that of repairing and keeping radar systems operational, he spent an appreciable amount of his time tracking unidentified incoming aircraft. This assignment occurred at the onset of the Korean War when most soldiers completing basic and advanced training were being assigned to combat and combat support units in Korea. In his case, it is believed that his prior education was perhaps higher than normally required for high-tech training assignments such as radar, electronics, and similar skill areas. Prior to radar school, all of his military experiences had been in all-Black units. The makeup of the radar school students was practically all-White. He learned that attendance by Blacks and other minorities had only recently begun.

Christy's military training and experiences in electronics and electrical systems application had prepared him well for the civilian labor market. However, highly saleable skills that he gained during his high-tech radar schooling and practical experience were never used as a vocation. Upon his discharge from the army in March 1953, at Camp McArthur, California, he returned to his job of teaching at the Prairieville Elementary School. He also taught in the Prairieville High School, and eventually became the principal of the Prairieville Elementary School. Later, he was elevated to the superintendent's staff as the supervisor of Federal Programs.

On a Personal Note

South Korea was still recovering from the war that had ravished parts of that country a decade earlier. My first assignment there occurred in 1963 when I became the chief of the Warehousing and Transportation Division for the Transportation Depot Activity Korea (TDAK) located in Bupyeong, near Kimpo Air Base and Seoul. TDAK's mission involved ordering, warehousing, issuing, and/or shipping transportation repair parts, including aviation, from the Bupyeong location and TDAK sub-warehouses located in Pusan, Taegu, and Uijongbu, the latter serving the combat and combat support units (mainly the Second Infantry Division) guarding the 38th parallel line. The job took me to each of the locations at least once monthly. During the Cyprus crisis in 1964, TDAC's purpose was amended to include supporting U.S. troops in that effort also.

In December 1969, I had the good fortune to return to Korea on an assignment to Headquarters, Korea Support Command (KORSCOM). My job was that of chief for Transportation Division, assistant chief of staff for transportation and services. As such, my job was to keep current plans and procedures to provide transportation support services to all U.S. Army units in Korea.

Three years after the 1968 assassination of Martin Luther King and the resulting riots in the Watts District of Los Angeles, in Harlem and elsewhere in the United States, a series of race riots began to surface in the U.S. military community internationally. During February 1971, a riot involving Black and White soldiers erupted at Camp Humphreys, located on the outskirts of Pyeongtaek village. Reports were received at KORSCOM Headquarters that a dozen White and several Black soldiers had received personal injuries and several buildings and heavy equipment were set afire. One soldier was reported to be seriously injured and two buildings badly burned. I had been appointed the KORSCOM equal employment officer (EEO) earlier that day, just in time to accompany the KORSCOM commander, Major General Holmes, on a flight to Camp Humphries to investigate firsthand the causes of these problems.

Darkness was setting in as we approached the Camp Humphrey's landing strip. Several smoldering buildings were still visible from the air. Once on the ground, we were told by the post commander that two soldiers had been seriously injured, with twelve others treated at the dispensary for cuts and abrasions and restricted to quarters. Damage to equipment included one helicopter and two trucks destroyed and four trucks badly damaged. Several buildings had been badly damaged by fire also. Following the briefing, the general and I talked with several top staff officers and senior noncommissioned officers (NCOs) to get their views on the probable causes of the disturbances. (There were no Black staff officers and only two junior NCOs assigned to the headquarters, although a small number of Black officers and senior NCOs were included in the camp's census.) They all stated that tension between the soldiers was a surprise to them. Later that night, after activities had settled down, the post commander and his senior staff officers escorted the general, his aide, and me to the Officers' Club for dinner. As we approached the club, the jukebox was so loud that it could be heard a block away. The jukebox was playing "Dixie."

I remained on site for two days, interviewing staff and other officers and NCOs, including two Black officers and several Black NCOs and approximately thirty-eight lower-grade enlisted men, both Black and White.

After collecting and reviewing signed statements from those interviewed, the tenor of my after-action report to General Holmes was that the major cause for the incident was a complete lack of leadership on the part of the commander and his senior staff as well as the tenant commanders and their senior staffs. The Blacks, including NCOs interviewed, stated the following:

- A club in the town of Pyeongtaek had been placed off-limits to Blacks by White troops. Several Blacks had been beaten up by Whites for trying to get into the club. Blacks complained to the NCOs, but no action was taken by the post commander.
- White leaders, including the commander, were insensitive and nonresponsive to the needs of Black soldiers. Blacks had requested two hours off to celebrate a church service honoring Martin Luther King's birthday in January. The command refused the request without explanation.
- White commanders in tenant units promoted unqualified White soldiers ahead of qualified Blacks with outstanding performance records.
- The curfew policy for having local women on post after midnight was being violated by some of the White officers and NCOs. Korean women were being entertained in the bachelor officers' quarters and NCO quarters long past midnight.
- Morale among the Blacks assigned to the command headquarters and tenant units on post was extremely low.

Most of the White soldiers interviewed validated these accounts.

On the day General Holmes received my report, he relieved the post commander of his duties, and a major shifting of senior staff officers and NCOs out of the Camp Humphries command headquarters was effected during the following week.

The Vietnam Engagement

About the same time U.S. military troops were being deployed to the Republic of Korea in 1950, the United States' involvement in the Republic of South Vietnam (RVN) had begun. It started with the U.S. government sending military aid to the French military establishment that had been engaged in war with the North Vietnamese military system for four years. In four more years, the French would surrender to the Viet Minh and withdraw from Vietnam.

During early August 1964, the United States charged that North Vietnamese forces had attacked American warships in the Gulf of Tonkin. That incident was determined serious enough for the U.S. Congress to pass a Joint Resolution on August 7, 1964, which was followed by President Lyndon B. Johnson's signed approval. The Joint Resolution, made into Public Law, stipulated, in part, that,

> the Congress approves and supports the determination of the President, as Commander-in-Chief, to take all necessary measures to repel any armed attack against the forces of the United States and to prevent further aggression.

With that resolution, the United States entered into what became known as the Vietnam War. During my twenty years of service in the United States Army, my only wartime encounters came during my tour of duty in Vietnam. Some of the most sobering experiences of my life happened during that assignment, several that I will share here.

Veterans' Stories

The soldiers and airmen whose stories appear below represent examples of the varied experiences reported by a few of those Blacks who served during the Vietnam War. These stories pertain to roles played by each veteran during their tours in Vietnam. It is noteworthy that two of the four with combat experiences (Brimmer and Smith) were volunteers inducted after the war had started, knowing that they could be candidates for combat. The third (Burd) was drafted and spent part of a tour during the Korean War as well as two tours in Vietnam. Finally, Raymond Walters was drafted for a two-year tour; however, he voluntarily extended his duty for one additional year so that his two brothers would not have to serve there.

Combat Veterans

Raymond Walters, Vacherie (St. James), Army

Raymond Walters left Saint James Parish with his parents when he was six years old. The family relocated to Marrero, Louisiana, where Walters attended public schools and graduated from Lincoln High School. Reportedly, many people from Saint James and Saint John parishes were relocating to Marrero which, at that time, was a developing city. Folks were leaving the plantations for work in the Johns Manville Asbestos and Celotex fiberboard plant and several other large plants recently built in Marrero.

Walters graduated high school in 1963 and spent the next four years at Grambling University, where he majored in chemistry. During his stay at Grambling, the role of the United States in the Vietnamese war intensified; however, Walters was granted a deferment because of his academic work. After graduating, he received his draft notice to report to the Custom House in New Orleans for induction. In February 1968 at the tail end of the Tet Offensive in Chu Lai, Walters was transferred to Fort Polk, Louisiana, for basic training. From there, he went to Fort Lee, Virginia, near Petersburg, for advanced individual training in accounting, bookkeeping, and supply handling. His first unit assignment was with the Cam Ranh Bay Supply Depot operations in the Republic of South Vietnam. Several months later, he was reassigned to the Americal Division where he worked in accounting for managing warehouse operations. However, that assignment soon changed to convoy duties making supply and equipment deliveries to division units scattered about in a twelve-mile radius.

Viet Cong Rifleman

CURTIS J. JOHNSON

"Convoying was worse than infantry duties. Although you had armor escorts with MPs leading and trailing and choppers flying overhead, you were always like sitting ducks out there," he said. Fortunately, they were able to complete all trips with minimum damage. His next assignment would be different.

He was then transferred to a missile and reconnaissance unit in Chu Lai for ten months. Although his responsibilities included those of a helicopter courier between Chu Lai and Da Nang, his main duties involved being dropped off in patrol teams by Huey helicopters to recon areas to spot the movement of Viet Cong troops. Occasionally, and unknowingly, they would land in zones occupied by the VC and would have to call in for artillery and air strikes, many times leading to destruction that was "too close for comfort," he said.

He spent ten months in recon patrols before being sent to Fort Hood, Texas, where he managed the military clothing store for the remainder of his enlistment time. Upon his discharge, he was offered a full-time job as the store manager. He declined the offer in favor of returning to his native Saint James.

Before leaving Fort Hood, he successfully completed the test for postal workers. However, he never had time to apply for a postal position because his degree in chemistry paid off. He was hired as a research and development chemist at DuPont Manufacturing Company in Saint James Parish.

Clarence J. Brimmer, Sr., Donaldsonville (Ascension), Army

For a boy who started elementary school when he was ten years old, Clarence Brimmer learned at an early age that success in school was paramount to success in life. He began to prove this theory by the time he received his high school diploma—in ten years. He was the first in his family to complete high school. When he graduated from Lowery High School in 1960, his vision for his immediate future was to have a successful tour of duty in the United States Army. Brimmer volunteered just out of high school, and his recruiter requested that he be assigned to the communications field. He would soon learn that his assignment would be to the infantry instead, which was his last choice of service assignments. He decided then that when it was time to reenlist, he would definitely request to be discharged.

His first assignment after basic and advance training was to Company E, Seventh Cavalry, First Cavalry in Monsani, South Korea, arriving in November 1960. His job was to be a rifleman (Browning automatic) and team leader. He was selected to serve on the division's honor guard, a team of highly motivated soldiers who took pride in their appearance. Their duties involved funeral services for fallen comrades and escort duties for the national flag, an honor in itself of sorts.

Due to the Berlin Crisis in 1961, Brimmer's tour of duty was extended to sixteen months. He returned in 1962 to Fort Gordon, Georgia, where he was assigned to Company C, Ninth Battalion, First Training Regiment as a platoon sergeant for the third and fourth platoons involved in basic training. At that time, he was an E-4 assigned to assist in the training of the two basic training platoons, each with fifty men. Normally, E-4s were assigned to only one platoon. Additionally, he served as the training NCO and company clerk. After being there three and a half months, he was promoted to E-5. He was cited for willingly accepting all assignments and performing them in a manner that was noticed by the company commander and the battalion commander.

Brimmer's supervisor, a sergeant (E-5), was married with children. Whenever makeup training or a special class training instructor was needed, the supervisor would volunteer him for the job. Several months later, the company commander called him into his office. The captain acknowledged that Brimmer was doing most of the work in the company and deserved to go before the selection board for promotion to sergeant (E-6). The most unusual thing about this arrangement was that Brimmer was the most junior sergeant E-5 soldier in the organization with three other sergeants having six, seven, and thirteen years in service. Brimmer had only two years and eight months in service.

After appearing before the promotion board, Brimmer was quite pleased with his being able to answer all questions asked by the board. To him, the questions were "just a piece of cake." He stated his surprise that the other candidates knew very little about basic military subjects such as the colors used on a military map and their meaning or the effective range of the M-1 rifle or current events. Days later, the battalion executive officer came by while Brimmer was sorting the mail to assure him that when the next allocation for E-6 was received by the battalion, Brimmer would get it; and two weeks later, he was promoted to E-6. After two years and eight months in the army, he had accomplished something that normally required fifteen years!

Following the Fort Gordon assignment, he spent a year as a squad leader at Fort Hood, Texas, with Company B, Second Battalion, Forty-sixth Infantry Regiment, First Armored Division.

His next duty station was to Augsburg, Germany, where he was assigned to Company C, Second Battalion, Thirty-fourth Infantry Brigade, Twenty-fourth Infantry Division, and was accompanied by his family for a four-year tour. His job was that of squad leader and physical training instructor. In this assignment, he was also assigned to temporary duty (TDY) for three months in Berlin as a regimental instructor to prepare our troops for the Expert Infantry Badge. The battalion was in Berlin to augment the Berlin Brigade. He also attended a one-month course at the Mines and Demolition School in Murnau. This assignment was terminated after two years because of the need for cadre at Fort Leonard Wood, Missouri, for training replacements for Vietnam. Arriving at Fort Leonard Wood in April 1966, he was assigned to Company C, Fourth Battalion, Third Basic Combat Training Brigade. In addition to duties as a platoon sergeant, he performed other duties as drill instructor and training NCO. He also graduated from Drill Sergeant School. After eighteen months as a replacement trainer, he became a replacement.

Brimmer arrived in the RVN in December 1967 and was assigned to Company A, Second Battalion, Eighth Infantry Regiment, Fourth Infantry Division, a mechanized infantry platoon. Initially an assistant platoon sergeant, he was soon elevated to platoon sergeant. Their area of operations was the Central Highlands with the rear base camp at Pleiku and forward base camp at Oasis. His was the only mechanized battalion in the division.

Brimmer stated that his platoon sergeant had developed a bad habit. Whenever the platoon stopped for a rest, the platoon sergeant would take off his helmet and light up a Winston while standing on top of a personnel carrier (PC). One day while on a routine patrol, they received incoming fire that lasted but for a few seconds. Brimmer was standing on his PC about ten yards to the right of the platoon sergeant's PC. The platoon sergeant was hit in the face by a sniper's bullet that exited the back of his head.

Because of a shortage of platoon leaders, Brimmer doubled as platoon leader and platoon sergeant. It was now April 1968, and he was invited to appear before a promotion board with a waiver because he didn't have enough time in service to be promoted to E-7. A chopper transported him back to the rear area camp located at Pleiku where he appeared before the board. The scenario was much like before: all other candidates had extensive service time. Without word of promotion, he was returned to the forward area to his unit. Within several months, he graduated from the U.S. Military Assistance Command Vietnam (MACV) Recondo School, the only school in the army that was conducted in an actual combat environment.

On August 31, 1968, while moving through the jungle (his platoon served as point guard for the company), the unit was ambushed by the enemy using numerous 40 mm rockets and small arms fire. Brimmer was wounded when his PC was hit with three rockets, two of which entered the engine compartment and one landed under his seat. When the firing stopped, and although he was wounded, he determined that the platoon was short one man. With the help of a team leader, the two men set out to recover the missing soldier from behind the enemy line. Within minutes, the missing soldier was rescued without further incident. Brimmer was evacuated to a rear field hospital. The company executive officer visited him in the hospital and congratulated him on his promotion to E-7, effective August 15, 1968. He was now twenty-nine years old. After eight days in the hospital and ten days in base camp, he was returned to his platoon. In November 1968, Brimmer rotated to the States and was assigned for his terminal tour of duty to Company A, Sixteenth Battalion, Fourth Training Brigade, Fort Knox, Kentucky. Like times before, he was a platoon sergeant and drill instructor for about six months. Prior to his discharge, Colonel Armstrong, the battalion commander, offered him a promotion to E-8 if he reenlisted; but staying on active duty was not in Brimmer's plans. He was discharged in June 1969. But his record of achievement did not stop there.

During his transition from the army, he accepted a job with the Coca-Cola Bottling Company in Baton Rouge, Louisiana. Two days later, he received an offer from the postal service for which he had taken the entrance exam earlier. He opted for the postal job because it would bring him back home. He was not discouraged by having to work many hours of overtime along with attending Southern University at night pursuing a college degree. He was awarded the bachelor of science degree in business administration.

In retrospect, Brimmer attributes his successes to his applying a basic value passed on to him by his mother, Mrs. Orelia Cox: "to treat people with respect, the way you wish to be treated," he stated. "I never used a curse word against anyone, especially the men under my responsibility. I spent a lot of time reading field manuals, technical manuals, and other military literature to learn and apply knowledge and learned skills in daily interactions with the troops. My nine years of interacting and training men under my supervision taught me that, when you respect men, they will work *harder* for you. I tried to be the best soldier that I could be." And he was a "best soldier" in many respects. His records speak volumes. Among his many medals and honors received were the Purple Heart and the Bronze Star Medal (for meritorious service) from his Vietnam experiences.

He credited his successes following his separation from the military community to the discipline and core values instilled in him by his years in the army.

Earl Burd, Belle Rose (Assumption), Army

Earl Burd was drafted seven months after completing his senior year at Reed High School in Napoleonville (Assumption) in June 1952. Following army basic and advanced infantry training at Fort Lewis, Washington, he was assigned to Korea as a replacement to join the Thirty-second Infantry Brigade, First Infantry Division. Burd was a rifleman on the demarcation line at Panmunjom for one "uneventful" year. The war was drawing down during his entire assignment.

Instead of rotating to the States at the end of 1953 as was normally expected, he was assigned to an armored infantry unit in Munich, Germany, as a squad leader, responsible for six men under his charge. The unit had a mission of patrolling the Czechoslovakia border in armored personnel carriers, providing continuous surveillance of the border that would signal a change from the cold war into an active one.

In 1957 upon leaving Munich, he was sent to Fort George Meade, Maryland, and joined the Second Armored Division. His stay at Meade would be limited, as the division personnel "gyroscoped" (replaced personnel in another division) six months later to Hol, Germany, near Nuremberg. There, his duties duplicated those on the Czech border, only this time as a platoon sergeant, for "another uneventful tour," he said. In 1959, Burd returned to the States to Fort Ord, California, as a drill instructor providing basic training for recruits. After a year, he was reassigned to Korea to the same organization (Thirty-second Infantry Brigade) as before near Panmunjom. This time, he was a platoon sergeant and tank commander in a reconnaissance (recon) platoon charged with scouting to locate areas for the battalion's forward movements in the event of future warfare.

At his next assignment at Fort Knox, Kentucky, to the Second Armored Division (*Hell on Wheels*), a veteran sergeant in the personnel office told Burd he was "too branded" to be in the infantry, since most of his time in service had been in armor units. He offered Burd a chance to change his branch from infantry to armor, a change Burd welcomed. His MOS (military occupational specialty) was changed to tanker (tank operator). This change would play an important role in his experiences in one of his two tours in Vietnam. In the meantime at Fort Knox, his duties changed from combat soldier to command and staff NCO, training young second lieutenants attending officer basic training course at the Armor School.

Burd's was one of the first armored battalions to arrive in Cam Ranh Bay, Vietnam in June 1962. There, they helped to clear the city of Viet Cong troops as well as snipers and helped to build and secure the military airport there. Soon, they moved on to Bear Cat where they built a tent city and remained there for several months, then on to the American Division. From there, the battalion began running convoy escort to Chu Lai using M-48 tanks. The tanks were also used at night for running checkpoints to guard against the enemy installing mines in the roadways. In spite of the tanks, the enemy would occasionally succeed in planting one or two mines. The escort services continued for another eleven months when he received orders to report to Fort Riley, Kansas.

At his new duty station near Junction City, Kansas, Burd was assigned to the Twentieth Infantry Brigade where he performed duties as a platoon sergeant and tank commander of the recon platoon. After about a year at Riley, he returned to Fort Hood, Texas, to join the recon squadron in the Second Armored Division Cavalry Battalion with a training mission. Little did he realize that this training would come in handy for his next assignment: his second tour in Vietnam.

The battalion arrived in the Saigon area in July 1967, with the mission of securing the road between Saigon and Bien Hoa using armored vehicles to keep the road open for American and Allied troops. Burd's unit, Company A, First Squadron, was assigned the night shift, from 6:00 p.m. to 6:00 a.m., along the route.

On May 4, 1968, Saigon came under heavy attack by enemy forces. Burd was the commander of an armored cavalry assault vehicle with his troops during operations in defending sectors on the edge of Saigon that were experiencing heavy enemy assault. His unit had been battling determined enemy troops throughout the previous night and morning. At approximately 1400 hours, a call came in with a mission to retrieve the bodies of twelve men lying in an alleyway on the edge of the city. Burd and his assault vehicle and two tanks made up the recovery force. Arriving at the recovery site, Burd backed his vehicle into a narrow pathway so that the dead could be loaded onto it. The recovery forces received heavy sniper fire, but he remained in an exposed position on top of his vehicle placing rapid and accurate machine gun fire on the enemy positions. As the other crew members worked quickly to retrieve the bodies, he directed covering fire on the nearby buildings, allowing the retrieving forces to escape without harm.

For his actions, Burd was awarded the Bronze Star Medal with V-device for heroism "in connection with military operations against a hostile force in the Republic of Vietnam." His citation further read, in part, "Sergeant Burd's display of aggressiveness, devotion to duty and personal bravery is in keeping with the finest tradition of the 1st Infantry Division and the United States Army." He also received the Purple Heart. During the skirmish with the snipers, his left hand was hit by an enemy bullet that mangled the hand, which was later repaired. He stated that VC bodies around the area were piled six to seven feet high after the attack.

In June 1968, Burd left Vietnam for another tour at Fort Knox, but only for one year before he headed back to Germany, this time, to the Third Armored Division Area near Frankfurt. However, this assignment would be short-lived. His wife needed exploratory surgery. He applied for an emergency leave, but higher headquarters denied the leave, saying that he had just returned from a Christmas leave several months earlier. His commanding officer told him he would approve his leave because by the time the division learned about it, he would have returned to his place of duty. He returned to his hometown and decided, due to his wife's illness coupled with only seven months remaining in service, to visit the armor branch at the Pentagon and inform the assignment officer of his situation. Understanding clearly Burd's desires, the officer assigned him to Fort Polk where he retired from the army in February 1973 after twenty-one-plus years of honorable service.

James Smith, Donaldsonville (Ascension), Army

"There was nothing to do, no jobs or anything else," said James "Mailman" Smith. And because of this, in June 1963, he volunteered for the U.S. Army and was sent to Fort Polk in Leesville, Louisiana, for basic training and advanced infantry training. When he heard that airborne jump training was offered for an additional pay allowance of $65 per month, he quickly signed up for parachute training at Fort Benning, Georgia, and successfully earned his jump badge. However, his main military occupational specialty (MOS) training was that of a ground soldier learning to "fight as infantry." His first assignment was to Company C, First Battalion, 506 Infantry Regiment, Fort Campbell, Kentucky. His job was that of a 50-caliber machine gunner. Little did he realize that his stay at Fort Campbell would be short, and that he would soon be headed for the Republic of South Vietnam.

He was chosen to be a member of the advance party for his company. At age 19, he and his battalion mates traveled to Oakland, California, where they boarded the USS Eltin. It was 18 days later when they arrived at the Port of Cameron Bay on the east coast of South Vietnam. After their gear and equipment were off-loaded, his convoy headed for Phan Rang, about three miles away, which became their base camp. There they would remain for 12 months. Their mission was to be flown by helicopters to suspected Viet Cong (VC) locations and to form patrols to seek out and destroy the enemy.

Combat puts a heavy strain on soldiers, especially the younger ones who were 18 and 19 years old, like Smith. "At first, shooting the VC soldiers stayed on my mind constantly. But as time passed on, you become used to it and your silent motto becomes "Dog eat dog," he said.

On one particular early evening on the beach at Phan Rang, Smith's platoon sergeant came over to the tent area yelling, "Saddle up!" About 20 minutes later, 25 Huey helicopters arrived and Smith's company began loading. Ten minutes later, the first of a series of helicopters headed for the designated drop zone "in the middle of nowhere" in a rice field. The men quickly off-loaded. As soon as the last helicopter was out of sight, the unit was attacked by VC soldiers who surrounded the drop zone using machine guns in crossfire maneuvers along with a hoard of snipers. Company C, then over strength with 285 men, returned the fire as best they could. They were scattered mostly in the open area, and many of them took cover behind a dike. Later that night after the firing stopped and a head count was taken, the company had been reduced to 60 men standing.

Huey Helicopter in Landing Zone

All during the night, they could hear wounded American soldiers throughout the area screaming and calling for their mothers. What they later learned was that the VC soldiers would push their fingers into the open wounds of fallen young soldiers to make them scream out, "Mama, oh, Mama!" It was an effective psychological tactic, considering the Americans were already scared and tense from the earlier attack.

The next morning, helicopters brought ammunition, rations, and other supplies and evacuated the dead and wounded. There were a few leaders remaining in the company, several platoon sergeants, and other sergeants. All of the commissioned officers had been killed or wounded. "We caught hell and I was lucky," Smith said. Replacements trickled in slowly, about five to eight per day. In the meantime, patrols were formed with seasoned troops as point guards to detect booby traps which consisted of punji stakes, trip wires connected to grenades, antipersonnel mines, and other explosive devices as they searched for VC pockets. Eventually, the unit gained its full strength of 270 men.

Smith stated that he was sitting on the beach at Phan Rang just after the drop zone "massacre" when "My prayers came to me in a vision on a Sunday morning," he said. He experienced a scene in which God was sitting in front of him talking to him, saying, "Our Father, who art in heaven," while he thought, *Yes, God is in heaven.* God continued, "Hallowed be thy name," while he thought, *Yes, always praise his name,* and the prayer continued in this manner until the end. "I had never thought about my prayers in that light, and as the prayer was ended, I heard the first sergeant yell, "Smith, pack your bags. You're going home!" He went to his tent and started packing.

Smith was now a specialist E-4 with less than five days left in the army before discharge. His replacement in his patrol was a sergeant (E-5). On that same Sunday when he received the going-home news, his old patrol headed out toward the Cambodian border. The sergeant was the point man. The patrol received incoming fire, and the first shot from the enemy hit the sergeant in the elbow. The bullet passed through his right arm and ripped off a part of his head. Because the others in the patrol were not seasoned, the sergeant became the patrol point man, which had been Smith's position before he was relieved.

It was hard for Smith to return home and find Vietnamese people walking around in the streets who he thought could have been the same people who shot at him in Vietnam. He said he had to adapt by staying away from them. On the other hand, he was certain that some of those

Vietnamese people who came to the United States were good people. "But the idea of them being able to borrow money from banks with ease while I still had to prove who I was and had to give the value of my relatives' property and a whole lot more information to get even the smallest loan was hard to take, almost like being shot at again in Nam," he concluded.

Combat Support Veterans

On the "combat support" side of the war, experienced non-combative participants told stories of a different nature. Perhaps the largest support activity in any war zone relates to logistics, a combination of supply and transportation services to combatants directly involved in warfare. The First Logistical Command had that responsibility in Vietnam. It was an organization whose mission was to supply Free World Military Forces in the six hundred mile long II, III, and IV Corps sectors of Vietnam with the items they used in common.

Stories of combat support U.S. Army and Air Force veterans are below.

Irvin Jones, Thibodeaux (Lafourche), Army

Irvin Jones was inspired by his father who was known as the "neighborhood barber" and who thought that he might one day make barbering his future work. This thinking began to become a reality when he was selected in 1967 as one of several students graduating from C. M. Washington High School to receive a scholarship to a barbering college in Nashville, Tennessee. However, upon receiving his barbering certificate, he did not start his work life using hair clippers. Instead, he went to Chicago where his uncle, who was a supervisor with Western Electric, helped him get a job making telephone parts. He was doing quite well at the job when he received his draft notice in February 1968 from the War Department to report to the Custom House in New Orleans for induction.

Jones and six other recruits from Chicago boarded a bus to Fort Polk, Louisiana, by way of New Orleans. Following the induction at the Custom House, and since they would not depart until the next day for Fort Polk, the Chicagoans, four of whom were White and who had heard so much about Bourbon Street, asked Jones to escort them there.

Arriving there, they decided to visit a bar for a beer. A doorkeeper, whose other job it was to stand on the street and invite people to the bar, told them, "We don't serve niggers here, but you four [Whites] can come in." The White soldiers told him that if the Blacks could not enter, then they wouldn't either. Jones considered reporting the incident to the authorities at the Custom House but reconsidered after later being advised by more seasoned Black soldiers that similar complaints had resulted in Blacks being sent to "hot spots" in the DMZ (demilitarized zone), a notoriously dangerous area in Vietnam.

At Fort Polk, Jones completed his introductory infantry training and immediately received orders for Vietnam. He reported to the Cam Ranh Bay Replacement Center. After remaining there for several weeks, he received orders to the Sixty-eighth Medical Group in Long Binh. Upon reporting there and taking his gear to his "new home in a new tent city," he learned that the Sixty-eighth was a medical supply depot for units scattered throughout the southern portion of South Vietnam. After a week of on-the-job training, he became a medical supply clerk, responsible for filling medical supply requisitions to be picked up by these units using helicopters as well as trucks. In some cases, he had to visit units at sites along the Saigon River or make a helicopter trip to isolated locations to investigate "lost" shipments or to attend to administrative matters. These became routine duties, with the biggest customers being the medical evacuation hospital in Saigon eighteen miles away and the hospital at Bien Hoa Air Force Base, a three-mile distance. His daily chores differed. On one occasion, while driving a two-and-a-half-ton cargo truck from his base station to Bien Hoa, "rockets and grenades exploded all around the truck as we sped through to safety. Once we drove by an intersection in a village where the heads of several American guys were displayed on top of ammo cans. You had to tell yourself to 'toughen up' and keep going,'" he said.

He described a loading incident involving a Conex container, the stackable steel boxes that were the army's shipping mainstay, that almost cost him his life. "The heavy steel container was filled with medical supplies, and the Chinook was the only available vehicle capable of delivering them to an isolated field location. I was a section leader, a sergeant E-5 after being promoted with less than two years in grade. As the helicopter hovered over the Conex, one of my men tried unsuccessfully to hook the helicopter to a cable bridle secured to the container. I got up on the container to make the hookup as the ground chief was signaling to the crew chief. But the crew chief evidently gave the pilot the signal to lower the chopper, causing it to begin pinning me down. I felt the weight of the helicopter pressing me against the container. For some unknown reason, I felt something move me out of the way. The next thing I knew, I woke up on the ground. I know it was God who saved me. It wasn't my time."

Jones talked about other lingering experiences that were nerve-wracking, such as traveling to deliver supplies on the Saigon River in open boats with jungle growth on both banks. "We were like sitting ducks. You didn't know what to expect from day to day. And after seeing guys with arms and legs shot off, you began to rationalize, 'If you gotta go, you gotta go,'" he said.

On many occasions, he drove a two-and-a-half-ton cargo truck in a convoy on many occasions to Saigon and towns such as Bien Hoa, Tan Son Nhut Air Base, and other locations surrounding Saigon. On one occasion while in a convoy, he dismounted and told his assistant driver that he would walk down to see what was holding up the convoy. As he walked to the front of the convoy, he saw and talked with several brothers. "It was always good to see and greet them with the *dap* and wear the multicolor [red, green, and black] shoestring bracelets," he said. They talked about how the Black soldiers had banded together since they were often treated poorly by their White counterparts.

Jones left Vietnam in April 1970 via the Bien Hoa airport to report to Fort Leonard Wood, Missouri. In this new assignment, he worked for the first time in his military occupational specialty as a company clerk in an engineering company for about a year until it was time for his discharge. He considered reenlisting for the $10,000 bonus he would receive to help his parents with the siblings, school expenses, and other family needs. He was ready to sign the papers when he realized, "I had made it out of Nam in one piece, but I may not be so lucky next time." With that, he put down the pen, stepped back, told the captain he had changed his mind, saluted, and asked to be dismissed.

During one trip when he rode the Greyhound bus while wearing his uniform from Missouri to his home in Thibodaux, he had to stand for the entire trip. He was tired, but no one would offer him a seat. In addition, the company lost his luggage; and when he went to the bus station to inquire about it, he was treated "as if I had committed murder. It was like we were fighting two wars, one in Nam and one here at home."

Again he traveled in uniform standing on a crowded Greyhound bus en route to his home in Thibodaux. During the trip, a White woman left the bus, and Jones took her seat. Some ten years after the Freedom Riders ended segregation in interstate transportation, the driver told him he couldn't sit there and to move to the back of the bus, where there were no seats available. Jones said he felt betrayed in the country he had risked his life to defend.

In another incident while taking a bus from Fort Polk to Thibodaux for a weekend holiday, the bus stopped for a lunch break at a bus stop. Everyone got off and walked in line to the counter to order lunch. He became disturbingly bitter as he approached the counter and saw the Whites Only sign and was told that he could not order from the counter and had to go outside to the back and order from the "colored" window. As he walked out, an older Black woman said to him, "Son, you're about to get in trouble in here. Go to the outside window, and you will be served there." He took her advice. but when it came time for him to place his order, he had lost his appetite and boarded the bus feeling betrayed *again*. From then on, he took ham and cheese sandwiches, chips, Vanilla Wafer cookies, and drinks whenever he traveled. "I'll never forget that," he said.

He applied for jobs in his hometown but soon learned that jobs of any consequence could not be found. "When Vietnam veterans applied for jobs, they were referred to as baby killers, an indication of the unpopularity of the war," he said. He tried several jobs but had to start at the bottom. That's when he decided to start his own business and work for himself.

Sergeant Irvin Jones opened his barbershop in 1976 in Thibodaux where he continues to operate today. He is a member of American Legion Post 513 and has served as the post finance officer.

Earnest Harris, Bertrandville (Assumption), Air Force

A native of Belle Rose, Assumption, Earnest Harris was drafted into the army in 1964 at a time when the United States was "gearing up" for the war in Vietnam. He completed basic training at Fort Polk, Louisiana, and his advance individual training course in finance and accounting at Fort Ord, California. He was then assigned to a special unit on board a navy ship at Fort Roberts, California. The unit was selected to attend an eleven-month helicopter repair course in Corpus

Christi, Texas. Upon their return to Fort Roberts, the ship departed for an "unknown destination" which was later announced to be Vietnam.

Once in country, the ship's ports alternated between Cam Ranh Bay to the north and Vung Tau to the south, providing helicopter repair services to aviation units in the two areas. His ship also traveled from the South China Sea to the Philippines for resupply each six months.

Harris traveled by helicopter between the ports as necessary to conduct the unit's accounting business. On one such occasion as he traveled with his commanding officer, the helicopter took on Viet Cong machine gun fire. Although he remained in Vietnam for six additional months, that incident was the only time he had experienced danger. Upon rotating to the United States from Vietnam on October 26, 1967, he was discharged from the army at Oakland, California.

Harris was hired immediately by the Corps of Engineers in New Orleans as a finance clerk at twenty years old, and remained in that job for seven years during which time he continued taking courses in the human resources field. In 1973, he was hired by Hughes Aircraft Company, Culver City, California, as the human resource manager and served in that position for thirty-two years.

Harris retired from Hughes to return to Belle Rose, he said, "to take care of my mother and father due to their illnesses, and to live in the house where I was born after leaving thirty-eight years earlier." For Harris, who left home at age eighteen to serve his country, "what goes around really does come around."

Preston J. Landry, Donaldsonville (Ascension), Army

Preston J. Landry was commissioned a second lieutenant in the Army Transportation Corps at Fort Eustis, Virginia, in August 1954, upon completion of the Reserve Officer Training Corps (ROTC) Summer Camp exercises. He also received orders to attend the Transportation Officer's Basic Course (TOBC) at Fort Eustis. Upon completing the course, he was assigned to the 582nd Transportation Company (Army Aircraft Heavy Maintenance and Supply) as a Platoon Leader. The mission of the unit was to provide third-, fourth—and fifth-echelon maintenance services to the Seventh Aircraft Maintenance Battalion stationed at Fort Eustis and other regional aircraft units.

While on temporary duty to the Second Terminal Command at Fort Eustis, the unit shipped out aboard the troop ship SS *Spiegel Grove* from

Norfolk to the Distant Early Warning (DEW) Line, a series of arctic radar installations in Goose Bay, Labrador, for a training mission to resupply units supporting U.S. Air Force personnel. While en route through the icy North Atlantic Ocean in April 1957, the ship hit an iceberg that ripped a forty-foot gash in the bow at the waterline, causing the stern to lift the propellers from the water, stalling the ship. The two ice breakers that accompanied the ship transported the troops via Greenland on to their destination without further incident.

Upon completion of the TDY assignment, the unit returned to Fort Eustis in September 1957. There, he was assigned to the Forty-eighth Transportation Battalion (truck) as commanding officer of the Sixty-second Transportation Company (medium truck) with the mission of supporting the Transportation Regiment of the Transportation Corps School.

Seven months later, he was assigned to the United States Army, Europe (USAEUR) Army Ordinance Depot in Captieux, a small village in South West France. Landry spent the next three years there as the post transportation officer involved in supporting the depot mission of storing and shipping ammunition to army bases in France and Germany. His family accompanied him on this tour. One of his fond memories was the experiences of living in the village among the people who were warm, friendly, and embracing. At about the time French president Charles de Gaulle began talks to remove the United States military forces from France, Landry returned to the United States and was reassigned in 1961 to the Fortieth Transportation Battalion (army aircraft maintenance), Fort Eustis, where he served as adjutant until 1963.

Beginning in August 1962, Landry received orders for the Forty-sixth Transportation Group in Bupyeong, South Korea, where he served as adjutant for a year. Upon completion of this assignment, he was sent to Fort Campbell, Kentucky, as the adjutant of the Seventh Transportation Battalion (truck) in support of the One-hundredth Airborne Division. There he was responsible for administrative functions and personnel matters. From 1963 to 1966, Landry served two units at Fort Campbell, Kentucky: as commander of special troops and as executive officer of the Seventh Transportation Battalion (truck). In 1965 after the announcement of the country's involvement in the Republic of Vietnam, his battalion began training truck companies at Fort Campbell to package and load supplies and equipment for deployment. His next overseas assignment would come quickly, as his battalion headquarters began pre-deployment actions.

During July 1966, Landry, as acting commanding officer, deployed the battalion's headquarters troops and equipment and sailed from San Francisco en route to Vietnam. (The battalion commander had preceded the headquarters as a member of a group advance party.) The trip, which involved multiple stops along the east coast of Vietnam, took thirty days.

After spending two months with the battalion in the Bien Hoa area, he was transferred to the Saigon Support Command as the motor transport officer. In this position, he supported the greater Saigon area with administrative sedans, trucks, and buses, over seven hundred vehicles, a job that occupied practically all of his waking hours. He kept boxes of C-rations under his desk because he didn't have the time to travel to a mess hall for lunch.

He rotated to his next duty station at Fort Eustis in July 1967, where he was awarded the Bronze Star Medal "for service in connection with military operations against a hostile force in the Republic of Vietnam."

Before his first assignment at Fort Eustis in 1954, Landry had completed three and a half years of studies in the industrial arts curriculum at Southern University, Scotlandville, Louisiana. After leaving Vietnam in 1967, he was again assigned to Fort Eustis where he was reassigned to temporary duty at the University of Omaha, Nebraska, where he completed his college requirements and was awarded the bachelor's degree in general studies with a concentration in history.

Returning to Fort Eustis, he was assigned to the Transportation School where he worked as the foreign liaison officer. Upon his promotion to lieutenant colonel (O-5), he was assigned as the chief of Academic Records and Student Affairs officer and assistant secretary of the Transportation School. He insisted that none of his military assignments had been skewed by negative racial treatment until this one.

One of his duties was to brief his boss, a full colonel (O-6) on potential problems and incidents involving students so that his boss could, in turn, inform the school commandant. On one such occasion, Landry went to the colonel's office to report a student incident. The colonel responded heatedly, "Boy, what do you mean by . . ." or words to that effect. Landry, now a lieutenant colonel, responded in kind by saying, "What do you mean by calling me *boy*," and walked out of his boss's office. Later that day, the colonel stopped by Landry's office and apologized repeatedly for his "poor choice of words."

The assignment to the Transportation School was followed by a second duty station in Korea, this time in Pusan, the country's most southeastern port city, where he served as the deputy commander of the Second Transportation Group with units scattered about the country, including port operations in Inchon and Pusan, the Twenty-fifth Transportation Battalion Movement Control in Seoul, and the Sixty-ninth Transportation Battalion (truck) in ASCOM City, Bupyeong. Returning to his final army tour of duty at the Transportation School, Landry was assigned as the assistant secretary for Student Affairs and school adjutant. He retired on September 30, 1974, after twenty years of active service with several medals of commendation for meritorious service, including the Bronze Star Medal, three Meritorious Service Medals, and the Army Commendation Medal.

Herman Reynard, Modeste (Ascension), Pre-Vietnam Era, Army

After graduating from Lowery High School in 1962, Herman Reynard, was drafted for a two-year army tour of duty. He was sent to Fort Polk, Louisiana, near Leesville for basic training. His advance individual training (AIT) was completed at Fort Hood, Texas, in an infantry battalion. This training consisted of completing instructional modules in operating armored personnel carriers, qualifying on the 50-caliber machine gun and other light weapons, and fighting in infantry battle simulations.

Reynard was assigned to the Seventh Infantry Division in Manheim, Germany. There, his full-time job was preparing for combat. He stated he was able to complete all training assignments and got along well with his fellow soldiers. He attributed his success to family love and respect that was demonstrated by his parents, and credited Wilbert "Coach" Huey, his high school basketball coach and my sister Odile's husband, with teaching him the fundamentals of teambuilding skills that were transformed into army life skills.

Reynard finished his tour after twenty-two months in Germany and was returned to the United States before being discharged in 1964.

Realizing that his acquired skills as an infantryman were not marketable among local employers, Reynard attended a preparatory course in building construction under the GI Bill and, later, a course in bricklaying that was sponsored by the Bricklayers' Masons' and Marble Masons' Union #1 Keep as is in New Orleans. Armed with these skills, he spent twenty-eight successful years in the building trades, the last eleven as superintendent.

Gerald Theriot, Schriever (Lafourche), Vietnam Era, Air Force

As a sophomore at Nicholls State College in Thibodeaux, Louisiana, in 1967, Gerald Theriot continued to receive draft notices. The frequency of these notices led him to volunteer for the air force in August 1967. He was inducted into the air force at the Union Station in New Orleans at a time when U.S. troop strength was leveling off in Vietnam.

Following basic training at Lackland Air Force Base (AFB), San Antonio, Texas, he graduated from a six-week French language course at the Defense Institute (operated by the army), Presidio, Monterey, California. He then graduated from basic cryptographic training in the application of the French language at Goodfellow AFB, San Angelo, Texas, which served as a holding place between tours for airmen assigned to emergency reactionary units with sensitive intelligence-related MOSs, such as cryptic specialists, linguists, Morse code specialists, etc. These achievements marked the beginning of an interesting twenty-one-year career, mostly in air force intelligence.

Theriot's first assignment was to a radio intercept squadron at Iraklion AFB, Crete, Greece. He was primarily a French/cryptologist linguist who collected and routed information related to military activities in North Africa to the appropriate agency sources for their action. He was one of a few people of color in the field at this time. In the air force, this was considered one of the "tighter" fields and required mostly college graduates.

From Crete, he was assigned again to Goodfellow AFB. After a short stay, Theriot returned to the language school at Monterey and completed the six-month advanced French course. His career assignments continued as noted below:

- Returned to Goodfellow AFB to complete the cryptologist language course to apply his advance French training.
- Returned to Iraklion AFB in Greece for twenty months. This tour included his wife and two sons. It was during this time that his daughter was born in a military hospital in Germany.

- Returned to Goodfellow AFB in 1973 and was assigned to an emergency reaction unit. He volunteered for cross-training in North Vietnamese dialect and returned to Monterey and completed the nine-month course.
- Returned to Goodfellow for practice training in the use of the North Vietnamese dialect in military application of the language.
- Assigned to the U.S. Air Force Base, Taipei, Taiwan. Their area of surveillance concern was North Korea.
- Transferred to Sheppard AFB as a training manager for base and squad-level monitoring training in all career fields.
- In 1974, returned to the language school, graduating after six months' training in basic North Korean
- Following the tour at Sheppard, he returned to the language school and completed the nine-month course in advanced North Korean.
- Sent to Osan AFB located about thirty miles north of Pyeongtaek, South Korea, for a year in the intelligence field.
- Returned to the training management field at Buckley AFB in Aurora, Colorado.
- Returned to Osan for one year, again serving in the intelligence field.

During his military career and in addition to his many stateside locations, Theriot lived in Germany, Greece (twice), South Korea (twice), Taiwan, and Thailand and visited Laos. He spoke three foreign languages fluently. Few airmen in the history of the air force can match or exceed his language competency when one considers all of his language courses were gained through *volunteering*.

He was assigned to the National Security Agency at Fort George Meade, Maryland, at a time when international problems began stirring in North Korea. He was appointed the leader of a team of linguists to translate incoming fragmented reports and create a composite report on actions being planned or taken by the North Korean government. A highlight, and perhaps the biggest achievement in this assignment, was to lead the crafting of an intelligence report for the then-Secretary of State Robert McNamara and his interest in China.

After retiring from the air force, his leisure time is spent as an amateur photographer and a member of the American Legion Post 513 in Thibodeaux. He currently serves as the chaplain at the Louisiana Department level.

On a Personal Note

During mid-1965, President Lyndon B. Johnson announced his decision to increase the American presence in South Vietnam. Since my unit, Headquarters and Headquarters Company, Eleventh Transportation Battalion (Terminal), was well trained in logistical operations (supply, transportation, and maintenance) as well as deepwater port operations, we were selected to deploy to Saigon, Republic of Vietnam (RVN) in August 1965 to support the buildup of U.S. combat units soon to follow.

Viet Cong Welcoming Party

At the appointed time, the battalion headquarters personnel and equipment departed Langley Air Force Base in Hampton, Virginia, aboard an Air Force C-130 cargo plane. After two days and nights of flying with stops in San Francisco, Hawaii, and Okinawa, our plane headed for Tan Son Nhut Air Base on the outskirts of Saigon.

It was a little past midnight when the well-lit runway appeared in the distance. During our approach, the plane, without decelerating or warning, began a rapid descent at a steep angle. Flares from the ground lit up the entire approach area, and tracer bullets were coming from a dozen locations on the ground. Our flight had come under Viet Cong (VC) machine gun fire. The dive took less than five minutes, although it seemed more like an hour. Luckily, our plane was not hit.

A security guard told us the airborne fusillade was the VC's way of welcoming us. "They do it all the time," he said.

After gathering our gear, we were herded into a thirty-eight-passenger bus that took us to Tent City Bravo about a mile from the airport. As we approached the camp, a Military Police sergeant stopped us, told us to quickly dismount, and take cover in a ditch along the road. We did immediately. He told us the guards believed several VC soldiers had infiltrated the camp and the security guards were searching for them. At that moment, a machine gun positioned at the far end of the tent city opened fire, and tracers actually lit up the roadway! A perimeter guard had thought he had seen the intruders crossing the road and decided to end the manhunt with several bursts of fire that passed less than six feet from my head!

While I regained my composure, another guard told us the captured intruders were actually two teenage boys scrounging for food at the mess tent. Miraculously, no one was injured. However, I had begun to feel like a seasoned veteran, having been in country for less than an hour and already survived two "enemy" attacks!

Mission and Monsoons

My battalion arrived in South Vietnam on the night of August 5, 1965. A temporary headquarters was established at Tent City Bravo, located near the combined RVN civilian and military airport that was shared by allied military forces. The battalion immediately assumed the mission of operating the Saigon Port by taking charge of all U.S. military and State Department cargo shipped in and out of the port. During that same time, the battalion also assumed responsibility for the Army Air Cargo Operation at the Tan Son Nhut International Airport, a facility that served the South Vietnamese civilian airline, South Vietnamese Air Force units and military services of the United States as well.

By mid-August, a light truck company and a medium truck company had been assigned to the organization. By the first week in September, another light truck company and a terminal service company (a stevedoring unit) had joined our battalion. By the end of November, four additional Transportation Corps cargo handling companies were assigned.

Together, these manpower and equipment resources were engaged in daily port clearance at the Saigon Port along with highway long—and short-haul cargo delivery operations to designated destinations. The battalion headquarters and most of the units moved from the Saigon area to Long Binh, about sixteen miles northeast of Saigon. With the help of soldiers from the assigned transportation units, construction of the Long Binh Transportation Camp began. Within a month, all battalion units had moved to TC Hill (as it was called by truckers) where all of the trucks, trailers, and other equipment were kept when not in use, except for several truck companies that were now camped at Camp Red Ball located several miles to the north of the airport. TC Hill included living quarters complete with raised wooden floors and other necessities of home, such as a kitchen and messing tent and a recreation tent. There were administrative, operational, and maintenance tents as well as an outdoor covered latrine and shower, all having wooden floors which were necessary when monsoon season sent daily rains. Our road construction supplies included laterite, a type of hard soil that drains and dries quickly without forming the mud that impedes movement of trucks and soldiers on dirt roads.

The battalion ammunition discharge operations took place at U.S. flag cargo ships on anchor offshore in the Saigon River at Nha Be, about ten miles downstream from Saigon. Our job was to deliver to five dedicated ammo depots scattered across an area of about one hundred square miles. With the danger of "sappers" (enemy assault soldiers) lurking at practically any location, cargo ships carrying explosives were not permitted to dock in the Saigon Port.

The month after I arrived in country, while en route from Long Binh to the Saigon Port, I drove my Jeep past a large crowd of people, many of whom were standing in the main street. Although the RVN army military police were directing traffic, I was able to pull to the curb on the opposite side of the street and see General William Westmoreland, commander of the Military Assistance Command, Vietnam (MACV), and General Nguyen Cao Ky, the prime minister of South Vietnam in conversation. Heavily armed American and RVN army guards were scattered about the crowd. It was fascinating to be so close to the two most powerful and well-regarded military figures of the world. In his capacity, Westmoreland was viewed by many contributing countries as the commander-in-chief of all Allied forces in the war effort. General Ky, a comparatively young general officer at 36, was also the commander of the South Vietnamese Air Force at the time. His uniform was adorned with a purple scarf that he traditionally wore and a swagger stick which supported the flamboyant style for which he was known. Although there were as many as forty countries contributing to supporting the South Vietnam war effort, only seven countries, in addition to the United States, provided *military* assistance, including Thailand, South Korea, New Zealand, Spain, Australia, and the Philippines. These nations comprised the Free World Military Assistance Forces that was headquartered in Saigon.

Units continued to be assigned or attached to the Battalion Headquarters until a strength of 37 officers, 48 warrant officers, and 897 enlisted men was realized by May 1966 and was now made up of several additional units with varying specialty supporting missions (dock and floating cranes, deep sea divers, petroleum tankers, tugs, and LCMs [landing craft medium]). The battalion headquarters had now moved into the Le Lai Hotel in Saigon.

Sampan Ammo Delivery Operations

A *field expedient* delivery system was established by our Battalion Headquarters to transport ammunition from the ships to the U.S. Army/Vietnamese army depots for temporary storage and to be picked up by using units. A Vietnamese civilian transport company with sampans was contracted for this purpose. The sampans were loaded at ship's side and, powered by inboard diesel engines, were maneuvered through the tributaries to the five inland dispersed ammunition depots. All of these storage facilities were guarded by South Vietnamese army soldiers and were located at the water's edge where the contractor used mobile cranes to off-load onto small piers. Forklifts facilitated placing the pallets of ammo in the depot for storage.

Security for the depot facilities became a major challenge for our supervisory personnel as well as the RVN soldiers and civilian guards who provided surveillance around the clock. Periodic attacks by VC underground cells to overrun the guards were unsuccessful. According to some reports by RVN forces, the main purpose of such attempts was to disrupt the flow of ammo to Allied forces. Another equally important reason for the attacks was to obtain ammo and explosives to be used to disrupt the travel routes used by Allied forces to and from resupply depots.

When the contractor hired on sampans, he not only hired the skipper of the boat but his family as well. These boats also served as home for three to six family members, including women and children. Male teens and adult members served as stevedores and deck hands. Female members prepared meals and did "house" work, but served as deck hands when needed.

There were inherent dangers in the ammo transport business, and no one knew this better than the families involved. Some VC operatives threatened to blow up the sampans unless they were rewarded for not doing so. The skippers reported the threats to Mr. Khai, the owner/contractor, who usually informed us but ignored the threats. But on November 2, 1965, the VC captured one of the loaded sampans with four family members on board. A ransom handwritten note (below) was received by Mr. Khai from a North Vietnamese army organization containing the following message:

Translation:

To the owner of the barge #4365

We caught your barge loaded with American merchandizes, but, because of the generosity of our army, we kept this barge and we will release it after you give us 100.000$.
At 12 o'clock of the 4th of November 1965, meet us at Vam Mon.
If it is later than that date, we cannot take charge of [be responsible for] the people on this barge.

Sincerely,

Army of Liberation in
South of Vietnam.
Thu Duc Province
Mai Ba

The contractor took no action, as usual; however, this time the consequences were tragic. The sampan was completely destroyed by fire, and the family members were never found by search parties from the Vietnamese army and navy and civilian police forces, at least not during the remaining ten months of my tour.

Body Bags and B-52s

The Battalion S-3 (operations officer) was inundated with routine daily port discharge and highway transport operations in an oversized organization. Therefore, supervision of the air cargo activity was added to my responsibilities as the Battalion executive officer. This job entailed troubleshooting for the three-man operation involved in receiving and shipping by air critical small machinery components and repair parts to get much-needed army equipment back in operation. The air cargo activity served the entire southern portion of South Vietnam.

I was on the phone with the sergeant in charge several times each day and would visit the unit, located at the Tan Son Nhut Air Base, at least twice each week. These visits were mostly for morale boosting, since the team was as professional and competent as I'd ever seen and did not need supervision.

Adjacent to the air cargo activity was the U.S. Quartermaster Graves Registration Unit. Each time I visited our activity at any time of day, I observed the QMGR men moving body bags containing corpses of American military personnel from the helicopter landing area to the buildings where the bodies were prepared for return to Stateside. This operation had eventually taken its toll on several of our men, and necessitated having to replace those who had been mentally and physically fatigued by a combination of the continuous graves registration operation and the extended working hours of the air cargo operations. This was the first of two most troubling experiences for me during my twelve months in RVN.

While stationed in Long Binh, an almost nightly recurrence was also troublesome to me, and probably to others as well. Beginning around 10:00 p.m., sounds of two-thousand-pound bombs being dropped in suspected VC-occupied areas twenty to twenty-five miles away by U.S. Air Force B-52 bombers could be heard for several hours. Although the bombs were intended for military targets, the thought of destruction and death in the villages containing nonmilitary women, children, and elderly people caused by the bombings was impossible to ignore.

Games the VC Played

Treacherous Sappers

Several months before the battalion arrived in Saigon, the My Canh Restaurant located adjacent to the Saigon Port was badly damaged by two sappers who left plastic explosives in the restaurant after finishing a meal. The *St. Louis Post-Dispatch* dated June 25, 1965, reported at least 29 and as many as 50 were killed, incuding five U.S. servicemen and three American civilians. Pictures of the destroyed restaurant were seen on international television broadcasts and served as a wake-up call to military personnel who were deploying for Vietnam. That incident was my introduction to sappers and plastic explosives and the danger of not being able to distinguish the Viet Cong from any other Vietnamese on the street.

Due to a lack of real estate suitable for quarters, civilian hotels in Saigon were used to house American troops. These facilities were secured with fences complete with concertina wire and bunkered with sandbags, with security guards at the entrances to discourage sappers on motorbikes and sometimes bicycles, from riding past and throwing explosive satchels at the facility. Several hotels were badly damaged by sapper explosives that killed American and Allied soldiers, sailors, and airmen as well as Vietnamese soldiers and civilian security guards. Each time following such an event, steps were taken to better fortify the facilities. In spite of these efforts, the sapping continued and was seemingly accepted by American troops as one of the perils of the war.

Destructive Rubber Bands

Occasionally, units were directed by higher headquarters to reinforce security around motor pools and other areas where vehicles were staged overnight. Additionally, everyone was to be on the lookout for strangers in these and all other areas of administration and operations so that proper security steps could be taken to prevent destructive incidents. One such maneuver reportedly used by infiltrating VC was the placing of a rubber-banded-hand grenade in the gas tank of trucks.

The VC would pull the pin on an incendiary grenade while holding down the release lever. With the free hand and using a rubber band made from a truck inner tube, the handle was then secured in place by the rubber band to prevent detonation, and the grenade dropped into the gas tank of a truck. The explosive reaction from the gas gradually eating away at the rubber band was predictable.

Aromatic Jasmine or Hand Grenade?

While our headquarters cadre lived in the Lei Lai Hotel in downtown Saigon, traveling to and from the Saigon Port by Jeep and truck became a daily routine for our personnel. Often, officers drove their section vehicles because assigned drivers were occupied by other mission-related chores.

On one such occasion, I was driving a Jeep while en route to the port. As I was stopped for a traffic light, a slightly built Vietnamese boy of perhaps fourteen years approached me on the driver's side of the vehicle. He held a small cloth bag and a bouquet of flowers.

He said, "Hey, Joe, you buy?"

"No, thanks, "I answered.

"I sell you cheap," he continued.

"No, thanks," I repeated.

"Joe, you look like nice guy. I sell you for one dollar," he offered.

I countered, "No, thanks."

Just as the traffic light turned amber to allow pedestrians to cross, he started telling me how the Vietnamese people appreciated all that the Americans were doing to help his country. Mine was the first vehicle in line, and before the light turned green, the boy began walking across in front of the Jeep; and as I was about to drive off, he turned toward the Jeep and said, "For you, Joe!" as he tossed *something* into the front passenger seat. In the second that it took me to glance at what that *something* was, I had already envisioned it to be a hand grenade. I quickly grabbed the bundle to toss it from the Jeep when I realized it was the jasmine bouquet!

Black Women and the Military System

Introduction

American women have participated in defending this nation in both war and peacetime. Their contributions, however, have gone largely unrecognized and unrewarded. While women in the United States Armed Forces share a history of discrimination based on gender, Black women have faced both race and gender discrimination. Initially barred from official military status, Black women persistently pursued their right to serve. Once in service, they began to gain more respect as the public in general and men in particular realized that women could work successfully outside of the house.

Documentation of the history of Black women participating in the military forces of our country appears sparse. However, there is written evidence that shows these women played major roles in both peacetime and during each major war.

The Revolutionary War

During the Revolutionary War (1775-1783), Black women worked for the American cause against England in the country's first war on native soil. They worked as caretakers, nurses and nursemaids, and spies and helped build forts for protection against the Indians as well as the British.

The War of 1812

There is little surviving documentation on Black women's roles during the War of 1812, which was primarily a naval conflict, again with England. Records do show that Black women managed farms to replace the White men who were called to service. These women further supported the war effort by making bandages and being nursemaids for the sick and wounded sailors.

The Civil War

By the Civil War, Black women's presence had greatly increased. They nursed, cooked, and did laundry for soldiers. Black nurses served in both the Union and Confederate hospitals. Records show that as many as 180 Black nurses—male and female—served in convalescent centers and hospitals in Maryland, Virginia, and North Carolina during the war.

Civil War Cannon

CURTIS J. JOHNSON

No history of the Civil War would be complete without mentioning Harriet Tubman who served in the Union Army as a nurse, a soldier, a scout, a spy, and an abolitionist who helped to destroy Confederate supply lines. She was also a freedom fighter, and the conductor of the Underground Railroad who led over three hundred slaves to freedom in the North and into Canada.

After the war, she became an active advocate of woman suffrage and was one of the founders of the African Methodist Episcopal Church. She was unsuccessful in her fight to get a military pension; however, she did receive a pension because of her husband's service. She was buried with full military honors.

The history of Cathay Williams serves to support the involvement of Black women immediately following the end of the Civil War. Williams was the first female buffalo soldier. According to a feature article in the *Armed Forces News*, Spring. 1998,

> *Cathay Williams was born into slavery near Independence, Missouri, in 1842. As the Civil War began, Cathay was pressed into service as a cook for the 13th Union Army Corps. Cathay followed the troops to Arkansas where she learned to cook . . .*
>
> *Cathay was at the battle of Pea Ridge in Arkansas. As they moved throughout the South, she watched as the Union Army burned the cotton fields and captured rebel gunboats on the Red River in Shreveport [Louisiana]. In 1864, she was sent to Washington to be a cook and laundress for General Phil Sheridan and his staff. She was with Sheridan on his raids in the Shenandoah Valley . . .*
>
> *On November 15, 1866, in St. Louis, Missouri, Cathay Williams enlisted as "William Cathay." With no physical examination required to enlist and less than flattering uniforms to disguise any hint of her female form, Cathay Williams spent her military service as William Cathay . . .*
>
> *In 1876, she stated to a St. Louis newspaper reporter, "I was never put in the guard house, no bayonet was put to my back. I carried my musket and did guard and other duties while in the Army."*
>
> *William Cathay's date of discharge was October 14, 1868. There are some accounts that she feigned illness in order to receive a discharge and that upon visiting the surgeon, her gender was discovered . . .*
>
> *While the papers for Williams' discharge are proof of her service, the fact that she was not compensated for her contributions to the*

military with a pension is unfortunate. It is easy to want more for her measureable acts of courage and visible signs of bravery. Although we know little about Cathay Williams, we do know this: she is the kind if hero we all have the capacity to be. She is an example of the profound capacity that exists to this day, not just in the military, but our daily lives as well.

Cathay endured!

The Spanish-American War

Black women served mostly as nurses during and after the brief engagement. The greatest challenges to the American army were the typhoid, yellow fever, dysentery, and malaria that reportedly resulted in over 75 percent of all recorded deaths. Black nurses were favored for service during the war because the surgeon general believed that their darker and thicker skin provided immunity from the diseases. That belief was unfounded, as several of these nurses died from typhoid fever.

World War I

World War I (1914-1918) was almost over before Black women were allowed to enlist. Initially, Black nurses enrolled in the American Red Cross, hoping to gain entry into the Army or Navy Nurse Corps. As the war escalated, public pressure increased to enlist Black women.

In 1917, the Red Cross invited Black nurses to enroll in the American Red Cross. However, it was not until September 1918 that Blacks were accepted into the Nurse Corps, two months before the war ended in November 1918.

Shortly after the war ended, eighteen Black Red Cross nurses were sent to Army Nurse Corps assignments in Illinois and Ohio. They lived in segregated quarters and cared for German prisoners of war and Black soldiers. All Black nurses had been released from service as the corps was reduced to its peacetime levels. Aileen Cole, one of the pioneering nurses, later wrote:

The story of the Negro nurse in World War I is not spectacular. We arrived after the Armistice was signed, which was alone anticlimactic. So we had no opportunity for service above and beyond the call of duty.

But each of us . . . did contribute quietly and with dignity to the idea that justice demands professional equity for all qualifications.

World War II

The Great Depression had been economically hard on everyone, especially Blacks. At the onset of World War II, Black people still faced systemic racism that continued to inhibit them from getting good-paying jobs. Together, these two conditions placed many Blacks at the very bottom of the economic ladder, particularly in Jim Crow states.

As the men left the home front to join the war effort, many White women moved outside of their traditional jobs and filled jobs vacated by these men. The shortage of men had advanced the opportunities for woman to enter nontraditional fields.

During late 1940, hiring was increasing in plants that manufactured war materials that were intended to support our country and allies overseas. At the same time, efforts were underway by the U.S. military to prepare for war that would soon involve this country. However, Blacks were excluded from this hiring process as well.

Women Army Corps (WAC)

The Women's Army Auxiliary Corps (WAAC) was established on May 15, 1942. Almost a year later, on July 3, 1943, the WAAC became a part of the army, and was renamed the Women's Army Corps (WAC). It was no longer an "auxiliary" and members were accorded the same pay, allowances, and privileges as their male counterparts.

Black women were included in the WAC since its inception in 1942. The corps started with 400 White and 40 Black women, the latter limited to 10 percent, matching the Black proportion of the national population.

The approximately 6,500 Black women who signed on in the WAAC/WAC joined an institution in which segregation was the official policy. Black enlisted women served in segregated units, participated in segregated training, ate at segregated mess facilities, and used segregated recreational facilities. Officers received their officer candidate and technical training in integrated units but lived in segregated quarters. Specialists and technical training schools were integrated in 1943.

WACs in Formation

CURTIS J. JOHNSON

Charity Adams was among the 40 Black and 400 White women in the WAC first class, whose platoons were separated by race. At the end of the officer candidate training, she was commissioned a second lieutenant and became the commanding officer of a training unit. Later in her career, she would command the 6888th Central Postal Directory Battalion, a one-of-a-kind army unit created to boost troop morale in the European Theater by making sure the mail reached its intended destination.

The 6888th, consisting of more than 850 members, was formed during WWII to clear a backlog of mail heading overseas to soldiers. The women underwent basic training in Georgia and then boarded a ship for Europe.

The number of U.S. personnel in the European Theater of Operations was staggering—a total of about seven million. Many had the same name; there were more than 7,500 Robert Smiths, for example. But the Six Triple Eight broke all records for redirecting mail. They knew the importance of their job in maintaining morale. The unit worked around the clock to finish the job in half the time. After handling seven million pieces of mail at a base in Birmingham, England, they were then sent to Rouen, France, for a similar job.

Adam's unit faced the typical disparagements of Black soldiers. The American Red Cross wanted to establish a separate hotel for Black WACs in London. Adams refused this "generosity," and her unit stood behind her. In Birmingham, the Black women had a curfew of 11:00 p.m. (instead of the 12:30 a.m. curfew for White soldiers), because English residents had been told that Blacks had tails that appeared at midnight, and these tails were especially apparent below the skirts of women.

One general was apparently bothered at seeing some of the unit's women in their bathrobes (even though it was explained to him that the unit worked in shifts and the women in bathrobes were not on duty). "I'll tell you what I'm going to do, Major Adams," said the general. "I'm going to send a White first lieutenant down here to show you how to run this unit." Adam's response: "Over my dead body, sir." Before the day was over, word came that the general was drawing up court-martial charges against her. In turn, she considered court-martial charges against him (for stressing racial disharmony among the troops, an action specifically cautioned against in a special directive from higher headquarters). Within a few days, the general had dropped the charges, and Adams, too, dropped her plans. Some months later, when they came across each other again, he apologized to her. She had outsmarted him, he said, and he was proud to know her. She had also been quite an education for him, especially about Negroes, he also said.

When the air force was created in 1947, a number of former Black WACs continued serving in the army but performed air force duties, as the air force did not admit women in its first year.

On June 12, 1948, the Women Army Corps became a permanent separate corps of the army.

Semper Paratus—Always Prepared (SPARs)

On November 23, 1942, Public Law 771 created the Women's Reserve of the Coast Guard (WRCG) that became known as the SPARs. Its purpose was "to expedite the war effort by providing for releasing officers and men for duty at sea and their replacement by women in the shore establishment of the Coast Guard and for other purposes." Four years later in October 1944, the Secretary of the Navy ordered the WAVES and SPARs to begin accepting Black recruits. The first Black SPAR was YN3 Olivia Hooker. By then, the SPARs' initial goal had almost been achieved, and the service had stopped accepting civilian women for officer training.

A few Black women enlistees did go through Officer Candidate School and were commissioned as ensigns before the end of the WWII. According to a Coast Guard report, Coast Guard personnel records do not indicate the total number of Black SPARs who enlisted in the three months before the recruiting effort began shutting down.

Women Airforce Service Pilots (WASP)

In 1940, famed White aviator Jackie Cochran lobbied Eleanor Roosevelt to establish a women's division of the air force to ferry planes from manufacturing plants to military bases. Cochran's efforts brought about establishing the Women's Flying Training Detachment (WFTD). Soon after, Nancy Harkness Love was successful in establishing the Women's Auxiliary Ferrying Squadron (WAFS).

On August 5, 1943, the efforts of these two women resulted in the merger of their proposed organizations—the WAFDS and

WFTD—becoming the Women's Airforce Service Pilots (WASP). Most people looked upon the WASP as a department/division of the air force; however, it was not. At best, it was a paramilitary organization formed to ferry military planes from manufacturing plants to military bases. The WASPs were considered civil service employees.

The literature shows occasional references to Black WASPs, such as Betty Budd of Concord, California; but Budd was an exception. Few Black women were qualified to join because the entrance requirements included holding a civilian pilot's license.

The Women Accepted for Volunteer Emergency Service (WAVES)

In November 1944, Harriet Pickens and Frances Wills, both from New York City, graduated from the Naval Reserve Midshipmen's School (Women's Reserve), Northampton, Massachusetts. They were commissioned as WAVES and became the first Black women to be assigned to the navy and the military, Pickens as a lieutenant junior grade and Wills as an ensign. They were members of the school's final class.

Although the navy intended to increase the number of Black women to 10 percent, there were fewer than fifty Black women by 1945. At the end of WWII, there were eighty-six thousand WAVES serving in the navy, and among them were two Black officers and seventy-thousand Black enlisted.

The Marine Corps began accepting Black males in 1942, one day after the navy's decision to do so. Black women would have to wait until 1949 to enlist. That year, Annie Graham (later Gillard) became the first Black female to enlist. The following day, she was followed by Anne Lamb (later Ellis). Annie Grimes became the third to enlist in 1950 and became the first Black woman officer to retire after a twenty-year career. Like their sisters before them in the other military branches, they were not welcome in off-base business establishments and public places.

Colonel Adele Hodges became the first Black woman to command Camp Lejeune, North Carolina, a base that once contained Montford Point Camp, the site of the first Blacks to join the Marine Corps from 1942 to 1949. Hodges said women like Grimes made it possible for many people, both male and female, to become marines today.

WAVE Officer

CURTIS J. JOHNSON

The Korean War

During WWII, women entered military service in unprecedented numbers, serving in all branches, thus freeing up men for combat.

The size of the military establishment had not fully recovered from WWII when the Korean War began in 1950. When it was realized that a shortage of combat-trained men existed, the War Department sent out a call for nurses and for women to replace men in administrative-type jobs. The call was again answered; however, not in the numbers that were targeted by the military hierarchy.

The American cultural climate of the time relegated many women to nonprofessional, low-paying jobs. The armed forces reflected this attitude, offering women "pink collar" jobs with little room for advancement.

Unlike restrictions imposed during WWII on the number of Black women who could enlist in certain branches of the service, no such quotas were imposed during the Korean War.

Black women of the WAC served at military bases in Japan, Okinawa, and the Philippines in direct support of the Korean War. Corporal Airline Hayward Wall was assigned to the Yokohama Engineer Depot helping United Nations soldiers get the supplies they needed to fight. Estella Ehelebe of the U.S. Army Special Services sometimes wrote letters of condolence to the next of kin of soldiers who had died in Korea.

Almost six hundred military nurses served in hospitals established in the Korean Theater. African American nurses were among this number, including Lieutenant Martha E. Cleveland (later colonel) and Lieutenant Nancy Greene Pease, both of whom were with the Eleventh Evacuation Hospital, and Lieutenant Evelyn Decker of the 8055th MASH unit. Other Black nurses were assigned to hospitals in Japan, Hawaii, and the West Coast of the United States.

Army nurse Captain Eleanor Yorke was another of the few Black nurses to serve on Korean soil during the three years of the war. Speaking to a reporter from the *Baltimore Afro-American* in May 1952, she provided the following information:

"It was a terrible eight months, but I was too busy to be scared. We received the wounded twenty to forty-five minutes after they were hit, treated them on the spot, and then shipped them to the rear depending on how badly they were wounded. They came by helicopter and ambulance. The helicopters flew continuously from dawn to dusk, and the ambulances rolled on constantly. It got pretty rough at times, working under artillery bombardment, and many times I was rocked to sleep in my army cot from the reverberations."

Black women who volunteered in the military during this period stepped over dual barriers of race and gender.

The Vietnam War

The Vietnam War saw the highest proportion of Blacks ever to serve in an American war. Black women were an important component of the intake of women into the All-Volunteer Force (AVF). At the outbreak of the war, increasing numbers of women, including Blacks, volunteered for duty.

Black members of the WACs also served in Vietnam. WACs on duty at Long Binh were stationed in an area that was frequently attacked during the TET Offensive. Chief Warrant Officer Doris Allen recalled, "As a senior intelligence analyst, I was recognized for having been responsible through the production of one specific intelligence report for saving the lives of at least 101 marines fighting in Quang Tri Province."

During the TET offense in 1968, Staff Sergeant Edith Efferson was stationed at Long Binh as a supply sergeant. The ammunition depot at Long Binh was a primary target of the enemy. WACs on duty in the orderly room would hit the floor frequently during the months of January and February to avoid the shattering glass, flying gravel, and other debris kicked up by the explosions. Sergeant Efferson's calm demeanor throughout this difficult period helped the younger women in the office to better deal with their own concerns.

Veterans' Stories

Daisy Calvey Brown, Donaldsonville (Ascension), Vietnam War Era, Army

Daisy Calvey Brown graduated from Saint Catherine of Sienna High School in 1965. After being discouraged by her priest and teachers from pursing her longtime goal of joining the army (a desire that came after she saw the Hollywood movie, *Francis* [the talking mule] *Joins the WACs*), she enrolled at the Louisiana State University, where she remained only one semester. She transferred to Southern University for two additional semesters before leaving Louisiana—ambitious and broke—to live with family members in Kentucky. When job prospects there proved disappointing, and after having reached age twenty-one, she no longer needed letters of reference from her priest and teachers. She decided to fulfill her dream and enlisted in the U.S. Army. On May 5, 1967, during the heat of the Vietnam War, she joined the Women's Army Corps (WACs). Following basic training at Fort McClellan, Alabama, she was transferred to Fort Benjamin Harrison, Indiana, where she prepared for a career as a finance specialist in the Finance Corps.

Her first assignment was in the Finance and Accounting Office at the U.S. Army Garrison, Fort Devens, Massachusetts, where she began to put her newly acquired skills to work as a disbursing clerk and cashier. She was responsible for accounting for and disbursing thousands of dollars in government monies directly to soldiers for basic and advanced pays as well as travel allowances. Using these basic skills as a foundation, Brown continued in a series of assignments with increasing responsibility that included:

- Pay Clerk, Finance and Accounting Office (FAO), U.S. Army Garrison, Heidelberg, Germany
- Pay Clerk, FAO, U.S. Army Garrison, Frankfurt, Germany
- Non-Commissioned Officer in Charge (NCOIC) and Pay Clerk, Travel Division FAO, Walter Reed Army Medical Center, Washington, D.C.
- NCOIC Travel Division, FAO, Eighth U.S. Army, Seoul, Korea
- NCOIC Travel Division, FAO, Military District of Washington, D.C.
- First Sergeant, FAO, Eighth U.S. Army, Seoul Korea
- Chief, Quality Assurance Branch, FAO, Third Infantry Division, Wurzburg, Germany
- NCOIC Finance Policy Branch, Office of the Assistant Chief of Staff, Comptroller Seventh Corps, Stuttgart, Germany
- NCOIC Finance Operations, Seventh Corps Regional FAO, Stuttgart, Germany
- Command Sergeant Major, Eighteenth Airborne Corps Finance Group, Fort Bragg, North Carolina

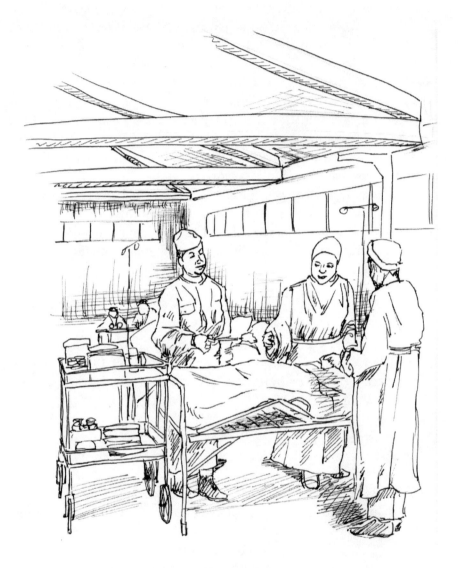

Operating Room Nurses

CURTIS J. JOHNSON

In short, Brown was able to gain competence in all phases of army finance and accounting operations at every level in the army's largest finance and accounting offices and at a wide variety of military installations worldwide. She graduated from the NCO academy at Fort Dix, New Jersey, in 1972 and later from the Sergeants Major Academy. When asked about her most challenging military experiences, Brown had this to say, "There were many. The most recent came as I worked as the army's first female command sergeant major to serve at the Eighteenth Airborne Corps at Fort Bragg, North Carolina, a bastion of more than three hundred male sergeants major. I demanded that the language be kept clean during the many meetings and gatherings I was required to attend. Of course, this did not merit me many friends. However, that did not stop me. I also demanded changes to protocol during dining-ins and dining-outs that recognized the presence of senior women soldiers. For example, the toast intended to recognize the invited guest read, 'To the lovely ladies.' I suggested it be changes to state, 'To the invited guests.' And the one which stated, 'Gentlemen, seat your ladies,' I suggested it be changed to, 'Members of the mess, seat your guests.' This, too, caused me to be talked about. In retrospect, I could have had an easier life had I chose to be passive."

Brown credits spiritual guidance for her ability to confront the racial and gender challenges that complicate Black women soldiers' daily lives. She said, "God was my friend. From everyone else, I only demanded and received respect. I did not seek association, and I did not miss them. I studied to show my self-worth, worked as if Jesus was my supervisor, and received promotions and accolades all along my journey. I knew my job and was not shy about making that known. Some said that I was mean, outspoken, or militant. My response was that I was competent.

"With regard to race relations, I did not seek friendships, just respect and advancement. The few who chose to befriend me, and my bosses who chose to promote and reward me were White, Black, Asian, German, and Spanish. I have no horrific racist stories to tell. I was too mean to be liked, and perhaps this was my defense mechanism. I can say, however, that affirmative action standards and principles made it possible for the records of minority soldiers to be looked at and given equal treatment. Consequently, we—the minority soldiers—were able to compete on a level playing field."

As a final analysis, Brown was asked about her overall rating of her life in the military service. She stated, "It was all good—no, it was excellent! The service fulfilled all of my needs. It provided shelter, food, clothing, reasonable pay, continuous training, valuable work experience, opportunity for advancement, worldwide travel, professional educational opportunities, international relationships, and most importantly, an opportunity for religious expression. I am grateful to God for infusing into my head and heart the desire to serve our country. I am also grateful to my wonderful husband who has been standing by my side since May 25, 1971."

She concluded the interview with these words: "To God be the glory, for the great things he has done in my life."

Her citations for commendable service included the Defense Legion of Merit, the Meritorious Service Medal (four awards), the Army Commendation Medal (two awards), and the Army Achievement Medal. She completed her education at the University of Maryland, European Division. This plus her twenty-three years of finance and accounting experiences had prepared her well for the civilian workforce. Her first job after retirement was that of chief of a Contracts Accounting Operation Division at the Defense Finance Service, Columbus, Ohio, in grade GS-11. She retired from the Defense Finance and Accounting Service in Arlington, Virginia, in grade GS-14.

Gloria Butler, Thibodaux (Lafourche), Vietnam War Era, Air Force

For most of her teenage life, Gloria Butler had chosen the airline stewardess field as a career. Near the end of her senior year at Thibodaux High School, she attended a school-sponsored job fair. When she shared her career choice with an airline recruiter, he told her that she would have to learn to fly an airplane before she could attend school to become a stewardess. He justified his statement by telling her that this was a basic requirement since the stewardess was the next in line to fly the plane in case the pilot became disabled.

With traveling as one of her career goals and considering herself an adventurous type of person, she wanted to try new things. She decided the military would be her second career choice. She methodically planned her military career by deciding to first join the air force to experience what it was like. Following that enlistment, she would switch to one of the other services (army, navy, or Marine Corps) and continue switching until she had experienced them all before retiring.

Butler initiated her career plan by volunteering for the air force and was inducted on February 13, 1973. Following basic training at Lackland Air Force Base (AFB) near San Antonio, Texas, she was sent to Sheppard AFB where she was trained as an aircraft mechanic. Her first assignment was to Cannon AFB in Clovis, New Mexico, where she became a part of the flight line transit alert unit involved in basic ground assistance and maintenance of the aircraft including pre-and post-flight inspections, directing them in parking, refueling, and performing maintenance as needed. With regards to aircraft maintenance, Butler said, "If there was a maintenance problem, it was your job to determine what was the problem and fix it. An aircraft mechanic would only work on one aircraft, whereas a transit alert mechanic worked on any aircraft that landed at the base, including helicopters and show birds (Thunderbirds)."

When asked about her most challenging experiences at Cannon, she stated it was learning detailed information about two specific aircrafts, the F-4 and F-111. "Working in transit alert, you didn't have to know about the complete aircraft. Therefore, when I was tested for a promotion, I couldn't pass the test. I was tested three times but never got beyond airman first class."

During her assignment at Cannon, she experienced a back injury, making mechanical work difficult for her. After about two years at Cannon, Butler was assigned to the Forty-eighth Operational Maintenance Squadron, Tactical Air Command (OMS/TAC) at Lakenheath AFB, Lakenheath, England. At first, she was assigned as a flight line crew member. However, the injury she received at Cannon began to take its toll. Her back became extremely uncomfortable considering the contorted positions she had to assume as a mechanic. Tests proved that she would no longer be able to do such work. She was asked by her new commander what skill field training she wished to undertake. She chose to cross-train in the clerical/secretarial field. "I wanted to work in an office setting. My back injury allowed me the opportunity to train and work in my dream job. I learned basic secretarial techniques so that when I completed my tour, I would be able to go into the regular workforce doing what I loved."

After two years in England, Butler was returned to McGuire AFB, New Jersey, where she received an honorable discharge on July 31, 1978. She returned to Thibodaux but was unsuccessful in getting a clerical job. She discovered a job opportunity in Midwest City, Oklahoma; however, she learned she needed computer skills and clerical/secretarial skills to qualify. Under the GI Bill, she enrolled in and completed an eight-month vocational and technical center course in office management. She spent the next three months working for the Midwest City Police Department in the Neighborhood Watch Program before returning to Thibodaux in February 1980 due to the illness of both her mother and father. Here, she worked for the Louisiana Department of Labor, Office of Employment Security (a.k.a. unemployment office).

When asked about her personal air force experiences, Butler said, "Contrary to most people's experiences, I had a wonderful time in the service. I may not have been assigned my choice of bases, but I got along well with everybody. I mean, almost everybody. But I had the time of my life!"

Airman First Class Gloria Butler, a disabled veteran, currently lives in Thibodaux.

The Ultimate Heroes

The heroes of all wars are identified as those men and women who participate with distinguished valor under combat conditions or those who perform roles in combat support service in a war zone. Those who are cited for heroics in combat are usually awarded high performance medals for valor and given places of honor in our society, especially by the military community. Those serving in combat support roles are also awarded the same medals as their combat comrades; although, the purpose is for service performance under unusual conditions against a hostile force. However, both roles, the combatant and the combat supporter, are dependent on nonmilitary forces—manufacturers, suppliers, communities, and families—to be successful.

As in most wars, everyone does not return unscathed. In every war, some do not return alive. I have always been convinced that these are the heroes who pay the ultimate price. These soldiers, sailors, airmen, and marines have been returned to their families from around the world for proper burial during and after wars.

The quad-parish area servicemen and women participated fully in WWII, the Korean War, and the Vietnam War. In the Louisiana Square fronting on the Ascension Parish Court House in Donaldsonville stands a War Veterans Memorial. The fitting inscription states,

This monument dedicated in memory of all veterans who served the United States Armed Forces in defense of freedom and peace, having fought bravely against tremendous odds on land, sea, and air, were no less honorable, valiant, and victorious men and women, were killed-in-battle, wounded-in-action, missing-in-action, or were held as prisoners-of-war. Dedicated May 20, 1990.

The monument was sponsored by the VFW Montalband-Sentilles Post 3766 and the American Legion Babin-Haynes Post 98. The names of veterans listed on the memorial are the following:

<u>World War II, 1941-1945</u>

William F. Bridewell
Bonnie J. Cedotal
Joseph Cedotal
James A. Crawford
Lawless C. Falcon
Joseph L. Frey
Howard J Guidry
George P. Haynes
P. A. Hernandez
Ulysses J. Hidalgo
Andre J. Landry
Isaac Landry
Claude P. LeBlanc
Samuel A. LeBlanc, Jr.
George Millet, Jr.
Milford J. Morales
Deena Motton
Walter S. Ricardo, Jr.*
Ezekiel Robinson
Oldin R. Sanchez
Roy F. Sentilles
Joseph L. Smith
Sherel J. Talbot
Herbert Thomas
Adrian D. Williams
Macellan Williams

John Winfrey*
Euclid J. Roger, Jr.
Delmayne E. Veron

Korean War, 1950-1953

Reginald L. LeBlanc*
Reginald A Riley*
Leon S. Jones*

Vietnam War, 1965-1973

Edmund Ferman
Victor Johnson, Jr.*
Eddie L. Landry*
Charles A. McKinney*
Arman Stein

*Black

During my early military years, I was inspired by the poem "In Flanders Fields," although, I admit, I did not have a thorough appreciation for the message at the time. That is, until my first visit many years ago to the Arlington National Cemetery in Arlington, Virginia, where the scenery caused me to reflect deeply on the poem. The thousands of aligned white crosses were reminders of those warriors who sacrificed their lives for our freedom.

The poem was written by Lieutenant Colonel John McCrae, then a major and surgeon in the Canadian Army, following the death of a friend during the battle of 1815 in the Ypres Salient area of Belgium.

The poem reads:

In Flanders fields the poppies blow
Between the crosses, row on row,
That mark our place; and in the sky,
The larks, still bravely singing, fly
Scarce heard amid the guns below.

We are the Dead. Short days ago

CURTIS J. JOHNSON

We lived, felt dawn, saw sunset glow,
Loved and were loved, and now we lie
In Flanders fields.

Take up your quarrel with the foe:
To you from failing hands we throw
The torch; be yours to hold it high.
If ye break faith with us who die
We shall not sleep, though poppies grow
In Flanders fields.

What a fitting challenge to those who would follow one day to also throw the torch ...

The poem was composed while McCrae sat in the back of an ambulance, near a cemetery filled with poppies and rows of white crosses marking the final resting place for soldiers passing the torch of national defense. It is said that this poem established the basis for the annual tradition for the sale of poppies handmade by veterans, spouses, and Women's Auxiliary and sold in memory of those warriors who gave their lives to defend their country.

Roll Call . . . and Taps

The appendix contains the names of over 1,800 veterans, living and dead, from the quad-parish region, who participated in the military service during and between WWI, WWII, the Korean War, and the Vietnam War. There are also several from the Spanish-American War. In addition to the names of each veteran and whether they are alive or dead, the lists show their branch of service, if their service was under combat conditions or during a war era, and comments such as unit assignment, rank, years of service, and special medals received.

The lists may not contain the names of every veteran from each parish, as the names were obtained by word of mouth and from files of American Legion Posts in each parish (except West Ascension) and collected from cemeteries scattered throughout the region. I apologize for omitting any veteran's name.

Taps

CURTIS J. JOHNSON

APPENDIX

Roll Call . . . and Taps

ST. JAMES PARISH VETERANS

		Combat Service				Combat Era			
	Branch	WWI	WWII	Korea	RVN	WWI	WWII	Korea	RVN	Comments
Adams, Norwood J.	A				X					
Albert, Lewis Sr.	A		X							
Alex, Columbus (D)	A	X								
Alexander, Norah (D)	A		X							PVT, Casual Det.
Alexis, Oscar (D)	A	X								1894-1966
Ambros, Felician, Jr.(D)	N									
Ambros, James P.	A				X					
Armant, Craig	A									
Arrington, Phillip (D)	N				X					
Aubert, Edgar, Sr.(D)	A									
Aubert, Louis, Sr.(D)	A		X							
Aubert, Roland A.(D)	N		X	X	X					
Baily, James (D)	MC									
Baptist, John (D)	A	X								PVT, Co B, 349 Labor Bn.
Barker, Sam (D)	A		X							PVT
Barnes, Albert (D)	A	X								PVT, 524 Eng Svc Bn.
Barney, James (D)	A			X						
Batiste, Barry R	A									
Batiste, Edward (D)	A			X						
Batiste, Wallace J.	A				X					
Wallace, Norwood	A				X					
Bejoile, Freddie (D)	A									
Bell, Herbert, Sr. (D)	A		X							

		Combat Service				Combat Era				
		WWI	WWII	Korea	RVN	WWI	WWII	Korea	RVN	Comments
Bell, Herbert, Sr. (D)	A		X							
Berry, Lawaller (D)	A	X								PVT
Bottom, Melvin B. (D)	A				X					
Bourgeois, Harry (D)	N									
Bourgeois, Joseph (D)	A		X							
Bourgeois, Landry (D)	A	X								PVT
Bowser, Morris E., Sr. (D)	A		X							
Bowser, Morris, Sr. (D)	A		X							1915-1976
Bowser, Willie (D)	A	X								
Bradley, John (D)	A		X							
Brooks, Joseph M. (D)	A		X							
Brown, Alfred (D)	A	X								
	A									
Brown, Chester, Jr. (D)	A				X					
Brown, Freddie (D)	N	X								
Brown, Johnny (D)	A	X								PVT, Casual Co, 1st Dpt Rep.
Brown, Zack (D)	N		X							PVT, 530 Eng Bn
Bujole, Freddie, Sr. (D)	A		X							
	A									
Burham, Arthur (D)	A			X						
Butler, Clarence (D)	A		X							
Butler, Joseph (D)	A	X								
Butler, Royal (D)										PVT, 335 Service Bn., QMC
Cantreell, Henry (D)	A		X							
Cantrell, Dave J. (D)	A		X							
Cantrell, Gerald F. (D)	N		X							
Cantrell, Walter (D)	A		X							
Carter, Jimmie (D)	A	X								
Cayette, Carrol J., Sr.	A		X	X	X					LTC; Served in 3 world wars
Cayette, Harden	N							X		
Cayette, John	A	X								
Cayette, Joseph H. (D)	A	A		X						
Cayette, Leroy J. (D)	A	A				X				

	Branch	WWI	WWII	Korea	RVN	WWI	WWII	Korea	RVN	Comments
Cayette, Milton, Sr. (D)	A									
Cayette, Robert (D)	A									
Ceasar, Calvin (D)	CG			X						
Ceasar, Edward (D)	A		X							
Ceasar, Herbert T. (D)	N		X							
Celestin, Lionel M. (D)	MC				X					
Celestine, August C. (D)	A									
Celestine, Louis (D)	A									Killed in training
Celestine, Louis J.	A					X				
Celestine, Othello O. (D)	A							X		Artillery; Japan
Cerrier, Leon (D)	N									
Certin, Henry (D)	A		X							
Chapiede, Theral (D)	A			X						
Charles, Edward (D)	A	X								
Charles, Jimmy (D)	A					X				
Chiquet, Harold	A									
Chiquet, Percy	N									
Clark, Joseph (D)	A					X				
Clark, Roland J. (D)	A					X				
Clayton, Charley (D)	A		X							PVT, 508 Eng Svc Bn.
Clayton, Losten, Jr. (D)	A				X					
Clement, Alexander (D)	N(R)				X					
Collins, Arthur (D)	A			X						
Cooper, Adam, Sr. (D)	A			X						
Cooper, Earl (D)	A			X						
Cooper, Lloyd (D)	A			X						
Cooper, Robert (D)	A			X						
Cooper, Welton (D)	A			X						
Cunningham, Whitney (D)	A			X						
Davis, Clarence M. (D)				X						
Davis, Clarence M. (D)	A			X						

	Branch	Combat Service				Combat Era				Comments
		WWI	WWII	Korea	RVN	WWI	WWII	Korea	RVN	
Davis, Earl (D)	A									
Davis, Elliot, Sr. (D)	A			X						
Davis, Sterling (D)	A					X				
Davis, Wilmer, Jr. (D)										
Dennis, Wilfred (D)										
Deontine, Clarence	A					X				
Dickerson, Herman (D)	A								X	
Dillons, Joseph, Sr. (D)					X					
Doyle, Edmond (D)	A					X				
Dumas, Dennis T.	A									
Dumas, Neil P.	A			X						
Dumas, Russell M.	A				X					
Ellis, Charles, Jr. (D)	A		X							
Ellis, Lloyd (D)	N									
Ester, Walter, Jr. (D)	A									
Ezidore, Eddie E. (D)	A			X						
Ezidore, Norman (D)	N									
Farchaud, Kern J. (D)	A			X						
Farchaud, Willis, Sr. (D)	N			X						
Farlow, Ernest (D)	A			X						
Ferchaud, James J. (D)	A		X							
Ferchaud, John A. (D)	A		X							
Ferchaud, John B. (D)	AF				X					
Finnel, Alton (D)	A		X							
Florence, Edward, Jr. (D)	A									
Florent, James L.	A			X						
Fluence, Elijah E. (D)	A				X					
Fluence, Versey (D)	A			X						
Francois, Houston, Jr. (D)	A				X					
Franklin, Isaac E. (D)	A			X						
Gaines, Ferdinand, Jr. (D)	A						X			
Garrison, Lonnie (D)	A		X							
Garrison, Melvin (D)	A		X							
Garrison, Royal (D)	N			X						
Garrison, Smith E., Sr. (D)	A		X							
Gauthreaux, Ulysses O., Jr. (D)	A									

| | | Combat Service | | | | Combat Era | | | |
Branch	WWI	WWII	Korea	RVN	WWI	WWII	Korea	RVN	Comments
Geason, Robert, Jr. (D)	A			X					
George, Joseph (D).	A	X							PVT, Co C, 801 Pioneer Inf
Gibson, Ransom (D)	A	X							
Gistiver, Johns E. (D)	A		X						
Gladstone, Richard J. (D)	A		X						
Grady, Alfred, Jr. (D).	A	X							Co D, 418 Svc Bn
Grady, George (D)	A		X						
Green, Leonard (D)	A		X						
Green, Wilson (D) A X									
Griffin, Clarence (D)	N		X						
Griffin, Henry, Jr. (D)	A								
Griffin, Joseph (D).	A	X							PVT, I Co, 104 Depot Bn
Griffin, Wallace A., Jr. (D)	A				X				
Gros, Raymond L.	A			X					
Grove, Anthony A.	A				X				
Guidry, John (D)	A	X							
Hanslay, Clarence (D)	A		X						
Harris, Eddie, Sr. (D)	A		X						
Harris, Ernie (D)	AF								
Harris, Henry (D)	A		X						
Harris, Oliver, Sr. (D)			X						
Harris, Samuel (D)	A		X						PVT, Co K, 25 Inf.
Hawkins, Algie (D)	A								
Hawkins, Hal J. (D)	A								
Hayden, Spencer (D	A								
Henderson, Lawrence (D)	A					X			
Henderson, Lewis (D)	A		X						
Hill, Jack B. (D)	A		X						
Hill, Ozemee (D)	A				X				

	Branch	WWI	WWII	Korea	RVN	WWI	WWII	Korea	RVN	Comments
Hilliard, Lewis (D)	A		X							
Himes, Larry P. (D)	N				X					
Himes, Octave (D)	A									
Hitch, Freeman (D)	A	X								
Hogan. Joseph (D)	A	X								
Hogan, Edwin B. (D)	A					X				
Hogan, Wilbert W. (D)	A					X				
Holmes, Thomas (D)	A			X						
Hooper, Oliver, Sr. (D)	N		X							
Howard, Dave, Jr. (D)	A			X						
Jackson, Howard (D)	A	X								
Jackson, Kelly (D)	A		X							PVT
Jackson, Ladis (D)	A		X							
Jasmin, Armon	A		X							
Jasmin, Clarence, Sr. (D)	A		X							
Jasmin, John J., Sr.	A				X					
Jasmin, Joseph S., Sr. (D)	A		X							
Jasper, Charley (D)	A						X			
Jasper, Peter (D)	A		X							
Jetson, Howard L. (D)	A							X		
Johnson, Alfred (D)	A		X							
Johnson, Eddie (D)	A									PVT
Johnson, Edward (D)	A		X							
Johnson, Gerald J., Sr. (D)	A				X					
Johnson, Henderson C. (D)	A			X						
Johnson, Herman (D)	A				X					
Johnson, Isaac (D)	A		X							
Johnson, John, Sr. (D)	A		X							PVT
Johnson, Joseph (D)	A		X							
Johnson, Kenneth	A			X						
Johnson, Warren M. (D)	AF									
Jones, Albert, Sr. (D)	A									
Jones, Hayward, Jr. (D)	A			X						
Jones, Joseph J.	A			X						
Jones, Ulysses (D)	N							X		
Joseph, Alton (D)	A	X								

		Combat Service				Combat Era				
Branch	WWI	WWII	Korea	RVN	WWI	WWII	Korea	RVN	Comments
Joseph, August (D)	A	X								Co A, 508 Engr.
Joseph, Clarence (D)	A	X								PVT, 114 Svc Bn., QMC
Joseph, Edward (D)	A									
Joseph, Henry, Jr. (D)	A		X							SGT
Joseph, Herbert (D)	MC				X					
Joseph, Isaac	A									
Joseph, Jackie (D)	N									
Joseph, Raymond, Sr. (D)	A		X							
Joseph, Raymond, Sr. (D)	N		X							
Joseph, Samuel, Sr. (D)	A		X							
Joshua, Clifford, Sr. (D)	A		X							
Joshua, Clinton (D)	AF			X						
Joshua, Edgar J. (D)	A			X						
Joshua, Frank, Jr. (D)	N			X						
Joshua, Raymond (D)	A		X							
Keller, Charles	A		X							
Keller, Gufielle	A				X					
Keller, Morris, Jr.	A			X						
Kennard, Kelly (D)	N				X					
Kennedy, Lawrence, Sr. (S)	A		X							
Kent, Willis, Jr. (D)	A									
Ketchens, Charles D.	A				X					
King, Edward M. (D)	A		X							
Kraemer, Edward C.	A									
Landry, Carl (D)	A	X								PVT
Landry, Clarence (D)	A		X							PVT, 65 Pioneer Inf.
Landry, Furman (D)					X					
Landry, Lattis (D)	A	X								Co A, 65 Inf.
Landry, Louis M.	A				X					
Landry, Melvin P., Sr. (D)	A		X							

| | Combat Service | | | | Combat Era | | | | |
Branch	WWI	WWII	Korea	RVN	WWI	WWII	Korea	RVN	Comments
Lawrence, Willie (D)	A		X							1911-1978
Lebray, Herman (D)	A		X							
Lee, Manuel, Sr. (D)	A		X							
Lewis, Freddie (D)	N				X					
Lewis, Horace (D)	A		X							PVT, 418 Service Bn.
Lewis, John (D)	A		X							
Lewis, Thomas	MC									Purple Heart
Linton, Frank, Jr. (D)	N	X								
Louis, Joe (D)	A	X								
Love, Thomas, Jr. (D)	N (R)		X							
Lowery, Lionel, Sr. (D)	A									
Luke, Darryl J. (D)	A									
Luke, Percey J.	A				X					
Macklin, Madison (D)	AAC		X							
Macklin, Matthew (D)	A		X							
Macklin, Paul (D)	A		X							
Maloncon, Larry	A				X					
Manuel, Alexander, Sr. (D)	A			X						24 Amphibian Trk Co
Manuel, Alexander (D)	A				X					
Martin, Sam (D)	A	X								PFC, 409 Svc Bn, QMC
Martin, Valsin (D)	A		X							
Mayho, Eugene (D)	A		X							
Meggs, Nathan, Jr. (D)	N		X							
Meggs, Sidney, Sr. (D)	N		X							
Meggs, Walter J. (D)	A	X								
Meghee, Charles (D)	A			X						
Michael, Alvin J. (D)	MC				X					
Miller, Arthur (D)	A	X								55 Depot Brigade
Miller, Arthur, Sr. (D)	N				X					
Miller, Wilton J. (D)	A		X							
Mitchel, Nathaniel (D)	A				X					

| | | Combat Service | | | | Combat Era | | | |
	Branch	WWI	WWII	Korea	RVN	WWI	WWII	Korea	RVN	Comments
Mitchell, Charles (D)	A	X								
Mitchell, Henry (D)	A	X								ASF Training Cntr
Mitchell, Joseph, Jr. (D)	A	X								Co A, Develop. Bn.
Mitchell, Joseph W. (D)	A		X							
Mitchell, Leon (D)	A		X							
Mitchell, Ned (D)	A		X							
Mitchell, Ridgley, Jr.	A				X					
Monconduit, Albert	A									
Monconduit, Marks J. (D)	A		X							
Morris Horace, Jr. (D)	A									1918-1996
Morris, Clayton (D)	A		X							PFC
Mumford, Henderson (D)	N		X							
Mumford, James, Jr. (D)	A		X							
Mumphrey, Isiah T., Jr. (D)	A		X							
Nailer, Murphy (D)	A			X						
Narcisse, Felix K.	A				X					
Nelson, Paul, Sr. (D)	A									
Nelson, Richard M. (D)	A		X							
Nicholas, Carol J., Sr. (D)	A	X								
Nicholas, Carol J., Jr.	A		X						X	
Nicholas, Earl (D)	N		X	X	X					
Nicholas, Lynn (D)	A		X							
Nicholas, Russell J., Sr. (D)	A		X							
Nicholas, Russell	A		X					X		
Nicholas, Warren	A		X					X		
Octave, Arthur	A									
Octave, Edwin	A			X						
Octave, Willis	A									
Oubre, Larry A.	A				X					
Oubre, Raymond J.	A				X					
Oubre, Ursin A.				X						
Parker, Curley (D)	N									

	Combat Service				Combat Era				
	Branch	WWI	WWII	Korea	RVN	WWI	WWII	Korea	RVN	Comments
Parker, Peter (D)	A	X								PVT, 803 Pioneer Bn., Inf.
Parnell, Clarence, Jr. (D)	A		X							
Parness, Royal, Jr. (D)	A									1952-2003
Parquette. Hilton (D)	A				X					
Paul, Walter J. (D)	A									
Pedescleaux, Clarence	A									
Perkins, Fred, Jr. (D)	A				X					
Perkins, Johnny (D)	A		X							
Phillip, Marcus (D)	A		X							
Pierce, Phillip L. (D)										IO, U.S.C. H.A.
Pierre, Elex J., Sr. (D)	A		X							
Pierre, Joseph U.	A							X		
Pittman, Drew R., Sr. (D)	A			X						
Pittman, Walter F. (D)	A				X					
Porter, James, Jr.										
Porter, Joseph, Jr. (D)	A				X					
Prean, Lestie	A									
Preyan, Lesley C. (D)	A		X							
Price, Eddie, Jr. (D)	A	X								561 Depot Bde., 1896-1970
Randall, Matthew	A		X							
Ranson, Joseph A. (D)	A			X						
Raphall, Leroy	A				X					
Ray, Lenny (D)	A	X								PFC, 11 Depot, Labor Bn., QMC
Richardson, Victor (D)	A	X								
Robinson, Clarence, Jr. (D)	MC	X								
Robinson, John (D)	N	X								
Robinson, Joseph (D)	A	X								
Robinson, McDonough (D)	A		X							
Rodriguez, Jimmy (D)	A		X							

	Branch	Combat Service				Combat Era				Comments
		WWI	WWII	Korea	RVN	WWI	WWII	Korea	RVN	
Rodriguez, Matthew B. (D)	N								X	
Rollins, Simuel (D)	N							X		
Rosemond, Earl J. (D)	A X		X							
Roucell, John (D)	A		X							
Rousell, Wayne P.	A									
Roussel, Warren P.	A				X					
Saul, Donald	A				X					
Schexnayder, John B.	A		X							
Schexnayder, Stanley	A		X							
Scieneaux, Landry, Sr. (D)	A		X							
Scioneaux, Alcide (D)	A	X								PVT, Co C, 325 Svc Bn., QMC
Scott, Ralph, Jr. (D)	A									1921-1996
Scott, Richard (D)	A		X							
Scott, Samuel (D)	N		X							
Scott, Steven (D)	A				X					
Seals, Morris (D)	A						X			
Seals, Sullivan (D)	A	X								
Sias, Willie (D)	A						X			
Smith, Earl, Sr. (D)	N						X			
Smith, Edward, Sr. (D)	A									
Smith, Israel (D)	A	X								PFC
Smith, Jimmy L. (D)	A				X					
Smith, Kitry (D)	A		X							
Smith, Stafford, Jr. (D)	A		X							
Soloman, Jerry (D)	A	X								523 Svc Bn., Engr. Corps
Sorrell, Harry J., Sr. (D)	N		X							
Stafford, George (D)	A	X								PVT, 419 Labor Bn., QMC
Stanton, Thomas (D)	A									
Steib, Joseph E.	A			X						
Stevens, Lawrence, Sr. (D)	A									
Stevens, Warren, Sr. (D)	A				X					PFC

		Combat Service				Combat Era				
	Branch	WWI	WWII	Korea	RVN	WWI	WWII	Korea	RVN	Comments
Steward, Nathan (D)	A	X								
Stewart, Edward, Sr. (D)	A				X					
Stewart, Willie (D)	A	X								Co G, 371 Inf. Bn.
Sutherland, Charles	A		X							
Sutherland, John J. (D)	A		X							
Taylor, Arthur A. (D)	A		X							
Taylor, Henry (D)	A	X								
Taylor, Henry W. (D)	A						X			
Theramafor (D)	A	X								
Thomas, Israel, Sr. (D)	A		X							
Tollins, Ben (D)	A	X								
Tribit, Henry A., Jr. (D)	A		X							
Ursin, Wilbert, Sr. (D)	N		X							
Variste, William A. (D)	A			X						
Vincent, James (D)	A		X							
Wallace, Henry (D)	A	X								
Waters, Raymond	A				X					
Watkins, Jesse, Jr. (D)	A			X						
Webber, Allen A.	A									
Weber, Joseph E. (D)	A		X							
Wells, Edmon (D)	A		X							
White, Joseph (D)	A	X								AB, Co B, 349 Maint. Bn.
Williams, Andrew (D)	A		X							
Williams, Charles (D)	A		X							PVT
Williams, Corneileus, Jr.	A									
Williams, Corneileus, Sr.	A		X							
Williams, James, Jr. (D)	A		X							
Williams, Joseph (D)	A		X							
Williams, Milton R. (D)	AF									
Williams, Nezar (D)	A		X							
Williams, Robert (D)	N		X							
Williams, Sylvester (D)	MC		X							
Williby, Sheridan, Sr. (D	A		X							
Wilson, Eddie (D)	A	X								
Wilson, Matthew (D)	A	X								PVT, Co C, 526 Eng

	Branch	Combat Service				Combat Era				Comments
		WWI	WWII	Korea	RVN	WWI	WWII	Korea	RVN	
Wilson, Matthew (D)	A	X								PVT, Co. B, 526 Eng
Wiltz, Adam (D)	A			X						
Winchester, Charles (D)	A		X							
Winchester, Clarence	A									
Winchester, John R. (D)	A				X					
Winchester, John, Sr. (D)	A		X							
Winchester, John	A									
Winfield, Arthur (D)	A	X								
Woodfolk, Eddie B. (D)	N		X							
Woodley, Clairiborne (D)	A		X							Casual Detachment
Woodly, Henry (D)	A		X							
Woods, Kermit, Sr. (D)	A		X							
Woods, Sidney	A									
Woodson, Dave (D)	A		X							
Woodson, James (D)	A						X			
Wright, William	A	X								PVT
Wyre, Willis, Jr. (D)	A						X			
Young, Vince C. (D)	A									
Young, Willis	A				X					

Legend:

AF	Air Force
A	Army
ASF	Army Service Forces
(D)	Deceased
Bn.	Battalion
CG	Coast Guard
Co.	Company
Dpt.	Depot
Det.	Detachment
Eng	Engineers
Inf.	Infantry
LTC	Lieutenant Colonel
Maint.	Maintenance
MC	Marine Corps
N	Navy
N(R)	Navy (Reserve)
PFC	Private First Class
PVT	Private
QMC	Quartermaster Corps
Rec.	Records
SGT	Sergeant
Svc	Service
Trk	Truck

ASCENSION PARISH VETERANS

	Combat Service				Combat Era				
Branch	WWI	WWII	Korea	RVN	WWI	WWII	Korea	RVN	Comments
Adams, Willie (D) A		X							
Adams. Ricky N									1986-2001
Aikens, Ardis (D) A		X							Tech SGT-5
Alexander, Joseph (D) A		X							
Anderson, Alfred (D) N									
Alexander, Joseph A				X					SGT-5, 1965-67
Armstead, Calvin (D) A				X					1931-1993
August, Robert (d) A		X							
Augusta, A. G. (D) A						X			
Augusta, Charles G. (D) A				X					SGT
Bailey, Alex A				X					
Bailey, Lawrence (D) A									519 QM Reg. 1920-43
Baily, Dauf (D) A						X			SGT
Baily, Dauf B. (D) A						X			SGT
Baily, Lawrence (D) A		X							1920-1943
Baily, Promise A						X			
Baily, Willie (D)									
Baker, Willie A. (D) A				X					
Bakerm Palmer L. A						X			
Banks, Joseph MC									1959-63
Banks, Spencer A									
Barrow, Robert (D)									
Bartley, Earnest, Sr. (D) A		X							
Batiste, Emile (D) A		X							SGT, 1928-1979
Batiste, Herbert (D) A			X						1960-63
Batiste, Herbert (D) A								X	527 Inf. 1941-1963
Batiste, Rougon N			X						
Baughn, Anaias J. (D) A		X							
Bedley, Lon V. A				X					
Bell, Charles B., Sr. (D) A			X						

	Branch	Combat Service				Combat Era				Comments
		WWI	WWII	Korea	RVN	WWI	WWII	Korea	RVN	
Bell, Clinton (D)	A				X					
Bell, Lloyd (D)	A			X						
Bennett, Alvin L. (D)	A			X						
Billy, Alton C. (D)	AF				X					
Bizer, Clarence (D)	A								X	
Blouin, Ray E., Jr.	AF		X							1973-1976
Blouin, Ray E., Sr. (D)	N		X							
Braudy, James (D)	A		X							CPL
Breaux, Albert B. (D)	A		X							
Breaux, Alfred J. (D)	A		X							
Brimmer, Clarence J., Sr.	A				X					BSM, PH
Brimmer, Lloyd, Sr. (D)	A		X		X					
Bringier, John D. (D)	A									1927-1964
Brisco, James B. (D)	A									SP4, 1950-2001
Brooks, Daniel (D)	A	X								PVT, 1886-1977
Brooks, Donald Ray	A			X						SGT-5, 82 AC, ACM, 1969-71
Brooks, Edward C. (D)	A								X	
Brooks, Ezzard	A								X	
Brown, Earl	A							X		
Brown, Henry L, Sr. (D)	A		X							
Brown, Henry L. (D)	A			X						
Brown, James (D)	N		X							
Brown, Johnny, Jr. (D)	A		X							
Brown, Jonny, Jr. (D)	A		X							
Brown, Joseph T., Jr. (D)										
Brown, Leslie	A		X							
Brown, Nelson (D)	A	X								Co C, 814 Pioneer Inf.
Brown, Ulyess (D)	A		X	X						KIA 1951
Burgess, Sam F. (D)	A		X							BSM; PH
Burl, Richard (D)	A								X	
Burnett, Joseph H. (D)	MC			X						
Burns, Alexander (D)	A		X							

	Combat Service				Combat Era				
	Branch	WWI	WWII	Korea	RVN	WWI	WWII	Korea	RVN	Comments
Burns, Frank (D)	N									
Burns, Joshua S. (D)	N		X							
Bush, Clarence B., Sr.	A			X						
Bush, Joseph (D)	A		X							24 In. Div
Bush, Vincent (D)	A		X							
Butler, Felton R. (D)	A				X					Major
Butler, Lawrence W. (D)	A		X							1922-1997
Campbell, Daniel (D)	A	X								Inf. 1898-1969
Canty, Albert, Jr. (D)	A		X							
Canty, Robert (D)										
Canty, Emile (D)										1916-1975
Capron, Clyde B.										
Carter, Frank (D)	A				X					
Castery, Lawrence A. (D)										
Castor, Lawrence A.										
Cato, James (D)	A	X								
Ceasar, Felton C.	AF								X	1955-59
Ceasar, Leonard	A									1955-58
Chapman, Clarence (D)	A									SP4 Med Co; 1955-1966
Chapman, Tyrone B. (D)	AF									1949-2008
Chapman, Vernon D.										
Chatman, Roy C.	A								X	SP-5, AAO Sig Bn., 1967-69
Chefney, Mitchell (D)	A	X								PVT
Christy, Larry	A								X	
Christy, Leo	A		X							
Christy, James P. (D)	A		X							
Clark, Buddy (D)	A	X								PVT 1893-1972
Clark, Royal, Jr. (D)	A	X								
Colbert, James E.										
Coleman, Alexander (D)	A	X								1890-1972 QMC

		Combat Service				Combat Era				
	Branch	WWI	WWII	Korea	RVN	WWI	WWII	Korea	RVN	Comments
Coleman, Eddie, Sr. (D)	A		X							
Coler, Clarence										
Collins, Ford (D)	A	X								
Collins, Lionel	A								X	SGT 11 Airbn. 1952-54
Collins, Percy (D)	A		X							
Collins, Rush, Jr.	A							X		PFC 1952-1954
Comeaux, Andrew (D)	A				X					
Comeaux, Ronald, Sr.	A									SSG (Ret.) 1979-2004
Cooker, Leslie (D)										
Cox, Frank H. (D)	A		X							
Cutno, Daniel (D)	A		X							
Daggs, Anthony (D)	A	X								348 Labor Bn. QMC 1895-46
Daggs, Wardell (D)	A		X							
Delaney, James (D)	A	X								1896-1984
Demesme, Elliot R. (D)	A		X							562 Port Co, TC
Dempsey, Rudolph	A		X							
Dennis, Stanford L. (D)	A				X					
Diggs, Frank	A									
Diggs, Thomas, Sr. (D)	A		X		X					SP4 ACM 1970-1977
Diggs, Willie, J. (D)	F		X							
Dixon, George, Jr. (D)	A		X							
Dominick, Edward, Sr. (D)	N		X							
Dominique, Roger J. (D)	A		X							
Domio, James (D)	A			X						
Dorsey, Robert	A			X	X					Retired
Dright, Albert	AF									1959-1963
Dright, Preston	AF									
Dudley, Leo	A			X	X					Retired
Dugas, Leonard (D)	A			X						

CURTIS J. JOHNSON

		Combat Service				Combat Era			
	Branch	WWI	WWII	Korea	RVN	WWI	WWII	Korea	RVN	Comments
Dunbar, Edward L. (D)	A			X						
Dupard, Alfred (D)	A		X							
Dupard, Freddie (D)	A		X							
Duplush, Thomas, Sr.	A		X							
Earl, Frank (D)										
Earl, Sampson (D)	A		X							
Earl, Samson (D)	A		X							
Earl, Woodrow	A		X							
Earl, Woodrow W. (D)	A		X							
Earvin, Heary (D)	A		X							
Edwards, Joe (D)	A		X							
Edwards, Vincent (D)	A	X								416 Res Labor Bn. QMC
Elam, Joseph, Jr. (D)	A		X							
Elliot, Emile (D)	A		X							
Elliot, Emile (D)	A	X								Engr. Svc Bn. 1894-67
Etienne, Hebert	A			X						
Etienne, Lawrence G. (D)	N		X							
Ewen, Earl J. (D)	A	X								2d Lt, 1895-1973
Fernandez, Cherie	A			X						CPL 1951-1956
Fletcher, Alfred M. (D)	A	X								1883-1946
Ford, Albion, Sr. (D)	A		X							
Foster, Jim (D)	A		X							
Francis, Herbert	A									
Francis, John E., Sr. (D)	N			X						
Francis, John, Jr. (D)	A								X	
Francis, John Edgar, Sr. (D)	N		X							1942-1945
Francis, Kenneth	N				X					
Francis, Lionel	A	X								
Francis, Lionel (D)	A							X		1960-63
Francis, Roland	N								X	

Name	Branch	Combat Service				Combat Era				Comments
		WWI	WWII	Korea	RVN	WWI	WWII	Korea	RVN	
Francis, Stanley	A							X		
Francis, William	A								X	
Francis, Williams	A							X		
Francis, Willie (D)	A		X							Under GEN Patton
Frank, Carter (D)	A				X					
Franklin, Clarence	A					X				
Franklin, Clarence	A		X							
Franklin, Douglas W. (D)	A			X						
Frazier, Lawson (D)	A	X								1890-1964
French, Kennet	A		X							
Gaines, Clarence (D)	A	X								1886-1967
Gallon, Clarence A. (D)	A									
Garnett, Albert (D)	A	X								1895-1973
Garret, Albert (D)	A	X								
Garrett, Albert (D)	A	X								1895-1973
Gauthreaux, Edward J.	A				X					SP4 1968-1971
Gibson, Curtis (D)	A									
Gilbert, James (D)	A		X							
Gipson, Clarence	AF									
Gipson, Ronald	A				X					SP4 1966-1967
Godcheaux, Benjamin	AF		X							
Gomez, August J.	A									SP-4, Panama, 1969-71
Gomez, Purcel (D)	A									
Goodwin, William E., Sr. (D)	N		X							
Gorden, Frank H.									X	2 RVN Tours; LOM
Grady, Nace (D)	A	Spanish-American War								US Vol. Inf.
Granderson, Garnett, Jr. (D)	A		X							
Graves, Nathaniel	A								X	MSGT ACM w/3OLC

		Combat Service				Combat Era				
	Branch	WWI	WWII	Korea	RVN	WWI	WWII	Korea	RVN	Comments
Gray, Charles, Sr. (D)	A		X							CPL
Gray, Charley (D)	A		X							
Gray, Charlie (D)										
Gray, Elvin, Jr.	A			X						
Green, Chester	A									
Green, Chester H.	AAC		X							
Green, Cornelius (D)	A	X								1891-1965
Green, Cornelius, Jr. (D)	A		X							
Hall, Lawrence A. (D)	N		X							
Hall, Cleveland (D)	A		X							
Hall, Daniel (D)	A	X								1895-1973
Hall, Lenix (D)	A	X								
Hardy, William M., Sr. (D)	A	X								
Harris, Herman, Sr. (D)	A	X								
Harris, John A. (D)	A									
Harris, John B. (D)	A	X								Bugler, 805 Pioneer Inf.
Harris, John H. (D)	A	X								
Harris, Leon (D)	A		X							
Harris, Will, Sr. (D)	A	X								PFC 1891-1979
Hawkins, Cantrelle, Jr.	A				X					SP4 1970-1976
Heary, Eirvin (D)	AAC		X							
Henderson, Leonard (D)	A							X		
Henderson, Leonard L. (D)	A									
Hendricks, Alphonse, Jr.	A			X						
Hendricks, Gary	A			X						
Henry, Warren (D)	A									
Hill, Joseph H., IV	A				X					SP5 1966-1968
Hill, Walter P. (D)	A		X							
Hilliard, Joseph, Sr. (D)	A		X							
Hilliard, Roberts D. (D)	A		X							PFC 169 Inf.
Hogaun, Joseph (D)	A	X								1889-1923
Holland, Joseph (D)	A	X								

| | Combat Service | | | | Combat Era | | | | |
	Branch	WWI	WWII	Korea	RVN	WWI	WWII	Korea	RVN	Comments
Hudson, Joseph (D)	A		X							
Huey, Wilbert (D)	N		X							
Irvin, Randolph (D)	A	X								CPL 518 Svc Bn. QMC
Irvin, Willie (D)	A		X							
Irvin, Willie (D)	A		X							
Irwin, Joseph H.										
Jackson, Aaron (D)	A		X		X					
Jackson, Edward (D)	A		X							
Jackson, Erin (D)	A		X							
Jackson, Ernest R. (D)	MC					X				
Jackson, Lucius M. (D)	A		X							
Jackson, Shredword (D)										
Jackson, Valsum	A		X							
Jackson, Vernel	AF									
Jackson, Wilson, Jr. (D)	A		X							
Jacob, Barnard (D)	A				X					1951-1953, Alaska
Jacob, Huber	A		X							25 Inf. Div
Jacob, Roland	A		X							1097 Combat Eng
James, Alma (D)	A		X							
James, Cleveland (D)	A									1921-1984
James, Eyvest J., Sr. (D)										
James, Eyvest J., Jr.	A		X							
Jenkins, John H. (D)	A		X							
Johnson, Alex (D)	A			X						
Johnson, Curtis J.	A				X			X		LTC BSM
Johnson, Earnest (D)	A		X							
Johnson, Emile, Jr. (D)	N		X							
Johnson, Emile, Sr. (D)	A	X								1895-1967
Johnson, Ernest (D)	A		X							
Johnson, Herman (D)	X		X							
Johnson, Gus (D)	A		X							
Johnson, Jack, Jr. (D)	A			X						

	Branch	WWI	WWII	Korea	RVN	WWI	WWII	Korea	RVN	Comments
Johnson, Joseph, Sr. (D)	A	X								49 Co, 161 Depot Bde
Johnson, Louis (D)	A									
Johnson, Matley (D)	A	X								415 Labor Bn. 1892-1961
Johnson, Natley (D)	A	X								Co D, 415 Res Labor Bn.
Johnson, Royal (D)	A		X							
Johnson, Victor (D)	A		X							
Johnson, Walter E. (D)	A		X							Allutian Islands
Johnson, Wellington										
Johnson, Willie (D)	A		X							
Jones, Eldriede I. (D)	A		X							
Jones, Eldriedge I. (D)	A		X							
Jones, Henry, Jr.	A			X						BSM
Jones, Henry, Sr. (D)	A		X							
Jones, Jerrold A. (D)	A									1961-2003
Jones, Larry										
Jones, Larry W. (D)	A									1949-1977
Jones, Lawrence R. (D)	MC									1957-1990
Jones, Leon (D)	A			X						1st LT
Jones, Paul (D)	A	X								PVT Co I, 805 Inf. 1896-71
Jones, Raphall O. (D)	A		X							
Jones, Sirley O. (D)	A		X							
Jones, Willie (D)	N		X							
Joseph, Albert, Jr. (D)	N									
Joseph, Clarence, Jr. (D)	N		X							
Joseph, Clifton, Sr. (D)	A		X							
Joseph, Edward, Jr. (D)	A		X							
Joseph, Edward, Jr. (D)	A		X							
Joseph, Jessie	MC								X	1960-65; Hawaii
Joseph, Junior, Sr. (D)	A		X							
Joseph, Oliver	MC						X			Gunnery SGT

| | Combat Service | | | | Combat Era | | | | |
	Branch	WWI	WWII	Korea	RVN	WWI	WWII	Korea	RVN	Comments
Joseph, Vernon A., Sr. (D)	MC		X							
Joshua, Claude	A								X	1960-1963
Joshua, Subert B. (D)	N		X							
Julien, Clifford	A			X						
Julien, Floyd	A							X		SP5 1960-1963
Julien, Januile (D)	A	X								1890-1958
Julien, Junius	A			X						CWO-04 Helicopter Pilot
Julien, Leonard, Jr.	A				X					Germany
Julien, Mack	A									
Julien, Michael, Sr.	N				X					Germany
Julien, Oscar J.	MC									
Julien, Raymond (D)	A									
Julien, Romel	AF			X						SGT 1967-1971
Keller, Eddie (D)	A		X							
Kenner, Nicholas (D)	A	X								Co C, 416 Res Labor Bn.
Kinsey, Ben (D)	A	X								306 Labor Bn. 1894-72
Kinsey, Lionel	A	X								
Knight, George (D)	A						X			
LaBlanc, Clevelamd (D)	A									
Lacey, Isaiah (D)	A		X							
Landry, Edward (D)	A		X							SFC
Landry, Frank (D)		X								1888-1979
Landry, Kernel (D)	A	X								1887-1979
Landry, Paul H. (D)	N									
Landry, Preston J.	A				X				X	LTC, BSM
Landry, Ulysses	A						X			
Lang, Adam (D)	A		X	X						
Larks, Earnest	A		X							
Larks, Horsey S. (D)										

| | Combat Service | | | | Combat Era | | | | |
Branch	WWI	WWII	Korea	RVN	WWI	WWII	Korea	RVN	Comments
Larks, Robert J. (D) — A		X							SGT, 590 Port Co, TC
Lawrence, Robert (D) — A		X							Tech SGT-5
Lawson, Earnel (D)									
Lawson, Earnest (D) — A		X							Tech SGT-5
Lawson, Emmit — AF			X						
Lawson, Ernest (D) — A		X							Tech SGT-5
Lawson, John — A									Greenland 1961-63
Lawson, Joseph (D) — N									
Lawson, Leonard (D)									
Lawson, Woodrow (D)									
Leban, Gerald (D) — A		X							SFC, 1945
LeBlanc, Cleavlen — A		X							Tech SGT 5
LeBlanc, Alton — A									
LeBlanc, Alton — AF									
LeBlanc, Bernard — A									
LeBlanc, Clifford — A		X							
LeBlanc, Edward J. (D) — A		X							
LeBlanc, Gerald (D) — A									
LeBlanc, Martinel — A									
LeBlanc, Murphy									
LeBlanc, Reginald (D) — A			X						KIA, PH
Lee, Eddie — A		X							
Leggett, Johnson, Sr. (D) — A		X							
Lemann, Arthur (D) — N									
Lemay, Sylvester (D) — A		X							
Lemay, Sylvester (D) — A		X							
Leon, Claudell (D) — N									
Levy, Arthur — A					X				PH
Levy, Rufus A. — A			X						
Lewis, Clarence D. (D) — N		X							
Lewis, Isiah (D) — A		X							QMC
Lewis, Johnny, Jr. — A		X							

	Branch	Combat Service				Combat Era				Comments
		WWI	WWII	Korea	RVN	WWI	WWII	Korea	RVN	
Lewis, Lilton J. (D)	N		X							
Lewis, Lilton, Jr. (D)	N		X							
Lewis, Mckinley	A			X						
Lewis, Michael	A									
Lewis, Thomas	MC				X					PH; '69-'70 Disabled-Ret
Little, Joseph H. (D)	A	X								CPL, Co C, 24 Inf. 1888-62
Lomas, Eddie L.										
Lonas, Walter (D)	A		X							
London, Joseph, Sr. (D)	A		X							
London, Lawrence H. (D)	A		X							
Lotten, Eugene	A			X						
Lotten, Huit E. (D)	N		X							1942-1944
Lotten, Sterling (D)	A		X							
Marks, Robert (D)	A		X							
Martin, Leander	A			X						
Materre, Freddie L., Jr. (D)	A		X							
Mattere, Alfred (D)	A		X							
McGalliard, Claude, Jr. (D)	N									
MaGalliard, Floyd (D)	N		X							1927-1988
McGee, Allie (D)	A	X								1896-1977
McKinney, Charles A. (D)	A			X						25 Inf. Div, SP-4, KIA, PH
McKinney, Edward (D)	A		X							
McKinney, Wayne	A									
Medise, Herman (D)	A		X							
Megee, Allie (D)	A	X								1896-1977
Melancon, Joseph, Jr.	A		X							
Meyers, Henry (D)	A	X								
Meyers, Julius (D)	A	X								PVT 1888-1975

		Combat Service				Combat Era				
	Branch	WWI	WWII	Korea	RVN	WWI	WWII	Korea	RVN	Comments
Milan, Curtis (D)	A	X								PVT 161 Depot Bde
Milan, Curtis P. (D)	A	X								PVT Depot Bde
Miles, Leander										
Miles, Leandrew										
Miller, Dave, Jr.	A			X						
Mills, Earnest (D)	MC		X							
Moore, George (D)	A	X								
Moses, Armsey, Jr.	A		X							
Moses, Frank, Sr. (D)	A									SGT 1928-2004
Motten, Irvin	A			X						CPL 1952-1954
Mulberry, Herbert	A		X							
Nabor, Charlie										
Nabor, Smith										
Nahur, Charles (D)										
Natrar, Smith, Sr. (D)										
Nelson, Scott (D)	A	X								
North, Clarence (D)	A	X								
Oliver, James (D)	A	X								PFC 1900-1961
Parms, Isaac, Sr. (D)	A		X							
Patterson, Kevin	AF								X	Europe 1970-1979
Patterson, Marion					X					
Paul, Irving E. (D)	N		X							
Pedescleaux, Charles	A		X							PFC 1942-1945
Pedescleaux, Clarence (D)	A		X							TECH-SGT E-5
Pedescleaux, Dennis (D)	A		X							
Pedescleaux, Earnest (D)	A									
Pedescleaux, Victor	A		X							
Peters, Herman (D)	A		X							
Pine, Richard (D)	A		Spanish American War							92 US Colored Inf.

	Combat Service				Combat Era				
Branch	WWI	WWII	Korea	RVN	WWI	WWII	Korea	RVN	Comments
Pinkins, Eddie, Jr. (D) — A		X							
Pinkney, Willard (D) — A		X							
Populars, Horace L., Sr. (D) — N		X							
Populars, Horace L., Sr. (D) — A		X							
Porter, Clarence — A		X							
Preston, Leroy I. (D) — A		X							SFC
Quezaire, Carl — N									1958-1962
Quezaire, Conrad — A									1960-1982
Reed, Owen H. (D) — A		X							
Reynard, Herman — A									Germany
Rhodes, Ronald R. (D) — A		X							
Ricard, Albert — MC						X			
Ricard, Leroy — A									1960-63
Ricardo, Charles R. — A							X		
Ricardo, Ralph E. — A									1st LT, Company CO
Ricardo, Walter, Jr. (D) — A			X						KIA; PH
Richard, Arthur — AF									1962-1966
Richard, Tyrone									
Riley, George D.									
Riley, Reginald (D) — A		X							KIA; PH
Riley, William D. (D) — A		X							
Robinson, Charles (D) — A	Spanish American War								US Vol. Inf.
Robinson, Clarence, Sr. (D) — N		X							
Robinson, Richard W. (D) — MC			X						
Rodrigue, Allen (D) — A			X						
Rodrigue, Emanuel (D) — A									PVT
Rodrigue, Wendell (D) — A									
Rogge, Fred (D) — A									1940
Rollins, Oscar — A		X	X						
Rome, Edward, Jr. (D) — A		X							
Rome, James A., Sr. (D) — A		X							

	Combat Service				Combat Era				
	Branch	WWI	WWII	Korea	RVN	WWI	WWII	Korea	RVN	Comments
Ross, Charles, Jr. (D)	AAC		X							
Ross, Charlie J. (D)	AF		X	X						
Russer, Richard (D)	A	X								
Sanders, Isom, Jr.	A		X							SGT
Sandres, Cleven	A		X							
Schomberg, Charles	N									1955-1960
Schomberg, Earl	A		X							CSM (Ret), 1961-1991
Schomberg, Errol					X					
Schomberg, Ralph (D)	A									
Scott, Earnest (D)										
Scott, Edward J.										
Scott, Ellery (D)	A	X								65 Pioneer Inf. 1891-1957
Shelton, Claude	A									
Shelvin, Willie (D)	MC		X							
Shelvin, Willie (D)	MC			X						
Simmons, Vallery L. (D)	A		X							
Simms, Vernon C. (D)	N		X							
Simms, Asa C., Jr. (D)	AF									LTC PHD 1919-99
Sims, Leroy	A									SP5 Alaska 1958-62
Sims, Percy	A		X							MSG, Airport Security, 1942-45
Sims, Wilmer S. (D)	A		X							
Singer, Berthold C. (D)	N			X						
Singer, Eddie J. (D)	N									1931-1958
Small, Vernon L. (D)	A		X							
Smith, Aaron (D)	A	X								1895-1996
Bringier, John B. (D)	A									1927-1964
Smith, Aaron (D)	A	X								Co. C, 913 Pioneer Inf.
Smith, Clinton (D)	A			X						
Smith, Henry	A	X								
Smith, Isiah (D)	A		X							

	Combat Service					Combat Era				
	Branch	WWI	WWII	Korea	RVN	WWI	WWII	Korea	RVN	Comments
Smith, Issac	A								X	SP-5, 1969-1973
Smith, James H.	A				X					PH
Smith, Joseph J. (D)	A		X							
Smith, Nabor, Sr. (D)	A		X							
Smith, Oscar J. (D)	MC			X						1927-1982
Spears, Pouylas										
St. Amant, Joseph (D)	A		X							
Stephens, Paris H.	A		X							
Stephens, Peter	A		X							
Stevens, Joseph	A		X							
Stevens, Peter (D)	AAC		X							PFC 1912-1987
Stevens, Phillip (D)	A				X					1921-1996
Stevenson, Ivory F. (D)	A		X							
Stevenson, Ivory F., Jr. (D)	A			X						
Stewart, Edward	A								X	
Stewart, Jerry (D)	A			X						
Stewart, John (D)	A	X								Co G, 92 US Col Inf.
Sykes, Bruce E. (D)	A									PFC; 1908-1989
Taylor, Arthur	A		X							
Taylor, Herman (D)	A			X	X					CSM, BSM
Taylor, James, Jr.	A			X						
Taylor, James, Sr. (D)	A		X							
Taylor, James, Sr.	AF			X						
Taylor, Robert, Sr. (D)	N		X							
Taylor, Ronald L.	AF				X					
Taylor, Shedrick M. (D)	A		X							
Thomas, Aldrich	A								X	SP4 1963-1965
Thomas, Curtis (D)	N		X							
Thomas, Willard (D)	A		X							
Thompson, Arthur (D)	A									1912-1989

	Branch	WWI	WWII	Korea	RVN	WWI	WWII	Korea	RVN	Comments
Thompson, Bryon	A									SGT 1921-1984
Nabor, Smith (D)	A		X							
Thompson, Earl (D)	A									1920-1995
Thompson, Earl (D)	A									1920-1995
Thompson, Edward	A		X							
Thompson, Edward (D)	A									1916-2005
Thompson, George, Jr.	AF									Spain, Japan 1959-63
Thompson, George, Sr. (D)	N		X							
Thompson, James	A			X						
Thompson, Lushon (D)	A									323 Trans Co, Mess SGT
Thompson, Oliver	AF									1960-64
Thompson, Robert	AF									1964-68
Tircuit, James C. (D)	A		X							Med Dept, 1914-1964
Traveler, Walter P., Sr.										
Valentin, John (D)	A									1912-1987
Vallery, William (D)	A		X							CPL
Vaughn, Anaias (D)	A		X							
Vaughn, Henry, Jr. (D)	A	X	X							
Veal, Albert, Jr. (D)	A			X						
Veal, Albert, Sr. (D)	A		X							
Veal, Ruffin (D)	A		X							
Victor, Isaac (D)	AAC		X							
Victor, James M., Jr.	A		X							TECH SGT E-5 1942-45
Victor, Valcin, Jr. (D)	A			X						
Walker, Booker T. (D)	A									
Walker, Claude H. (D)	A									1938-1994
Walker, Daniel (D)	A		X							
Walker, Joseph (D)	A			X						
Walker, Mansfield	N		X							
Walker, Stanford	A								X	1959-62

	Branch	WWI	WWII	Korea	RVN	WWI	WWII	Korea	RVN	Comments
Washington, Joseph (D)										
Washington, Melvin (D)	N		X							
Washington, Robert	A			X						
Watson, Willis P. (D)	A		X							
Webb, Robert (D)	A		X							
Welford, Buck (D)	A	X								Co A 7 Dev Bn. 1895-61
Wells, Lewelton (D)	A	X								
West, John	A		X							
West, John H.	A		X							
West, John H. (D)	A		X							
West, Joseph W. (D)	A		X							
West, Lee N. (D)	A									SP4; 1939-1988
West, Lionel	A			X						
White, Ernest L.										
White, Jimmy (D)	N		X							
Wilkins, Willie	AF									1960-64
Williams, Andrew (D)	A	X								Co H, 419 Res Labor Bn.
Williams, Angelin (D)	A	X								
Williams, Frank (D)	N		X							PFC 327 Inf. 1941-1963
Williams, Frank S. (D)	N		X							
Williams, Geary (D)										
Williams, Harris (D)	AF									1941-2007
Williams, Haywood (D)	A		X							
Williams, Haywood (D)	A		X							
Williams, Henry P. (D)	A	X								1888-1987
Williams, James	A									
Williams, John, Sr. (D)	A	X								Co A, 349 Labor Bn.
Williams, Leroy (D)	MC			X						
Williams, Louis, Jr. (D)	A									1920-1998
Williams, Louis, Sr. (D)	A									

| | Combat Service | | | | Combat Era | | | | |
	Branch	WWI	WWII	Korea	RVN	WWI	WWII	Korea	RVN	Comments
Williams, Ronald	A						X			1966-69; Germany
Williams, Thomas										
Williams, Thomas J. (D)	A			X						
Williams, Willie	A							X		
Williams, Willie (D)	A									
Willis, Hillious (D)	A	X								1896-1979
Willis, James G.	A				X					PH
Willis, Taylor (D)	A	X								1893-1968
Wilson, Davelin	A			X						PH; a.k.a. David Moore
Winchester, John, Jr.	A			X						
Winfrey, Raymond (D)			X							
York, Areluas	A	X								
York, Darryl L. (D)	A									1974-2000
York, Eddie, Sr.	A	X								
York, Orelious (D)	A	X								PFC, TC 1893-1966
Young, Ellis (D)	A	X								
Young, Eluies, Jr. (D)	A	X								
Young, James R. (D)										
Young, Lloyd	A		X							
Youngs, Joseph (D)	MC	X								
Zeno, Ayo (D)	A	X								162 Depot Bde

Legend:

A	Army
ACM	Army Commendation Medal
AAC	Army Air Corps
AF	Air Force
Abn	Airborne
Arty	Artillery
Bn.	Battalion
Bde	Brigade
BSM	Bronze Star Medal
CAV	Cavalry
CSM	Command Sergeant Major (-9)
CWO	Chief Warrant Officer
CSM	Command Sergeant Major
CPL	Corporal E-4
(D)	Deceased
Div	Division
Eng	Engineers
1st SG	First Sergeant E-8
Inf	Infantry
KIA	Killed in Action
LOM	Legion of Merit
LT	Lieutenant
LTC	Lieutenant Colonel
MAJ	Major
MC	Marine Corps
MSG	Master Sergeant E-8
N	Navy
OLC	Oak Leaf Cluster
Ord	Ordnance
PVT	Private E-1 or E-2
PFC	Private First Class E-3
PH	Purple Heart
QMC	Quartermaster Corps
Reg.	Regiment
Res	Reserves
RVN	Republic of Vietnam
SGT	Sergeant E-5
SSG	Staff Sergeant E-6

CURTIS J. JOHNSON

SFC	Sergeant First Class E-7
SM	Sergeant Major E-9
Sig	Signal
SP-4	Specialist E-4
Svc	Service
Tech	Technical
TC	Transportation Corps
WWI	World War I
WWII	World War II

ASSUMPTION PARISH VETERANS

		Combat Service				Combat Era				
	Branch	WWI	WWII	Korea	RVN	WWI	WWII	Korea	RVN	Comments
Adams, Levy (D)	A		X							PVT 1898-1988
Adams, Samuel, Sr. (D)	A		X							CPL 1918-1993
Adams, Williams (D)	A		X							CPL 866Port Co 1920-1966
Alcorn, Vernon (D)	A		X							
Alexander, James (D)	A		X							
Allen, Frank (D)	A		X							PVT 1921-1968
Allen, Raymond (D)	A	X								PVT 1892-1973
Allen, Thomas J. (D)	A									SGT 1947-1877
Allen, Timothy (D)	A									1922-2008
Alsay, Horace	A		X							
Anders, John J. (D)	A									1918-1975
Anderson, Edward (D)	A		X							
Anderson, Richard (D)	A				X					PVT 1845-2008
Arnold, George (D)	A	X								PFC 328 Svc Bn. 1896-53
Arnold, Westley (D)	A									PVT 1895-1971
Atkins, James (D)	A	X								PVT 1891-1958
Atrand, Elmo (D)	A		X							PVT 1923-1870
Aubert, Edgar										
Ausams, Zack (D)	A		X							PVT
Bailey, Joseph (D)	A		X							158 Depot Bde, 1922-2000
Banks, Purcel (D)	A				X					

	Branch	Combat Service				Combat Era				Comments
		WWI	WWII	Korea	RVN	WWI	WWII	Korea	RVN	
Banks, Williams (D)	A		X							Co E, 1330 Eng. Reg.
Barnes, Charles (D)	A	X								525 Eng. Bn. 1889-1963
Barnes, Herbert W. (D)	A									1940-2008
Barrio, Henry (D)	A		X							PFC 166 QM Truck 1922-65
Barrio, Richard J. (D)	A		X							PVT 1928-1994
Beasley, Ferman (D)	A		X							
Beasley, Harry (D)	A			X						
Bell. Victor (D)	A		X							1916-1992
Benjamin, Wesley (D)	CG									
Bias, Sidney (D)	A	X								PVT 437 Res 1896-161
Blanchard, Eldridge I., Jr. (D)	A	X								
Blanchard, Joseph (D)	A		X							PVT 1921-1969
Bolden, James (D)	N		X							1912-1994
Bolden, Wilfred	A			X						
Boskent, Walter (D)	A									1922-1989
Bougere, Matthew (D)	A									1915-1988
Bougere, Philip R. (D)	A		X							
Bougere, Wilson A. (D)	A		X							
Boutain, James, Sr. (D)	N									1923-1989
Boutain, Raymond (D)	A									1918-1984
Boutan, Curtis J. (D)	A									1920-1988
Boutan, Lewis (D)	N		X							
Boutan, Lyle (D)	A									1953-1997
Braux, Phillip	A		X							
Breaux, Cornelius (D)	A		X							SGT 1917-1984
Breaux, Phillips A. (D)	A		X							1922-2009
Breaux, Samuel (D)	A		X							PFC 1923-1980
Bridges, Lenear	A				X					

	Branch	Combat Service				Combat Era				Comments
		WWI	WWII	Korea	RVN	WWI	WWII	Korea	RVN	
Brook, Frank (D)	AAC		X							PVT 2515 Base Unit 1910-63
Brow, Clarence (D)	A	X								PVT 1892-1942
Brown, Clarence J. (D)	A	X								PVT 1896-1979
Brown, Ernest	A				X					
Bryant, Edward (D)	A		X							SGT 1921-1972
Buggage, Herbert (D)	AF									1932-2000
Buggage, Isaac J. (D)	A									18951980
Buggage, James, Jr. (D)	A				X					
Buggage, James, Sr. (D)	A		X							
Buggage, Lawrence B. (D)	N		X							
Buggage, Louis T. (D)	A			X						
Buggage, Matthew (D)	A				X					
Buggage, Milton J.	A	X								CPL, 367 Inf. 1896-1965
Buggage, Ulysses P. (D)	A		X							
Burd, Desmond										
Burd, Earl	A			X	XX					PH, BSM, Two tours in RVN
Burd, Lionel M., Sr. (D)	N		X							
Burd, Philip (D)	A		X							
Burd, Samuel J. (D)	MC		X							
Burrell, Johnny, Jr. (D)	AAC		X							PFC
Bush, Wilson (D)	A		X							
Butler, Willis (D)	A	X								PVT 1896-1979
Byan, Jos (D)	A		X							
Cadrick, Willis	A			X						
Carcy, Arthur (D)	A				X					
Carr, Nathaniel (D)	AF	X								CPT

		Combat Service				Combat Era				
	Branch	WWI	WWII	Korea	RVN	WWI	WWII	Korea	RVN	Comments
Carter, Alton (D)	A		X							PVT 510 Inf. Bn. 19211943
Carter, George (D)	A	X								PVT, 18951952
Castello, Clarence (D)	A		X							
Castello, Emile (D)	A	X								309 Svc Bn. 1891–1928
Charles, Henry (D)	A		X							PVT
Cheatham, Isial (D)	A	X								PVT
Clark, Soloman E. (D)	A									1936-1983
Clark, Spency	A			X						
Clark, Warren (D)	AF									SSGT, 1931-1958
Cola, Naymon (D)	A		X							
Cola, Roseman J., Sr. (D)	A				X					
Cola, Samson (D)	A	X								812 Pioneer Inf. 1896-56
Cola, Thomas, Jr. (D)	N		X							
Coleman, Raymond (D)	A	X								PVT 525 Eng, 1889-1971
Comeaux, John L. (D)	A		X							
Consonery, Joseph (D)			X							
Cooks, Ivory J. (D)	A	X								PVT 1892-1967
Coston, Eddie (D)	A		X							PVT 1919-1989
Crumes, Coles, Sr. (D)	A		X							
Cunningham, Ernest (D)	N									1925-1978
Cunningham, Isiah C. (D)	A		X							PFC 1923-2006
Cunnkin, George, Jr.	AF								X	SSGT
Dabney, Charles (D)	A		X							
Dabney, Willie (D)	A			X						
Dandridge, Lloyd (D)	A		X							

	Branch	WWI	WWII	Korea	RVN	WWI	WWII	Korea	RVN	Comments
		Combat Service				Combat Era				
Dansereau, Ernest (D)	A	X								164 Depot Bde 1893-58
Darensborg, Isakiah (D)	N			X						
Dave, Della (D)	A		X							PVT
Deggs, Joseph R. (D)	AF				X					SMGT
DeQuincy, Forester	MC									MSGT, 1 Bn., 26 Marines
Dominick, Cal (D)	A	X								1893-1984
Donsereaux, Carlo (D)	A		X							PFC 1922-1981
Donseroaux, Junidus (D)	A		X							PFC 1918-1996
Douglas, Harry (D)	A		X							
Dugas, Earl J. (D)	A									Tech 5, 1908-1998
Dyer, Joseph (D)	A	X								PVT, 1896-1978
Edwards, George C. (D)	A									1912-1974
Edwards, Louis H., Sr. (D)	A									Major, 1932-1999
Elliot, Walter H. (D)	A									X Tech-5, 1925-1997
Elphage, Thomas (D)	A		X							PVT, 269 Co, 5 Repl Dept
England, Jeffery (D)	A									2LT, 1933-2008
Ewell, Albert	AF								X	MSGT
Ewell, Sylvester	AF								X	MSGT
Fisher, James (D)	A	X								806 Pioneer Inf. 1902-66
Fortner, Edward (D)	A		X							
Fortner, Jesse, Jr. (D)	AAC		X							
Fortner, Munson (D)	A	X								1893-1945 "Cook"

	Branch	WWI	WWII	Korea	RVN	WWI	WWII	Korea	RVN	Comments
Fortner, Selvin J. (D)	A		X							SGT 1933-1988
Foster, Sterling R. (D)	A	X								CPL 1896-1978
Frances, Lloyd (D)	A		X							1918-1987
Francis, Clarence (D)	AF				X					1955-1994
Francis, Isiah (D)	A		X							PFC 1920-1994
Frank, Edward (D)	A	X								1899-1987
Franklin, Charles (D)	A		X							
Gardner, John (D)	A	X								Co D, 15 US Col. Inf.
Garnett, Frank (D)	A		X							
Gibson, Arthur, Jr. (D)	A									1930-1991
Gibson, Clarence	A		X							
Gibson, Tommy (D)	A		X							PVT 1912-19563
Granger, Arthur A. (D)	A	X								PVT Co C, 415 Labor Bn.
Granger, James (D)	A	X								PVT 1895-1973
Hall, Vincent J. (D)	A				X					
Harden, Wilbert (D)	A				X					
Hardin, Henry (D)	A	X								PVT 1898-1973
Hardrick, Jessie W. (D)	A		X							PFC 1554 Eng. Bn. 1924-1971
Harris, Andrew (D)	A	X								PVT 1896-1972
Harris, Earnest, Jr.	A				X					
Harris, Earnest, Sr. (D)	A		X							
Harris, Jacob (D)	A	X								1895-1965
Harris, Joseph (D)	A	X								814 Pioneer Inf. 1885-1965
Harris, Roy J.	A			X						
Harris, Tamos (D)	A		X							PVT 1922-1987

		Combat Service				Combat Era				
	Branch	WWI	WWII	Korea	RVN	WWI	WWII	Korea	RVN	Comments
Harvey, Freddie (D)	AF									SGT 1953-2008
Hawkins, Edward (D)	A	X								1895-1964
Haynes, Edward (D)	A		X							CPL QMC, 1912-1964
Henderson, Andrew (D)	A		X							PVT 1924-1987
Henderson, Cleveland (D)	A		X							MSGT 1923-1996
Henderson, Oliver	A									
Henderson, Raymond (D)	A									SP-3, 1933-1958
Henderson, Wilbert (D)	A			X						PFC 1930-1979
Herbert, Albert (D)	A		X							PVT 1924-1983
Herbert, Elois H., Sr. (D)	A		X							
Herbert, Gilbert (D)	AF			X						CPL 1933-1992
Herbert, Harold P. (D)	A		X							
Herbert, Henry H., Jr. (D)	A		X							
Herbert, Robert (D)	A		X							
Hill, James (D)	A			X						PFC 505 Abn. Inf. Reg. 192871
Hill, Sila (D)	A		X							PFC 1918-1967
Hirsh, Soloman (D)	A		X							
Holloway, Gus, Jr. (D)	A									1951-1990
Holmes, Jerome (D)	A				X					
Holmes, Joseph (D)	A	X								803 Pioneer Inf., 1887-55
Holmes, Tellesfhor (D)	A									1924-1992
Homer, Joe (D)	A		X							PVT
Honora, Wilfred (D)	A									Tech-5 1908-1986

		Combat Service				Combat Era				
	Branch	WWI	WWII	Korea	RVN	WWI	WWII	Korea	RVN	Comments
Howard, Calvin, Jr. (D)	N									Anti Acft 1947-1970
Howard, Clifford S. (D)	A				X					
Howard, Harold (D)	A		X							
Hubbs, Christopher (D)	A	X								162 2 Depot Bde
Hubert, Elious N. Jr. (D)	A				X					
Hughes, Alexander J. (D)	A		X							
Hughes, Isaac (D)	A		X							
Hughes, Marion I. (D)	A		X							
Hughes, Ricky (D)	N									1959-1983
Irvin, Joseph (D)	A		X							PFC, 37 Inf. 1917-1971
Jackson, Clarence (D)	A									PVT 1953-1980
Jackson, Rosemond (D)	A	X								PVT 1896-1974
Jacobs, Abraham, Jr. (D)	A		X							1919-1985
James, Alexander (D)	A				X					PVT, 3160 QM Svc Bn
James, Edwin O. (D)	A	X								PVT 1896-1964
James, Ferman P. (D)	A		X							
James, John	A					X				
James, Norman J. (D)	N		X							1937-1955
Jaruis, Lee A. (D)	A		X							PFC 1916-1978
Jefferson, Alex (D)	A	X								PVT 1824-1967
Smith, Ruben (D)	A	X								PVT 1874-1964
Jefferson, Charles E. (D)	AF									
Jelvia, Reginald H. (D)										
Johnson, August (D)	A	X								CPL, Eng 1895-1952
Johnson, Bernard D. (D)	A									1929-1986
Johnson, Charles C. (D)	A		X							
Johnson, Cleveland (D)	A			X						
Johnson, Gail A.	A				X					

		Combat Service				Combat Era				
	Branch	WWI	WWII	Korea	RVN	WWI	WWII	Korea	RVN	Comments
Johnson, Ivory	A								X	SGT
Johnson, Joseph (D)	A		X							SGT 1906-1991
Johnson, Louis (D)	A	X								PVT 1893-1970
Johnson, Morris (D)	A									
Johnson, Percy (D)	A		X							
Johnson, Raymond, Sr. (D)	AF									1936-1999
Johnson, Thomas R. (D)	N		X							
Johnson, Wilbert, Sr. (D)										PFC
Johnson, Willie (D)	A		X							Tech-5, 1921-1987
Jolevare, Malcolm (D)	A		X							1918-1988
Jones, Edward (D)	A		X							
Jones, James (D)	A		X							Tech-5 1927-2002
Jones, Nathaniel, Jr. (D)	AF				X					
Joseph, Henry, Sr. (D)	A		X							Tech-5 445 Port Co 1925-50
Joseph, Leonard (D)	A		X							
Jupiter, Lawrence (D)	A				X					SP4 1944-2004
Jupiter, Willie (D)	A			X						SP-4 1920-1975
Landry, Bobby	A				X					
Landry, Isaac (D)	A		X							PFC 1916-1983
Landry, Murry (D)	A			X						
Landry. Alfred (D)	A									SGT 1944-199
Laney, Leonce (D)	A	X								PVT 1895-1956
Larkin, Larry (D)	A	X								PVT 1888-1970
Larradian, Oscar (D)	A		X							
Lawkins, Oneil, Sr. (D)	A			X						

	Branch	Combat Service				Combat Era				Comments
		WWI	WWII	Korea	RVN	WWI	WWII	Korea	RVN	
Lawless, Pouis H. (D)	N		X	X						SDL 1918-1972
Lawrence, Cleveland (D)	AF			X						
Lawrence, Lawrence (D)	AF			X						
Lawrence, Ulysses J. (D)	A		X							
Leach, Simon (D)	A	X								PVT 1889-1958
Lee, Royal, Sr. (D)	A	X								PVT 508 Eng Bn. 1892-1952
Lemon, Willie (D)	N		X							
Lewis, Joseph (D)	N	X								M3C 1900-1981
Lewis, Leonard, Sr. (D)	A		X							
Lewis, Richard (D)	A	X								PVT 1890-1973
Lewis, Sam (D)	A		X							CPL 393 QM 1915-1952
Lewis, Wilbert (D)	A		X							PVT 1914-1985
Lewis, Wilbert B. (D)	A	X								319 Labor Bn. 1890-1963
Lewis, Wilbert	A			X						
Ley, Legistine (D)	A		X							PVT 1913-1985
Lockett, George	A		X							
Lovencie, Sonny (D)	A	X								PVT 1897-1968
Mack, Ben (D)	A	X								PVT 1893-1961
Mack, James P. (D)	A			X						PVT 1924-1992
Martin, Morris J. (D)	A		X							
Martin, Morris, Sr. (D)	A	X								1894-1967
Marts, Morris J. (D)	AF				X					SGT-5 1963-1979
McCrory, Robert (D)	A			X						PFC 1929-1992

Name	Branch	WWI	WWII	Korea	RVN	WWI	WWII	Korea	RVN	Comments
McGuire, March (D)	A	X								PVT 334 Svc. Bn. 1886-1960
Meads, Mack W. (D)	A		X							SGT
Meads, Ulis (D)	A		X							PFC 1923-1998
Melancon, Alfred, Jr. (D)	A			X						
Melancon, Cleveland (D)	A									416 Res. Labor Bn 1897-58
Melancon, Cleveland, Jr. (D)	N		X							
Melancon, Joseph, Sr. (D)	A		X							
Melonson, Clenard	A				X					
Merrimon, Cornelious (D)	A		X							PFC, Field Arty
Micken. Leonce R. (D)	A		X							
Miller, Clarence, Jr. (D)	A									
Miller, Isiah (D)	A		X							PVT, 65 Pioneer
Miller, Thomas (D)	A	X								PVT
Mills, Benjamin (D)	A									1928-2000
Mills, Hayward, Sr. (D)	A									1921-1984
Mills, Ivory, Jr. (D)	A		X							
Mills, Leonard C. (D)	A	X								PVT 1892-1974
Mitchell, Curtis L. (D)	A		X							
Mitchell, Joseph (D)	A				X					PVT 1923-1990
Mitchell, Melvin (D)	A	X								PVT 1895-1983
Molare, Murry, Sr. (D)	A		X							
Moore, James (D)	A		X							
Moore, James A. (D)	A		X							PFC 1922-207
Morand, Arthur W. III (D)	A									1963-1995
Morris, William S. (D)	A		X							PFC 1906-1989
Muse, Joseph (D)	A		X							

	Branch	Combat Service				Combat Era				Comments
		WWI	WWII	Korea	RVN	WWI	WWII	Korea	RVN	
Myers, David (D)	A			X						SGT
Myles, Clarence, Jr. (D)	A		X							Tech-5 1925-1997
Myles, Joseph, Sr. (D)	A	X								PFC 1896-1980
Narcisse, Joseph, Jr. (D)	A									
Nelson, Joseph (D)	N(R)									X SL 1912-1966
Nelson, Kenneth (D)	A X									SGT 1955-1997
Nelson, Oscar, Jr. (D)	A	X								PVT, 1919-1978
Nelson, Vernon (D)	A				X					
Nicholas, Lowney (D)	A			X						1923-1994
Nickerson, Junior (D)	A		X							
Nickerson, Samuel, Jr. (D)	A		X							
Oliver, Bernard, Jr. (D)	A			X						
Oliver, Wallace (D)	A									Tech SGT 1915-1989
Parker, Calvin B., Sr. (D)	A			X						
Parker, Irvin J. (D)	A		X							
Parker, Mitchell J. (D)	A									1954-1984
Parker, Ronald	A				X					
Patterson, James (D)	A		X							Tech SGT 1908-1974
Patterson, John, Jr. (D)	A		X							
Patterson, Joseph F. (D)	A		X							
Phillips, Willie (D)	A	X								PFC 1913-1987
Phoenix, Damsey (D)	A	X								508 Engr., 1896-1963
Plaisent, Hunory (D)	A	X								PVT, Pioneer Inf. 1887-51
Pleasant, Alfred K.	A			X						
Pleasant, Amos (D)	A	X								Co O, 92 US Inf.
Pleasant, Kernell J. (D)	A		X							

		Combat Service				Combat Era				
	Branch	WWI	WWII	Korea	RVN	WWI	WWII	Korea	RVN	Comments
Poret, Vincent P. Jr. (D)	A				X					
Prean, Kernell (D)	N		X							
Prean, Leonard (D)	AF									1947-2008
Pugh, Curtis E. (D)	A				X					
Pugh, Edward (D)	A									PVT
Rainey, Frank (D)	A		X							PFC 1923-1974
Randolph, James, Sr. (D)	A		X							PFC
Ranson, Beverly (D)	AAC		X							
Ribinson, Eric	A				X					
Ribiore, Theadore, Jr.	A	X								
Richardson, Joshua R. (D)	A		X							SGT Co E, 4 US Cav.
Riley, Melvin J. (D)	A		X							PVT 1918-1995
Riviore, Theoradore (D)	A		X							
Robertson, Matthew (D)	A		X	X	X					SP-5 1927-1981
Robinson, Derick	A				X					
Rohillard, Joseph (D)	N		X							STMI
Rousell, Richard	A				X					
Sanders, Colie, Sr. (D)	A	X								PVT 1894-1964
Sandies, Addison (D)	A		X							PFC 1910-1982
Sawyer, Jinel	AF								X	SGT 6940 Security Sqdn
Sheffie, Robert L. (D)	A									1922-1982
Sheffie, Thomas E. (D)	N		X							S-1 1924-1961
Sheffie, Charles B. (D)	A	X								
Shelby, Lawrence (D)	A	X								PVT 164 Depot Bn. 1888-44
Sherman, Charley, Jr. (D)	A									
Sherman, Sullivan J. (D)	A		X							
Sherman, Whittaker J. (D)	A		X							1910-1971

	Branch	WWI	WWII	Korea	RVN	WWI	WWII	Korea	RVN	Comments
		Combat Service				Combat Era				
Shields, Soloman B., Jr. (D)	A		X							
Simms, Clarence M. (D)	A			X						
Simoneaux, Roland (D)	A				X					
Sims, Byron K.	A									
Skidmore, Alfred A. (D)	A		X							
Skidmore, Favord B. (D)	A				X			X		
Skidmore, Frank G. (D)	A		X							
Skidmore, Fura (D)	A		X							
Skidmore, Gerald J. (D)	A		X							
Skidmore, Matthew F. (D)	A		X							
Skidmore, Matthew, Sr. (D)	A		X							
Skidmore, Richard	A				X					
Skidmore, Winston	A				X					
Skipper, Jason (D)	MC				X					PH, 1948-1993
Skipper, Silas (D)	A		X							PFC 1919-2003
Smith, Henry (D)	A	X								PVT 325 Svc. Bn. QMC
Soloman, Alfred (D)										
Southall, Johnson (D)	A	X								PVT 1897-1961
Southall, Samuel (D)	A	X								PVT 1893-1968
Southall, Samuel B.	A	X								
Southhall, Rolay L. (D)	A		X							
Southhall, Amos H., Sr. (D)	A		X							
Spark, Noan (D)	A		X							SGT 1922-1988
Spott, Sterling (D)	A		X							PFC 1928-1995
Stewart, Ike (D)	A		X							PFC 1926-1986

	Branch	Combat Service				Combat Era				Comments
		WWI	WWII	Korea	RVN	WWI	WWII	Korea	RVN	
Thomas, Albert (D)	A		X							Tech-4 1911-1967
Thomas, Irvin	A			X						SGT
Thomas, Roshia (D)	AF		X							Tech-4
Thomas, Rouden, Jr.	A	X								
Thomas, Sherley (D)	A		X							Tech-5 1920-2003
Thomas, Willie (D)	A			X						PVT 1951-1984
Thompson, Lloyd, Sr. (D)	A									PVT 1942-2009
Toussaint, Rayfield (D)	A		X							PFC, 539 Port Co TC
Toussiant, Edward (D)	A									PVT, 161 Depot Bde.
Trophi, John O. (D)	A	X								PFC 1898-1982
Tucker, Robert (D)	A	X								
Tunson, Donard (D)	A	X								PVT Co B, 6 Inf. 1877-1954
Tunson, Louis (D)	A	X								PFC 419 R. Labor Bn. 1890-64
Turner, Henry (D)	A	X								PVT 1990-1984
Tyler, Edwin (D)	N		X							
Tyler, Oliver (D)	A									PVT, 508 Eng
Wade, Clifton (D)	A									SP-4
Walker, Oscar (D)	A	X								VT 1889-1983
Washington, Alexander (D)	A									1944-1995
Washington, Andrew (D)	A									PVT 262 QM 1900-1945
Washington, Clarence (D)	A									PFC 1910-1991

	Branch	WWI	WWII	Korea	RVN	WWI	WWII	Korea	RVN	Comments
Washington, Edward (D)	A		X							Tech-5, 1926-1973
Washington, Ernest (D)	AF		X							PVT 1928-1972
Washington, Percy (D)	A		X							PFC
Watts, Harrison (D)	A	X								225 Svc Bn. Eng. 1890-1961
Watts, Joseph, Jr. (D)	N		X							
White, Norwood A. (D)	A	X								PVT 162 Depot Bde. 1896-68
Wiggins, Claude	A			X						
Wiggins, Claude W. (D)	A		X							
Williams, Albert (D)	A	X								PFC 319 Svc Bn. QM 1886-60
Williams, Andrew, Jr. (D)	A		X							PFC 1922-2001
Williams, Arthur (D)	A	X								PVT
Williams, Bartholomew J. (D)	A				X					
Williams, Cleveland (D)	AAC		X							1918-1974
Williams, Clifton, Sr. (D)	A		X							
Williams, Corneleus, Sr. (D)	A		X							
Williams, Dennis (D)	A		X							PFC QMC 1915-1948
Williams, Harry T. (D)	A				X					PH
Williams, Herd (D)	A		X							Tech-5, 1918-1977
Williams, Huey P.	A				X					
Williams, Isadore F. (D)	A		X							
Williams, Lawrence C. (D)	N									1924-1986
Williams, Lawrence, Jr. (D)	A			X						
Williams, Loyal G. (D)	A									1919-1993
Williams, Oliver (D)	A	X								PVT 1893-1984

	Branch	WWI	Combat Service WWII	Korea	RVN	WWI	Combat Era WWII	Korea	RVN	Comments
Williams, Oscar, Sr. (D)	A		X							PVT 1919-1992
Williams, Ralph (D)										1911-1992
Williams, Thamos (D)	A		X							PVT 1901-1992
Williams, Theodore, Jr. (D)	A			X						QMC
Williams, Walter (D)	A		X							1913-1978
Williams, Wash (D)	A		X							
Willis, James III (D)	AF									SGT 1952-1990
Wilson, Alphonse (D)	A	X								PFC 1895-1974
Wilson, Louvinia B. (D)										
Wiltz, Nolan (D)	A			X						CPL 1933-2008
Wise, Israel (D)	A		X							PVT 1917-1996
Wise, Jimmie E. (D)	MC				X					1943-1979
Wise, Walter (D)	A	X								PVT 1920-1994
Woods, Clarence, Sr. (D)	A		X							1925-1997
Young, Laroyal (D)	A									1934-2008

Legend:

A	Army
AAC	Army Air Corps
Abn.	Airborne
AF	Air Force
Arty	Artillery
Bn.	Battalion
Bde.	Brigade
CPT	Captain
CG	Coast Guard
CPL	Corporal E-4
(D)	Deceased
Eng	Engineer
Inf.	Infantry
LT	Lieutenant
MAJ	Major
M3C	Machinist 3rd Class
MC	Marine Corps
MSG	Master Sergeant E-8
N	Navy
N(R)	Navy Reserve
PVT	Private E-1
PFC	Private First Class E-2
PH	Purple Heart
QMC	Quartermaster Corps
Reg.	Regiment
Res	Reserves
RVN	Republic of Vietnam
SGT	Sergeant E-5
SSG	Sergeant First Class E-6
SP-3	Specialist E-3
Svc	Service
Tech	Technical
Sqdn.	Squadron

LAFOURCHE PARISH VETERANS

		Combat Service				Combat Era				
	Branch	WWI	WWII	Korea	RVN	WWI	WWII	Korea	RVN	Comments
Adams, Alvin	A	X								
Adams, Isaac (D)	A			X						
Adams, Joseph (D)	A		X							
Alcorn, Cleveland				X						
Alexandra, Lilas (D)	A		X							
Alexsee, John (D)	A	X								
Allen, George, Sr.				X						
Anderson, Alex, Jr. (D)	A		X							
Anderson, Alvin, Sr. (D)	A		X							
Anderson, Alvin, Sr. (D)	A		X							
Anderson, George (D)	A	X								Co I, 78 US Col. Inf.
Anderson, James C. (D)	A				X					
Anderson, John (D)	A		X							
Anderson, Philip (D)	A			X						
Anderson, Richard (D)	A			X						
Anderson, Wilbert (D)	A		X							
Anderson, Wilbert C. (D)	A		X							
Ansand, Herman (D)	A			X						
Arrow, Hasker, Jr. (D)	A		X							
Arson, Freddie (D)	A	X								
Ayrow, Hasker	A									
Bailey, Leon H. (D)	A			X						
Banks, Edward (D)	A	X								
Banks, Lawrence (D)	A		X							
Barrow, Joseph L.				X						

CURTIS J. JOHNSON

Name	Branch	Combat Service				Combat Era				Comments
		WWI	WWII	Korea	RVN	WWI	WWII	Korea	RVN	
Bartley, Heard C.		X								
Bartley, Herd J., Jr.			X							
Batiste, Lionel		X								
Billips, Noland, Jr.										
Billips, Noland, Jr. (D)	N			X						
Bolt, Lawrence J. (D)	A				X					
Bolt, Leroy B., Sr. (D)	A		X							
Boudreaux, Wilbert (D)	A								X	
Brickley, Earnest (D)	A			X						
Brisco, Arthur (D)	A		X							
Broom, Freddie (D)	A			X						
Broom, Harry (D)	A			X						
Broom, Junius (D)	N			X						
Broussard, Ernest (D)	A			X						
Brown, Alexander C. (D)	A	X								
Brown, Joseph (D)	A			X						
Brown, Nathaniel T. (D)	A		X							
Brown, Oliver (D)	A								X	
Brown, Ulyess Keep as is (D)	A			X	X					PH, KIA, Sep 1951
Bryant, J. C.		X								
Bryant, Robert			X							
Burgen, Elijah (D)	A	X								
Burrell, Luke, Jr. (D)	A	X								
Bush, Albert (D)	AAF			X						
Butler, Gloria	AF								X	
Butler, James (D)	A	X								
Butler, James, Jr.										

		Combat Service				Combat Era				
	Branch	WWI	WWII	Korea	RVN	WWI	WWII	Korea	RVN	Comments
Campbell, Curtis			X							
Campbell, Silas (D)	A	X								
Carter, Alfred	X									
Carter, Alfred, Sr. (D)	A		X							
Carter, Gerald		X								
Carter, Morell T. (D)	A				X					
Carter, Reginald (D)		X								
Catret, Reginald (D)	N		X							
Charles, Albert (D)	AAC			X						
Charles, Edwin F. III				X						
Charles, Edwin, Jr. (D)	A			X						
Coleman, Cleveland (D)	A	X								
Coleman, Ralph C. (D)	A				X					
Coleman, Warren (D)	A		X							
Collins, Ernest (D)	N(R)		X							
Collins, Harvey (D)	AF		X							
Collins, Jacob (D)	A			X						
Collins, Van (D)	A	X								
Cook, Alfred J. (D)	A							X		
Cook, Henry (D)	A	X								
Cook, Herbert T. (D)	A		X							
Cook, Levy (D)	A	X								
Cook, Thomas E. (D)	N		X							
Cooks, Lloyd E.			X							
Corbin, Daniel (D)	A	X								
Cox, Reuben (D)	A	X								Co G, 78 US Col. Inf.
Daggs, Leonce, Sr. (D)	A			X						

	Branch	Combat Service				Combat Era				Comments
		WWI	WWII	Korea	RVN	WWI	WWII	Korea	RVN	
Danferfield, Joseph (D)	A								X	
Davis, Edward (D)	A					X				
Davis, Floyd (D)	A			X						
Davis, Isiah (D)	A		X							
Davis, Johnny (D)	A						X			
Davis, Joseph Q. (D)	A	X								
Davis, Oliver (D)	A		X							
Desira, Drozan (D)	A	X								
Dickerson, Daniel (D)	A			X						
Dorsey, Albert, Jr. (D)	A			X						
Dorsey, Harry			X							
Douglas, Walter (D)	A							X		
Dunbar, Joseph, Jr. (D)	A									
Dyer, George (D)	A		X							
Dyer, Joseph (D)	AF		X							
Edward, Willie (D)	A			X						
Ellis, Samuel L., Sr.			X							
Everns, Willie (D)	A	X								
Every, Ernest		X								
Every, Norman, Jr.				X						
Every, Willie			X							
Flakes, Eddie (D)	A			X						
Fleming, Charles G. (D)	A								X	
Fleming, Clarence K. (D)	A			X						
Fletcher, Jack (D)	A		X							
Fletcher, Oliver (D)	A	X								
Folse, Leonard		X	X	X						
Frey, Arthur (D)	A					X				

| | Combat Service | | | | Combat Era | | | | |
	Branch	WWI	WWII	Korea	RVN	WWI	WWII	Korea	RVN	Comments
Frye, David (D)	A						X			
Frye, Joseph	A									
Frye, Junius (D)	A			X						
Frye, Roland (D)	A	X								
Garner, Sam (D)	A		X							
Goff, Garrison, Jr. (D)	A		X							
Gooseberry, Alex (D)	A		X							
Gramma, Lester P.T. (D)	AF				X					
Graves, Samuel (D)	A									Co M, US Hvy. Arty
Gray, Donald (D)	A					X				
Gray, Roy, Jr.			X							
Gray, Thomas (D)	A				X					
Green, George (D)	N			X						
Griffin, Robert			X							
Hadley, Andrew (D)	A	X								
Hadley, Elton, Sr. (D)	A			X						
Hadley, Henderson, Jr. (D)	A				X					
Hadley, Henderson, Sr. (D)	A	X								
Hadley, Irvin (D)	A			X						
Hadley, Jackson (D)	AF				X					
Hadley, Willie, Sr. (D)	A			X						
Harkless, Lawrence				X						
Hawkins, Rutherford M. (D)	A		X							
Hawkins, Rytherford M.										
Henderson, Cleveland		X								
Henderson, Eddie, Jr. (D)	A		X							

		Combat Service				Combat Era				
	Branch	WWI	WWII	Korea	RVN	WWI	WWII	Korea	RVN	Comments
Hester, Gustave (D)	A	X								
Hill, Edward S.			X							
Hill, Henry, Jr. (D)	A		X							
Hills, Andrew (D)	A			X						
Hills, Andrew			X							
Hogan, Cleveland, Jr. (D)	N			X						
Hogan, Eugene (D)	A							X		
Holly, Warner (D)	A	X								
Holmes, Bennie (D)	A						X			
Howard, John (D)	A	X								Co D, 75 US Col. Inf
Howard, Samuel, Jr.			X							
Hunter, Richard T., Sr. (D)	AF						X			
Hymel, Sterling L. (D	A			X						
Ingram, Benjamin, Jr. (D)	A		X							
Jackson, Ernest J. (D)	A		X							
Ingram, Benjamin, Jr.			X							
Jackson, Debra B.				X						
Jackson, Joseph (D)	A	X								
Jackson, Oglethroppe				X						
Johnson, Alvin P. (D)	A									
Johnson, Clifton J.			X							
Johnson, Donald L. (D)	A								X	
Johnson, Hubert			X							
Johnson, Isaac, Jr.			X							
Johnson, James (D)	A									
Johnson, Joseph (D)	A		X							

	Branch	WWI	WWII	Korea	RVN	WWI	WWII	Korea	RVN	Comments
Johnson, Kernell										
Johnson, Major (D)	A	X								
Johnson, Mervin (D)	A			X						
Johnson, Norman (D)	A						X			
Johnson, Oscar R., Jr. (D)	A			X						
Johnson, Oscar R., Jr.										
Johnson, Richard (D)	A		X							
Johnson, Richard		X								
Johnson, Samuel J., Jr.		X								
Johnson, Samuel J.	A		X							
Johnson, Thomas										
Johnson, Willie, Jr. (D)	A		X							
Jones, Donald (D)	AF			X						
Jones, Gerald B.		X								
Jones, Howard (D)	A			X						
Jones, Irvin	A					X				
Jones, Joseph T. (D)	A	X								
Jones, Larry J. (D)	A								X	
Jones, Leonard (D)	A			X						
Jones, Lois A (D)	A								X	
Jones, Lucien		X								
Jones, Oliver (D)	A		X							
Jones, Osben, Jr. (D)	A	X								
Jones, Porter (D)	A	X								
Jones, Tyrone			X							
Joseph, Alton B.	A									
Joseph, Ernest (D)	A	X								
Joseph, Ernest	A									

		Combat Service				Combat Era			
	Branch	WWI	WWII	Korea	RVN	WWI	WWII	Korea	RVN	Comments
Joseph, Henry (D)	A		X							
Joseph, Herman F. (D)	A				X					
Joseph, Herman A										
Joseph, Raymond, Jr. (D)	A							X		
Jules, Lawrence R. (D)	A				X					
Junius, Milton (D)	A				X					
Kane, Morris (D)	A				X					
Kane, Phillip E. (D)	A								X	
Kennedy, Columbus			X							
Kennedy, Henderson, Jr.					X					
King, Al S.			X							
King, Albert J.			X							
King, Willie, Jr. (D)	MC						X			
Kirk, James		X								
Lambert, John	A									
Lawson, Earl B. (D)	A			X						
Lawson, Joseph (D)	A			X						
LeBlanc, Arthur P. (D)	A	X								
Lee, Andrew (D)	A		X							
Lee, James (D)	A						X			
Lee, Joseph (D)	A		X							
Lee, Wilbert, Jr.			X							
Lemon, Paul			X							
Lewis, Anthony P.				X						
Lewis, John, Sr. (D)	A				X					
Lloyd, James (D)	A			X						
Lofton, Elijah, Jr.				X						

		Combat Service				Combat Era				
	Branch	WWI	WWII	Korea	RVN	WWI	WWII	Korea	RVN	Comments
London, Lawrence (D)	A				X					
Lowis, Bernard (D)	A			X						
Mason, Charles (D)	A	X								
Mathews, Andrew P. (D)	A	X								
Mathews, Clarence (D)	A				X					
Matthews, Harry, Sr. (D)			X							
Matthews, Willie (D)						X				
McAllister, Jacqueline S.					X					
McCloud, Steve (D)	A		X	X						
McGuin, Leo S.			X							
Meyers, Eddie (D)	A	X								
Miles, Marceline (D)	A	X								Co G, 78 US Col. Inf.
Miller, Alexander (D)	A	X								Co. K, US Col. Inf.
Miller, Charles J. (D)	A			X						
Miller, Leonard (D)	A			X						
Mitchell, Frank, Jr. (D)	A		X							
Mitchell, James (D)	A			X						
Monroe, Henry (D)	A			X						
Moore, Oscar (D)	A					X				
Moore, Willie, Jr. (D)	A		X							
Morgan, Albert, Sr.		X								
Morgan, Edward (D)										
Morris, Sidney (D)	A	X								
Morris, Willie (D)	A	X								
Mosby, Andrew (D)	A								X	
Murray, Ernest (D)	N							X		
Murray, Victor (D)	AAC			X						
Neville, Danny M. (D)	A								X	

	Branch	Combat Service				Combat Era				Comments
		WWI	WWII	Korea	RVN	WWI	WWII	Korea	RVN	
Nicholas, Edward C. (D)	A					X				
Odoms, Charley, Jr. (D)	A				X					
Owens, Lionel J. (D)	A					X				
Owens, Morell (D)	AF					X				
Pace, Alvin C. (D)	A	X								
Paige, James O. (D)	A									
Paige, Roland, Sr. (D)	A			X						
Parker, Marvin (D)	A							X		
Patterson, John L.				X						
Peltier, Gerald T.	A		X							
Peltier, Ramond J., Jr. (D)	A					X	X			Major
Perio, Joseph C., Sr. (D)	AF							X		
Perkins, Fulton (D)					X					
Phillips, James (D)	A							X		
Pierce, James E. (D)	A						X			
Pierre, Oliver (D)	A	X								
Pike, Charles R. (D)	A							X		
Pike, Welton (D)	A				X					
Powell, Boker T.			X							
Pratt, Theodore M.	A					X				
Price, Norman (D)	A	X								
Price, Willie, Jr. (D)	A			X						
Queen, Oliver			X							
Queen, Richard J.			X							
Randall, Elijah, Sr. (D)	A			X						
Rankins, Samuel (D)	A						X			
Reed, Calvin J. (D)	A		X							
Reed, Clarence (D)	A	X								

	Branch	WWI	WWII	Korea	RVN	WWI	WWII	Korea	RVN	Comments
Reed, Herman L. (D)	A			X						
Reed, Irby (D)	A						X			
Reed, Isaac Newton (D)	A				X					
Reed, Thomas J. (D)	A							X		
Reed, Thomas J. A										
Rhodes, Aaron E. (D)	MC								X	
Rhodes, James A. (D)	A	X								
Richardson, Daniel (D)	A			X						
Riggs, Thomas W. (D)	A			X						
Robertson, Leonard (D)	A			X						
Robertson, Warren (D)	A				X					
Robichaux, Cleveland B.	A		X							
Robinson, Arthur (D)	N(R)		X							
Robinson, Joseph (D)	A			X						
Robinson, Wortha (D)	A			X						
Rose, Clarence E. (D)	A					X				
Roy, Detroit (D)	A			X						
Ruffin, Freddie (D)	A			X						
Sanders, Charley (D)	A						X			
Sargeant, Reynard P.										
Sargent, Lloyd L. (D)	A				X					
Sargent, Lloyd			X							
Sauceberry, Wilbert (D)	A			X						
Scott, Clinton B. (D)	A			X						
Scott, Joseph (D)	A			X						
Scott, Monroe, Jr. (D)	A	X								
Seymore, Willie (D)	A			X						

	Branch	Combat Service				Combat Era				Comments
		WWI	WWII	Korea	RVN	WWI	WWII	Korea	RVN	
Shanklin, Carla M. (D)	A								X	
Shanklin, Early (D)	A	X								
Shanklin, Harold (D)	A			X						
Shanklin, Henry L. (D)	A							X		
Shanklin, Lester D. (D)	A				X					
Shanklin, Samuel			X							
Shaw, Cecila F.			X							
Shepheard, Solomon (D)	A		X							
Shields, Milton (D)	A		X							
Shortridge, Humphrey J.			X							
Skipper, Jason	A									
Skipper, Silas	A									
Smith, Kevin			X							
Smith, Roland V. (D)	A								X	
Smith, Willie (D)	N							X		
Southall, Michael			X							
Southall, Norman (D)	AAC							X		
Square, Andrew (D)	A						X			
Stafford, George		X								
Starks, George H, Sr. (D)	A					X				
Streams, Earl Jr. (D)	A				X					
Streems, Floyd		X								
Stringer, Walter (D)	A		X							
Tardiff, Joseph, Sr. (D)	A			X						
Theriot, Gerald	AF								X	
Theriot, Henry (D)	A			X		X				
Thibodeaux, Eddie (D)	A			X						
Thomas, Earl (D)	A			X						

	Branch	Combat Service				Combat Era				Comments
		WWI	WWII	Korea	RVN	WWI	WWII	Korea	RVN	
Thomas, Larry			X							
Thomas, Morris (D)	N(R)			X						
Thomas, Rufus (D)	A							X		
Thomas, Ulysses H., Jr.				X						
Thompson, Johnny		X								
Tucker, Edward M. (D)	N			X						
Turner, Earl (D)	A				X					
Turner, Earl	A									
Turner, James (D)	A	X								
Turner, Thomas J., Jr. (D)	A		X							
Valentine, Abraham (D)	A	X								
Valentine, Abraham, Jr. (D)	N			X						
Vanburne, Willie (D)	A							X		
Vicks, Freddie (D)	A			X						
Wagner, Isiah, Jr. (D)	MC							X		
Walker, Dilton (D)	N							X		
Walker, Edward (D)	A			X						
Walker, Emile			X							
Walker, Reginald (D)	A					X				
Walker, Reginald A., Jr.				X						
Wallace, Adam (D)	A					X				
Wallace, Lloyd H. (D)	A			X						
Waller, Leonard (D)	A			X						
Ward, Freddie (D)	A			X						
Ward, Horace (D)	A			X						
Ward, John				X						
Ward, Ulysses				X						

CURTIS J. JOHNSON

	Branch	Combat Service				Combat Era				Comments
		WWI	WWII	Korea	RVN	WWI	WWII	Korea	RVN	
Warner, Adam (D)	A		X							
Washington, Lawrence M. (D)	A		X							
Washington, Norman J. (D)	A						X			
Washington, Walter (D)	A	X								
Washington, Willie (D)	AF		X							
Watkins, Ernest (D)	A	X								
Watkins, Henry (D)	A								X	
Watkins, Louis, Sr. (D)	A			X						
Watkins, Manuel (D)	A	X								
Welton, Eugene (D)	A			X						
Wheiting, Joseph (D)	A	X								
Williams, Alexander (D)	A	X								
Williams, Alton (D)	A		X							
Williams, Charles				X						
Williams, Clarence (D)	A			X						
Williams, Dave (D)	A			X						
Williams, Earl (D)	A			X						
Williams, Edward (D)	A				X					
Williams, Ernest C., Jr. (D)	A						X			PH
Williams, Harry (D)	A	X								
Williams, Isiah (D)	A			X						
Williams, Isiah	A									
Williams, James S. (D)	A			X						
Williams, Joseph (D)	A				X					
Williams, Octave			X							
Williams, Robert (D)	A			X						

	Branch	Combat Service				Combat Era				Comments
		WWI	WWII	Korea	RVN	WWI	WWII	Korea	RVN	
Williams, Roosevelt, Jr. (D)	A				X					
Williams, Samuel G.				X						
Williams, Samuel		X								
Williams, Willie (D)	A	X								
Williams, Willie, Jr. (D)	A							X		
Wilson, Boveland, Sr. (D)	A			X	X					
Winston, Jake, Jr. (D)	A				X					
Winston, John, Jr.				X						
Winston, Nelson (D)	N			X						
Wood, Major (D)	A				X					
Woods, Clifton, Sr.			X							
Woods, James P. (D)	A		X							
Wright, Wesley D. (D)	A							X		
Young, Edward C. (D)	A			X						
Young, Freddie (D)	A	X								
Young, Horace (D)	A		X							
Young, Murphy (D)	A						X			
Young, Oliver (D)	N			X						
Young, Phillip (D)	A					X				
Young, Raymond (D)	A		X							
Young, Willie (D)	A		X							
Young, Willie, Jr. (D)	A			X						
Zeno, Herman R. (D)	A			X						
Zeno, Wendell P. (D)	N			X						

Legend:

A	Army	Inf.	Infantry
AAC	Army Air Corps	KIA	Killed in Action
AF	Air Force	MC	Marine Corps
Arty	Artillery	MAJ	Major
Bn	Battalion	PH	Purple Heart
Co.	Company	Res. or (R)	Reserve
Col.	Colored	RVN	Republic of Vietnam
CPT	Captain		
(D)	Deceased		
Hvy	Heavy		

Edwards Brothers Malloy
Thorofare, NJ USA
August 8, 2013